MW00397459

# ART'S CLAIM TO TRUTH

*Columbia Themes in Philosophy, Social Criticism, and the Arts*

COLUMBIA THEMES IN PHILOSOPHY, SOCIAL CRITICISM, AND THE ARTS PRESENTS monographs, essay collections, and short books on philosophy and aesthetic theory. It aims to publish books that show the ability of the arts to stimulate critical reflection on modern and contemporary social, political, and cultural life. Art is not now, if it ever was, a realm of human activity independent of the complex realities of social organization and change, political authority and antagonism, cultural domination and resistance. The possibilities of critical thought embedded in the arts are most fruitfully expressed when addressed to readers across the various fields of social and humanistic inquiry. The idea of philosophy in the series' title ought to be understood, therefore, to embrace forms of discussion that begin where mere academic expertise exhausts itself, where the rules of social, political, and cultural practice are both affirmed and challenged, and where new thinking takes place. The series does not privilege any particular art, nor does it ask for the arts to be mutually isolated. The series encourages writing from the many fields of thoughtful and critical inquiry.

Lydia Goehr and Daniel Herwitz, eds., *The Don Giovanni Moment: Essays on the Legacy of an Opera*
Robert Hullot-Kentor, *Things Beyond Resemblance: Collected Essays on Theodor W. Adorno*
John T. Hamilton, *Music, Madness, and the Unworking of Language*

# Art's Claim to Truth

## GIANNI VATTIMO

*Edited by Santiago Zabala* • *Translated by Luca D'Isanto*

COLUMBIA UNIVERSITY PRESS    NEW YORK

COLUMBIA UNIVERSITY PRESS
*Publishers Since 1893*
NEW YORK   CHICHESTER, WEST SUSSEX

Originally published in Italian as *Poesia e ontologia*
Copyright © 1985 Ugo Mursia Editore S.p.A.

Translation copyright © 2008 Columbia University Press

Library of Congress Cataloging-in-Publication Data

Vattimo, Gianni, 1936–
  [Poesia e ontologia. English]
  Art's claim to truth / Gianni Vattimo ; edited by Santiago Zabala ;
translated by Luca D'Isanto.
    p. cm. — (Columbia themes in philosophy, social criticism, and the arts)
  Includes bibliographical references and index.
  ISBN 978-0-231-13850-5 (cloth : alk. paper) — ISBN 978-0-231-51566-5 (ebook)
  1. Aesthetics.   2. Ontology.   3. Poetry.   I. Zabala, Santiago, 1975–
II. Title.   III. Series.

BH39.V34 13 2008
111'.85 — dc22                                    2007041079

Columbia University Press books are printed on permanent and durable acid-free paper.

This book is printed on paper with recycled content.

Printed in the United States of America

c 10 9 8 7 6 5 4 3 2 1

*For Richard Rorty*

# Contents

*Acknowledgments*

I would like to thank Luca D'Isanto for the extraordinary translation and Michael Haskell for helping me, once again, in revising the whole text. Special thanks go to Mario Cedrini, Ana Messuti, Alberto Martinengo, Wendy Lochner, and Robert Valgenti for their help throughout the various phases of the production of the book.

"Pareyson dall'estetica all'ontologia" was originally published in *Rivista di estetica* 40–41 (1993): 3–17; and "Arte, la verità ti fa male, lo sai," in *La Stampa*, 12 July 2005.

# Introduction

## The Hermeneutic Consequence of Art's Ontological Bearing

## Santiago Zabala

> Gianni Vattimo sees the phenomena which Hans Belting and I address
> from a perspective wider by far than either of us occupies: he thinks of
> the end of art under the perspective of the death of metaphysics in general,
> as well as of certain philosophical responses to aesthetic problems raised
> by a "technologically advanced society."
> —Arthur C. Danto, *After the End of Art* (1997)

The recent publication of *Weakening Philosophy: Essays in Honour of Gianni Vattimo* has induced us to translate and publish this early book of Vattimo's because the festschrift confirms not only that the Italian intellectual is one of the most important living philosophers but also that his early works deserve to be presented to Anglo-Saxon readers as much his later ones.[1] Although we are all well acquainted with Vattimo's understanding of postmodernity (educed in *The End of Modernity*, *The Adventures of Differences*, and *Beyond Interpretation*) and his interpretation of religion (in *Belief*; *After Christianity*; *The Future of Religion*, with Richard Rorty; and *After the Death of God*, with John D. Caputo),[2] *Weakening Philosophy*—through its critical essays by philosophers such as Charles Taylor, Nancy K. Frankenberry, Richard Rorty, Umberto Eco, Jean-Luc Nancy, and many others—has shown that Vattimo's philosophical position is not limited to his theory of postmodernity and his reformulation of the Christian message, but is also deepened by the studies he produced in the late 1960s, such as *Art's Claim to Truth*.[3] During these years, Vattimo taught aesthetics in the University of

Turin and published many books on Nietzsche, Heidegger, and aesthetics that laid the way for all these better known later texts and, most of all, for the formulation of his philosophy: *"pensiero debole,"* weak thought, which he first expounded in 1979. Weak thought is nothing other than the knowledge, acceptance, and recognition that philosophy, after the deconstruction of metaphysics, cannot capture the ultimate essence of its objects but must comply with a multiplicity of interpretations. As for religion, weak thought helps us to deal with the consequences and obligations of the death of God, that is, to weaken those ecclesiastic dogmas that stand as obstacles to the faith of believers and the agnosticism of nonbelievers. But how did Vattimo reunderstand philosophy as the modern description of static essences in order to recognize its postmodern, interpretative nature?

The answer to this question can only be found in those early texts by Vattimo, such as *Art's Claim to Truth* and the recently collected and translated *Dialogue with Nietzsche*, where weak thought took shape through an accurate analysis of Nietzsche, Heidegger, Luigi Pareyson, and Hans-Georg Gadamer, who have always been at the center of Vattimo's intellectual career.[4] But the current study on aesthetics not only prepares for weak thought and the well-known postmetaphysical interpretation of religion but also delineates, for the first time, Vattimo's own aesthetics, which is hardly known to the English-speaking audiences. Just like *Dialogue with Nietzsche, Art's Claim to Truth* is not simply a translation of the second edition of Gianni Vattimo's *Poesia e ontologia* of 1967, but a new edition, with two new chapters and a new order given to the original contents. All this has been done, with Vattimo's consent, because we felt the new chapters allowed a division of the book into three parts, "Aesthetics," "Hermeneutics," and "Truth," which indicate and constitute the core of Vattimo's aesthetic philosophy.

The best introductions to edited books are not those that summarize for the reader what she is about to read, but the ones that enable the reader to familiarize herself with the themes, authors, and vocabularies that constitute not only the structure of the book but also its thesis. This is valid not only for those introductions written by a collection's author (as in Vattimo's *Nihilism and Emancipation*),[5] but also for introductions written by the editors themselves (as in Rorty and Vattimo's *The Future of Religion*)[6]—which is the case here. Having said this, instead of summarizing all the essays that constitute this book, my brief introduction will try to delineate the book's main thesis by an examination of those authors upon whom Vattimo bases his aesthetic investigations: Martin Heidegger, Luigi Pareyson, and Hans-

Georg Gadamer. An introduction to these classic thinkers will enable the reader not only to work her way through Vattimo's aesthetical intuitions but also to understand the two themes (ontology and hermeneutics) that constitute the book's thesis: *truth as the hermeneutic consequence of art's ontological bearing*. This presupposes that art's ontological bearing (indicated by Heidegger) requires an interpretative process (delineated by Pareyson) that constitutes its truth (as Gadamer explained), which becomes the goal of art after the end of metaphysics. Although Heidegger, Pareyson, and Gadamer have specifically laid out their own aesthetic theories in their own texts, such as *Off the Beaten Track* (1950), *Aesthetics* (1954), and *Truth and Method* (1960), Vattimo uses their theories to overcome metaphysics, and this overcoming, according to him, is the necessary condition for understanding not only the general *conceptual* transformation of artworks in the twentieth century but also outstanding works of art, such as Marcel Duchamp's readymades, David Lynch's films, or Alfredo Jaar's projects, which are so often criticized as unaesthetic or incapable of fulfilling art's traditional function.[7] These artists' works are not only good examples for the reader to keep in mind in the different parts of the book (the *Fountain* for Heidegger's ontological bearing of art, *Mulholland Drive* for art's interpretative form according to Pareyson, and *Let There Be Light* for Gadamer's truth of art), but also indications that art's function is not to fulfill, perform, or entertain the demands of the public but, on the contrary, to require from the public an interpretation that allows the work's ontological truth to come out, hence, truth as the hermeneutic consequence of art's ontological bearing.

Although there have been many different theories of aesthetics since Alexander Baumgarten first gave the concept a modern meaning in 1735, most of them have either been limited to a philosophy of art or to the aesthetic nature of objects that are not art. This same distinction has been further divided in representationalism and formalism. This book situates itself beyond both understandings of aesthetics and, more important, as Arthur C. Danto correctly observes in my epigraph, "under the perspective of the end of metaphysics."[8] While Danto's view of the development of the history of art is inspired by Hegel, who claimed that art, through its growing consciousness of itself, eventually becomes philosophy and thus comes to an end, Vattimo instead interprets this end as an emancipation from the objectivistic-representational nature that limited art's creations. Such emancipation has repercussions not only on art but also on all the other disciplines, such as science (psychology) and politics (woman's rights), that contributed to liberating our culture from oppression. This is why, for Vattimo, the death of art also refers to the "constitution and modification of social structures and more specifically to the social conditions in which the artist lived throughout the nineteenth century,"[9] when the artist lost that direct contact with the restricted public that used to commission his works. In other words, for Vattimo the end of metaphysics also depends on the "philosophical responses" raised by its society or, as Danto says, by that "technological society" it inhabits. But how did Vattimo acquire this postmetaphysical perspective from Heidegger?

Vattimo's philosophy, weak thought, situates itself after Heidegger's destruction of metaphysics, that is, after the description of Being as "*parousia*" or "*ousia*," which ontologically and temporally means "presence," "*Anwesenheit*."[10] According to this metaphysical perspective, knowledge is nothing other than the correct apprehension of "something objectively present in its pure objective presence [*Vorhandenheit*], which, as Heidegger explained in *Being and Time*, Parmenides already used as a guide for interpreting Being."[11] As we can see, it was at the dawn of Western European thinking that Being was determined by time as presence, allowing it to be thought exclusively in terms of its relation to beings and their cause. This left the difference between Being and beings, the ontological difference, obscured, limiting the conception of Being exclusively to terms of its relation to beings as their cause: Being is only the permanent nominal presence determined as objectness. In this condition, Being has been forgotten in favor of what is called "the condition of the possibility," that is, the rational ground of beings, creating a metaphysical-scientific way of looking not only at the world but also at its artistic production. But where is mankind situated in this aesthetic relation?

Heidegger, in order to avoid the traditional tripartition of man into body, soul, and spirit—that is, in order to avoid locating its essence in a specific faculty, in particular that of Reason, of the rational animal—coined the term "Dasein," which is not the world, nor the subject, nor a propriety of both, but the relation, the in-between, which does not arise from the subject coming together with the world, but is Dasein itself. The central feature of Dasein, along with "thrownness"[12] and "fallenness,"[13] is "existence"[14] because it has to decide how to be. It is this essential characteristic that makes Dasein not a rational being but, more profoundly, a relationship to Being upon which humanity must decide if it wants to exist as "a metaphysical describer of objectivity" or a "postmetaphysical interpreter of Being." The best example of the describer of objectivity can be found in Descartes, for whom the world consists of objects that are already there *as such* even before they are investigated, that is, as if Dasein could only "understand its own being in terms of that being to which it is essentially, continually, and most of all closely related—the 'world' . . . in terms of what is objectively present."[15] If this were the case, our thought would only have to re-present objects in search of objective accounts, but such a philosophy would imply that we all have an impossible God's-eye view for which the truth of things exists in the form of a timeless presence. This is why metaphysics can be defined as the "age of the world picture,"[16] where the world is reduced, constituted, and presented as images.

As we've seen, metaphysics, and more specifically Descartes's conception of ontology, depended upon the images of the world reproduced by modern sciences, which aimed at a timeless description and representation of the way the world really is. If Dasein conceived itself on the basis of what is objectively present, this would imply it is finished, determined, and completed as an object might be; instead Dasein, as long as it exists, always remains open for the future because it implies *"Möglich-sein,"* being possible, possibilities. Heidegger insisted upon this ontological nature of objects, representing not the world as it is but rather as it could be, that is, by questioning the fact that it exists since in contrast to the rest of the objects of the world, as we already said, Dasein has a relationship with its own Being, called "existence." It is a self-relationship, hence a Being-relationship.

Heidegger's ontological recovery of Being showed how aesthetics after metaphysics cannot limit the problem of art by assigning it to either an a priori that legitimates it or to a simple alternative description of the world of art. Rather, aesthetics must seriously consider the question of the very *fact* of art. The recovery of ontology brought forward by the German master in *Being and Time* did not evolve, according to Vattimo, in the realm of philosophy only, but also in the artistic revolutions of the avant-garde of the nineteenth century, such as expressionism, surrealism, and dada. These revolutions arose to defend the fundamental meaning and importance of art for history and human existence; in other words, the artists rebelled against the aestheticism that is latent in every metaphysical theory that ignores the question of art's meaning as such. What constituted the elements for aesthetic reflection were no longer beautiful objects but rather the fact that in general there are works of art that do not satisfy any needs and whose existence is not required by any motive that could justify them. This is why Duchamp's *Fountain* is probably the best example of art's ontological bearing; it created a new world through the originality, novelty, and founding force of the work alone, that is, only for the virtue of art as such. The *Fountain*'s novelty consists in its suspending the public's habitual relationship not only with the world of art (within the boundaries of the museum and images of the world in paintings and sculptures), and also with the objects of the world (after all, *Fountain* was a real urinal, simply turned over onto its back and signed). It is only on the basis of Heidegger's destruction of Being as "something objectively present" that Duchamp was able to emphasize the ontological bearing of art because his *Fountain* is a "transfiguration of the commonplace,"[17] as Danto correctly states. It is also the first incarnation of Heidegger's ontological bearing of art. But how can such a work of art, which emphasizes only its ontological bearing, be created, evaluated, or even enjoyed?

The ontological bearing of art requires that we overcome traditional aesthetic-optical admiration and enter into dialogue with art because our consciousness has always consisted of spiritual contents that may only be realized in linguistic discourses. But why would ontological bearing allow us to enter into discourse with the new work of art if we cannot do so with, for example, a beautiful representation of a landscape? If the world, as Heidegger explained, is a system of meanings into which we are always already thrown, and a work of art founds a new world insofar as it founds a new system of meanings, laws, or links, then that work of art that represents a (recognizable) landscape we could see with our own eyes does not found anything new but only represents once again that system of meanings in which we are already thrown. Instead, a work of art such as the *Fountain*, which founds a new system of meaning, not only projects a new world but also becomes a new proposal, a way to arrange the world in a different manner. These are the sort of works of art that will oblige the public to enter into dialogue in order to possess and to be possessed by the work at the same time. After metaphysics, a work of art is beautiful if its wholeness is rigorously dominated by its own internal law, the law, explains Vattimo, "giving order to its structure, so that each part appears in its necessary links to the whole and the whole is revealed in each of its parts."[18] This internal law not only explains the single structure of each work of art but also demonstrates why all those attempts to find a canon of the beautiful in the past have failed; the internal laws of individual works do not allow for reduction to a norm that might transcend them and on the basis of which they could be evaluated.

It is through the destruction of metaphysics that Dasein becomes the "postmetaphysical interpreter of Being," forced to enter into dialogue with the work of art instead of recognizing the static perfection that it represents.

Heidegger's destruction of metaphysics, that is, the recognition of the ontological bearing of art, has not only allowed us to "question of the very *fact* of
art," but most of all demanded an *interpretative process* that is required to
enter into dialogue with the work. In this process, where the work of art
becomes a point of departure rather than a point of arrival, we can finally
stop asking what art means, what it refers to, or even if it is beautiful, in order to begin asking what it wants to say. But in order to enter into this dialogue it is necessary to understand the meaning of hermeneutics for ontology,
that is, its consequence. It is through Pareyson's hermeneutics that Vattimo
delineates not only the process for the work's interpretation but also its formation. Before venturing into Pareyson's theory of interpretation and how it
is related to Vattimo's aesthetic thesis, let's recall where it is situated in the
history of hermeneutics.[19]

Although hermeneutics, which today has become the *"koiné"* of contemporary thought,[20] has its etymological origins in the Greek god Hermes, the
reputed messenger and interpreter of the gods, it first developed systematically as biblical exegesis and then in a theoretical framework to govern such
exegetical practice.[21] But starting in the eighteenth and early nineteenth
centuries, theologians and philosophers extended it into an encompassing
theory of textual interpretation in general, regardless of the subject matter,
which could be God, the Bible, nature, science, or even art. From the narrow interpretation of sacred texts, hermeneutics became that modern concern of interpretation in general. Essential for Pareyson were Friedrich
Schleiermacher's and Friedrich Nietzsche's theories of interpretation. For
them there are no things (facts) "out there" that could subsequently receive a
certain shape by our (subjective) understanding of them; that is, neither the
interpreter not the interpreted depend on preestablished agreements but
only on an involvement that occurs during knowledge's natural interpretive
process. While Schleiermacher recognized how one always understands a
work "at first as well as and then even better than its author," Nietzsche instead insisted that "there are no facts, but only interpretations, and this is
also an interpretation." Both found in hermeneutics the "ontological dimension" that Heidegger would then transform in the "ontological relation" that
I point out above: Dasein as the in-between that does not arise from the
subject coming together with the world, but in a relationship with its own
Being. This is why for Heidegger Dasein "is in a hermeneutical relation,"[22]
that is, in an involvement in the world that takes the form of an interpretative process. Pareyson, following Heidegger in one of his fundamental

books, *Truth and Interpretation*, explains that the "original ontological relation is necessarily hermeneutic and every interpretation has a necessary ontological nature," meaning "that of truth there is nothing but interpretation and interpretation is only of truth."[23] But how does this process take place in order to acquire, for example, comprehension of a work of art? Pareyson explains this process through the "interpretative act," which is at the core of his philosophy.

The Italian master delineated his hermeneutics in the early 1950s in two of his major books: *Existence and Person* (1950) and *Aesthetics* (1954).[24] He defined interpretation as the "form of knowing in which receptivity and activity are inseparable, and where the known is a form and the knower a person."[25] In these texts he also demonstrated how the comprehension of a work of art does not consist in a panoramic contemplation of the work but only in an interpretation of the "artistic process" through which it has been formed. It is important to point out that by "artistic process" Pareyson does not refer to those technical aspects of the work such as, for example, the actors selected for the film, the screenplay, or the type of special effects used, even though these are, most of the time, the only elements of the work analyzed by critics. Instead, the "artistic process" that Pareyson has in mind is that interpretative process through which the artist has formed the work by pursuing his initial idea. At first this idea does not have a form, but then, little by little, within its forming process (through the artist's procedure) it gains a form that will constitute the internal law I mentioned above. The artistic process gives form to an idea that was unformed and hence indefinite, until it becomes recognizable through the internal law that the completed work indicates. Now, if the work of art is not the result of a sudden intuition of the artist but of that formed process, then, in order to interpret it, one must rethink its formation. This is why Gadamer, in *Truth and Method*, following Pareyson explained that an "aesthetic object is not constituted in the aesthetic experience of grasping it, but the work of art itself is experienced in its aesthetic quality through the process of its concretization and creation."[26]

For Pareyson the work of art is the "perfection of a formation" because the act of forming is "a making that, in making, invents a new way of making."[27] This theory, which he posited in *Aesthetics*, has received applause directly from artists because it recognizes the originality that belongs to each creation and how it cannot be presupposed by any law that could eventually be applied at ease, as Schleiermacher and Nietzsche noticed. Pareyson's theory invites the artist not only to form his work with his own procedures, which will vary through the production of the work, but also to recognize how his own making will also generate (invent) new procedures. A film such as David Lynch's *Mulholland Drive* is a good example of this theory not only because the movie does not follow a linear narration that would imply a previously dictated screenplay, but most of all since it actually started out as a pilot for a TV series and only during its process became a film.[28] In other words, the film *Mulholland Drive* was formed only during the making of something else (the pilot) and was not presupposed but only formed little by little through a concretization and creation, that is, through a "perfection of a formation." Now this perfection of formation is not a simple act of creation but also an act of interpretation because the materials of the film (actors, screenplay, and special effects) are somehow already present in the course of the process in which the "formed form" is revealed. All these elements converge to generate the "forming form," that intimate law of the productive process that, though only completely created at the end of the work, already somehow exists in the course of the process. Just as the production of the film already constitutes an interpretation by Lynch, his interpretative act is, above all, formative, where the form of the film is not only created but also grasped. Aesthetic experience, according to Pareyson, is not only the pleasure attained from the beauty of the made form but also the interpretation that recovers its formation. Such recovery is what often pushes spectators to contemplate the same work of art various times.

What Pareyson's hermeneutics theory underlines is that "making" is nothing else than pure creativity, that is, creation of forms during the same act of making. But isn't this common to all human making? After all, even a driver does not adhere to the letter of the traffic laws he is supposed to follow because there might be roads or situations in traffic that must be managed in different ways. These different and new situations will oblige him not only to invent new driving approaches but also to create his own *style* of driving, which is a permanent component of all practices and productions. It is interesting to notice that although styles are always recognizable, they are impossible to imitate without falling into mere replications because they always include new variables that make them unique within their own procedures. In fact, "making" is common to all human making, but in art it is more emphasized not only because the formative nature of the whole human existence comes to light but also because it is not (always) conditioned by moral, theoretical, or utilitaristic interest. This is why the best art does not create for the sake of morality, knowledge, or profit, but only for aesthetic purposes. But if every "making" contains an element of "risk," since works of art are not always successful (and car accidents do occur), how can the success of art be recognized?

As I explained above, the elements for aesthetical reflection after the end of metaphysics are not necessarily beautiful objects but rather those works of art that do not satisfy any needs and whose existence is not required by any motive that could justify them. Having said this, an interpretation (actualizing itself in the formation of the work of art) is going to be a success or a failure according to a destiny that is not in the hands of the artist but dependent on an "unpredictable element of congeniality," says Vattimo, which is always "involved. The success of the productive and interpretative process is then the model of the happening of truth, the coincidence of forming form and formed form, or image and thing."[29] But how does such happening or event of truth take place in art?

As we will see, Gadamer resolved this problem by radicalizing the aesthetical theory Heidegger exposed in "The Origin of the Work of Art,"[30] (*Der Ursprung des Kunstwerkes*) where for the first time art was defined as the "setting-itself-into-work of truth." But the problem with Heidegger's aesthetical theory was that it did not systematically develop that encounter between the spectator and the work or, as Pareyson would say, between the forming form and the formed form. How this concept of aesthetic enjoyment should be understood is an issue Gadamer solved by fusing together both Heidegger's ontological bearing of art and Pareyson's interpretative process. Such fusion not only explains why truth is the hermeneutic consequence of art's ontological bearing, but also why it is the actual goal of art.

It is no surprise that Gadamer was a direct disciple of Heidegger and an attentive reader of Pareyson. In *Truth and Method* he brought forward a hermeneuticization of ontology in order to displace the scientific conception of truth and method as the unique model for understanding; that is, he removed truth from the exclusive control of method. Although this control was defended by both historicism and positivism, which for decades insisted that the human sciences had to work out proper methods for themselves before they could attain to the status of science, it was a belief based on metaphysical grounds: methods as the sole guarantee and model of validity. But as Gadamer explained, the fact that we apply certain methods to particular objects does not justify the pursuit of knowledge; in other words, what "method defines is precisely not truth. It in no way exhausts it."[31] Method does not exhaust truth because understanding is never an act that can be

secured methodologically and verified objectively, as science tries to per-
suade us, but an experience that we must undergo. In this experience we
not only understand the object we are confronting but also become better
acquainted with ourselves because understanding always brings self-
understanding, and therefore a certain circularity, which Heidegger referred
to as the "hermeneutical circle." But the most important aspect of this process of circular understanding is not that it will never become absolute
knowledge (since Dasein is "finite," that is, conditioned by its historical situation), but that it occurs through the model of "dialogue." This model allowed Gadamer not only to defend the extramethodical truth of the human
sciences but also to avoid the danger of arbitrariness because the "question
concerning the truth of art is identical with that of the truth of the '*Geisteswissenschaften*,' that is to say, with the hermeneutical problem."[32]

This hermeneutical problem came up, as I explained above, once man recognized that he is not "a metaphysical describer of objectivity" but a "postmetaphysical interpreter of Being," since truth is not something that is already given
as an actual present structure but rather an announcement that "demands an
answer rather than an explanation."[33] An explanation would be required if the
meaning of art consisted in manifesting a propositional truth given prior to
and outside of the work, where the work would only be a contingent representation. Although such a propositional truth would somehow give information
regarding the state of things (such as the colors of a landscape, its emotional
condition, or the very structure of Being), it would not stimulate that further
interest that great works of art always produce. This is what Gadamer noticed
of those works of art that became classics: they are works that can never be
completely understood, not because of their complexity but because the "dura-
tion of a work's power to speak directly is fundamentally unlimited."[34] This is
why "understanding," Gadamer says, "is to be thought of less as a subjective act
than as participating in an event of tradition, a process of transmission in
which past and present are constantly mediated."[35] In this tradition the works
of art that will become classics are not those from which we may obtain information from their propositional truth in order to explain them but the ones
whose interpretation will never exhaust them. Such interpretive inexhaustive-
ness occurs in the dialogue with the work of art.

In this dialogue, where we are possessed, that is, led by the work of art
instead of leaders of it, "listening" and "responding" are the two major features that will constitute its truth because, as Vattimo explained, "the task
of art is not to represent the truth of the world but, rather, to take a stance in

the name of a project of transformation."[36] One of the best examples of this can be found in Alfredo Jaar's "Rwanda Project," which illustrates through photographs the struggles between Hutu and Tutsi before the genocide of 1994. His photographs are not really meant to grasp the reality of the massacre more faithfully or to better inform the public about this specific event but to understand "the truth of art as news rather than as the final revelation of human nature or of the world."[37] Jaar's works of art, insists Vattimo, are "an open datum calling for an active interpretation and a practical intervention"[38] since his projects (in the various forms his works take: photographs, postcards, installations) are messages of truth calling the spectator to "listen" and "respond," that is, to enter dialogue. In this dialogue, truth will not only change us but also demand actions that will not leave things as they were; the works are a call for emancipation from the objectivistic, static, and representational nature of metaphysics that limited our actions. But Jaar's art will hold us back from attributing eternal qualities not only to our own interpretations (which would transform them into descriptive and passive judgments) but also to his own works; in other words, it is an invitation to participate, modify, and, in a way, change his own works.

The fact that contemporary art after the end of metaphysics has actually produced works such as Jaar's "Rwanda Project" is a clear indication that aesthetics has overcome metaphysics and that the public is not conceived statically anymore (as a metaphysical describer of objectivity) but actively (as postmetaphysical interpreters of Being). Such postmetaphysical aesthetics not only presupposes that truth can never be secured methodologically but requires that it should be left to our contingent and independent responses. The works of Duchamp, Lynch, and Jaar have been useful not only in underlining the ontological and hermeneutical constitution of art but also in following the formation of Vattimo's aesthetical thesis (*truth as the hermeneutic consequence of art's ontological bearing*), which I uncover in these pages. Of the three works of art I commented on in this brief introduction, Jaar's has a special place in Vattimo's aesthetics, not only because it is the only one he dedicates a whole chapter to but because it is the only one that incarnates completely the two themes (ontology and hermeneutics) and the goal of art (truth) after the end of metaphysics. Jaar's works are points of departure rather than arrival and will help postmetaphysical aesthetics to instill a dialogue between the works and the public in order to engage "the person at all levels and" lead us "to speak of art's truth, of its cosmic nature, and of its ontological meaning."[39]

ART'S CLAIM TO TRUTH

# I *Aesthetics*

# 1 *Beauty and Being in Ancient Aesthetics*

## The "Modernity" of Ancient Aesthetics

The meaning of ancient thought for the history of aesthetics is still largely debated. The interpretative views on this topic have always oscillated between general observations to the effect that the antiquity of Greece and Rome did not develop a detailed inquiry of the question of art (hence the fragmentary presentation of isolated ideas that speak of a philosophical sensibility at a very embryonic stage for the question of art in regard to the beautiful), and the attempts to discover in antiquity the more or less explicit premises of the philosophical theories of modernity. Now, it is obvious that the confrontation of historical inquiry can only occur by means of "our prejudices," since this is the only and inexorable way in which we can "let the texts speak," as it is generally said, addressing to them questions and drawing from them answers so that we can reconstruct a meaningful ensemble rather than a disconnected jumble, giving shape to the figure of the author or of the epoch in question.

However, not every approach is right. This is not because it does or does not correspond to the object of our inquiry. Rather, the value of working hypotheses lie in their depth and completeness, in their degree of elaboration.

Recent studies of ancient aesthetics face precisely this problem with respect to an argument that is already problematic on its own.[1] Indeed, one can start out, like Warry in *Greek Aesthetic Theory*, with the general exigency of studying ancient aesthetics to discover solutions for contemporary problems.[2] The outcome, however, is a dull and narrow-minded representation of what classical Greece—limited to Plato and Aristotle, two of its most eminent representatives—supposedly produced in regard to the beautiful and to art. The basically informative purpose of the book, which is explicitly stated in the book's introduction, does not justify the insufficiency of the approach and the exposition of the theme, at least for the reason that it is accompanied by the claim to contribute to the solution of contemporary problems by recovering and rereading classical texts. The fact is that these supposedly contemporary problems are never clearly stated or defined. In Warry's account we can glean a general sensibility for themes that belong to the contemporary mindset, above all psychoanalysis. Based on such a shaky approach, the author gives an exposition of Plato's and Aristotle's aesthetics and abundantly reconstructs their systems (especially Plato's) through citations that are drawn here and there, and are not always employed correctly or with any sense of order.

Warry's own interest in his uncritically grounded "modernity" prevents him from truly understanding the question of the beautiful, especially in regard to Plato. From the point of view of modern aesthetics, which places the question of art and its subjective conditions at the very center, the writings of classical authors appear fragmented into a series of isolated and unconnected statements, so that it is necessary for the interpreter to intervene in order to give it unity and systematization, as Warry explicitly states.

Reading this book can be pleasant, even though it is not what the author intended. Take for example, the section where the story of the *Symposium* is told, where Alcibiades is called an Athenian playboy, and where the author devotes two pages to explain why the dialogue's title in English should be *The Cocktail Party* rather than *The Banquet*.[3] The same holds true for the psychoanalytical analysis (though it remains quite vague, even from this point of view) of Socrates' speech in the *Symposium*, and a few sophisticated remarks about the hypnotic value of art:

Despite much condemnation of existing poetry, it is stated that the right ideas can best be impressed on the mind of children through poetic fiction. It should have been only a short step from here to realizing that most men are children at heart and that for better or worse they are far more susceptible to inspiration through works of fiction and poetry than through utopian political systems such as kindled the imagination of Plato himself.[4]

In spite of all this, which may be attributable to the popular character of the book, Warry puts forth an interpretation of classical aesthetics that is formulated or implicit in the writings of Plato and Aristotle. According to Warry, such an interpretation may be summed up with the identification of two levels that are distinctly present in the Greek theory of the beautiful, the history of which is constituted by virtue of their manner of composition and discordance: the level of the subconscious and that of consciousness. Plato and Aristotle are fundamentally in agreement in regard to their dichotomous view of man and of aesthetic experience.[5]

In Plato, the dichotomy takes the shape of a juxtaposition between a romantic vision of the beautiful exemplified above all by the *Symposium* and a formal-intellectual vision found in the *Philebus* but running through the entirety of Plato's work, inasmuch as it is identical with the meaning of the beautiful as harmony, measure, and proportion. In Aristotle, the same dichotomy allows us to understand the concept of mimesis and its cognate rhythm. In fact, mimesis is not a principle that establishes art's dependence upon nature. Warry rightly observes that the verisimilitude or necessity of what happens in tragedy is measured with respect to the spectators' mindset rather than to nature, be it human or not, abstractly taken as an object of imitation. Mimesis is, therefore, a principle of external form, that is to say, the necessary proportion between tragedy and the spectators' mindset; it has its correspondent principle of internal form in the proportional structure of the work.[6]

It is here that rhythm is introduced.[7] Rhythm has the same proportional structure of tragedy, though it is considered at a rational (the event) or at an irrational level (meter, music, dance). The "form" that is proportionate to tragedy affects the spectators insofar as it is rhythm; it awakens catharsis. Catharsis is neither religious nor ritual; it does not consist in the purification of emotions: the two levels of the rational and the irrational (identical to the levels of the subconscious and of consciousness) correspond to the moral-intellectual and to the emotional levels of catharsis.[8] Put in these terms, what the author states in the conclusion is a bit unclear: while the conscious level is the site where moral and cognitive values are located and lived through, art, the beautiful, and the ugly regard the level of the subconscious (hypnosis or semi-hypnosis is produced by art). He leaves unanswered the question whether art and the artistically beautiful are to be seen in both levels as it seemed at first glance, or whether their activity is relegated to the level of the subconscious.

## Aristotle's Dissolution of the Ontology of Beauty

The works of Grassi and Perpeet are quite different form the preceding one with respect to their approach to the problem and style of thinking. They corroborate what we already saw, demonstrated in negative fashion, in Warry's reading: the more sharply formulated an approach in its systematic and theoretical aim, the more the texts allow us to grasp them in a more genuine manner, addressing us with an authoritativeness that can put them in dialogue with our contemporary questions.

The points of departure for Grassi and Perpeet are similar, even though in *Die Theorie des Schönen* Grassi formulates them more explicitly, occasionally giving in to the demands of "actuality" (his book, albeit of high value, belongs to a popular series of books). In Grassi's view, a genuine dialogue with ancient aesthetics, which would recognize it as what it genuinely wanted to be, can only start by acknowledging that aestheticism, the end point of all modern aesthetics, has failed, not only in the realm of aesthetics but also and foremost in that of art. Much of the nineteenth-century avant-garde, which for the author boils down to the technicity of Mallarmé and Valéry, consists in the manifestation, by now unstoppable, of a dissolutive process that began with Aristotle's theory of art as representation of the possible, that is, as a purely subjective interpretation of the world, which is entrusted to the will of the individual and to the sphere of emotions, deprived of any ontological foundation.

At the heart of this dissolutive process, however, there is the desire on the part of the avant-garde to recover an ontological foundation. With this observation Grassi distinguishes his position from the generic apocalyptic condemnations of modernity. In this respect, the pages Grassi devotes to the analysis of the philosophical views of nineteenth-century poetics are quite suggestive. These movements bear witness to the efforts made by contemporary art to retrieve an ontological rooting for the beautiful, a rejection of the "aesthetic sphere" as a zone of purely disinterested play and disengagement. Thus, the aim of exploring the aesthetics of antiquity—which the author no longer calls aesthetics but rather the theory of the beautiful, based on his premises—is to retrace the origin of the dissolution of the ontology of the beautiful that culminates with aestheticism to recover, possibly, the principle lines of another way of standing before the beautiful that would satisfy the ontological exigency manifested in today's art. Grassi's exposition—accompanied by a selection of texts[9]—unfolds along the lines outlined by his theoretical approach to the question, with a few occasional unhappy remarks on the opposition among the views of antiquity and modernity and contemporary times, though he is always sustained by a living theoretical interest and an original interpretation.

The classical origins of the beautiful are traced back to poetics and to Homer in particular. In this early stage of development, the notion of beauty still possesses vigorous religious roots: everything that belongs to a superior, even "divine" sphere of life is beautiful, and it is made manifest as luminosity and "evidence" (characteristics that will be important for its subsequent development). This is not to be confused with the evidence of logic, which refers instead to the imposition of the factually given and asserted as objectively present rather than being bound up, like conceptual evidence, with the activity of consciousness as evidence. The beautiful understood as luminosity has an implicitly transcendental character: it is the light whose manifestation lets appear whatever appears as such.

Grassi devotes a substantial analysis of his book to a few texts of Xenophone, where, outside of Plato, the doctrine of beauty developed in the poets and in the mythological-religious tradition took shape. In Xenophone, even more sharply than in Plato, the beautiful is formulated as an ontological predicate, Being's luminous manifestation in its perfection. "The dialectic of the beautiful, as it is developed by the *Phaedro* and the *Symposium* is an *ontological* rather an *aesthetic* dialectic" (author's emphasis).[10] Plato's insistence on *Eros*, too, does not refer to a fall into the sphere of emotions and of subjectivity, which would have no links with Being: "The links among Eros, Beauty, and the Being of things is not aesthetic; it is a metaphysical progression through the *degrees of being*, leading from the world of appearance to Being itself" (author's emphasis).[11] Plato's notion of mimesis does not imply an alternative between representation and imitation understood as copy: art represents ideas insofar as it imitates things. Needless to say, in Plato and in Xenophone the question of art in no way exhausts that of the beautiful; indeed, its constitutive element is nothing other than an aspect of it, so that whatever is said in regard to it can be understood in its distinctive meaning only when seen in the context of a general theory of the beautiful. Thus it retains a strong ontological or more generally religious intonation that, over the centuries, will have deeply shaped the Western tradition, in contrast with the latent aestheticism that comes from Aristotle's legacy, which will eventually culminate with the technological character of contemporary art.

Aristotle is the de facto founder of aesthetics—at least in the sense that Grassi attributes to this term—which by virtue of its identification with aestheticism echoes the meaning that Kierkegaard assigned to this term. Indeed, in Aristotle we see a clearly sharp separation between the beautiful and Being, in the sense that the work of art (i.e., tragedy) can be beautiful not to the extent that it is the luminous manifestation of a perfect character of Being; rather, it is so because it represents a possibility of man. The choice and determination of this possibility is entrusted to the will of the poet, as long as he obeys the law of coherency and completeness.

Grassi reaches this conclusion—which in its general outline can be agreed upon, especially insofar as it concerns the de facto significance of Aristotle for the Western tradition, above and beyond the letter of his texts—by means of a reading that does not always follow a linear path and gives impetus to systematicity at the price of the philological completion of interpretation. As a result, his hasty reduction of all the arts to the imitation of action (which, to be sure, does hold for poetry, even though it leaves out other arts like architecture and music) leaves out the notion of art as imitation of nature. This could have forced to author to set a limit—albeit not necessarily a decisive one—upon the meaning of his "aesthetic" interpretation of Aristotle; the same holds for his exclusive focus on the category of possibility in order to determine the types of actions that tragedy should represent. The category of the necessary, of which the *Poetics* speaks, is liquidated in a very unconvincing manner.[12] Here, too, the author stood before a possible ontological disclosure of Aristotelian theory but failed to grasp it.

Let me repeat that these observations does no in any way undermine to the general meaning of Grassi's interpretation of Aristotle, which he feels compelled to limit in some ways.[13] True, in contrast to the ontological effusion of Plato and of the pre-Platonic tradition, Aristotle affirms a theory of art as construction that succeeds not so much because it gives access to being as because it assumes control of productions that are endowed with internal coherence, whatever their relationship to nature or history. Aristotle reaches this conclusion, as mentioned earlier, by assigning to the poet the task of imitating the possible rather than nature: praxis, of which tragedy is an imitation, is just one among the possibilities of man. Not every action or event constitutes praxis: the only condition of poetic imitation is that praxis be an action endowed with completion and internal coherence. In replacing being with the possible (hence the poet's will, his subjective interpretation of reality) Aristotle reduces to the level of fable, of fiction, of arbitrary invention the original meaning of *mythos*, which instead referred to the indistinct unity of word and action.

A confirmation that Aristotle was the first thinker who separated the beautiful from the theory of being, is indirectly found in the classical theorists of antiquity (e.g., Quintillian) who concocted a didactic theory of art. Such a theory could arise only in order to find a justification for art once it had lost its original relation to being. The persistence of aesthetic theories of a didactic-pedagogical, moralistic, and *engaged* type throughout the Western tradition persuasively corroborates the progressive dissolution of the ontology of art, which began with Aristotle to culminate with the aestheticist and technical nature of modernity. Another, parallel phenomenon of late antiquity is the connection, increasingly stressed, between beauty and appearance, which is no longer the same appearance and self-manifestation of being as it had been up to Plato, for example, as it is exhibited in Stoicism. This degradation, too, of appearance is directly linked to the weakened meaning of imitation and fable in Aristotle. The two currents that came to light in ancient aesthetics had no mediation in antiquity whatsoever, nor at a later period; rather, they were persisted, separately, within our tradition, up to our epoch. Following these premises, the Aristotelian school did not generate aesthetic theories but poetic treatises: even the prevalence (when "ontological" aesthetics continued to live in metaphysics and theology) of poetics over the philosophical theories of the beautiful and of art in late antiquity and in the Middle Ages is due to Aristotle's influence, as well as to the gradually technical characterization of the beautiful.

It would be possible to give a more in-depth analysis of the mediation between these two currents of ancient aesthetics—the ontological and the technical—on the condition that one made clear the meaning of ontology and of the ontological character of the beautiful that appears in Plato. I have already said that Grassi's interpretation is a bit lacking in regard to certain aspects of Aristotelian thought, which could open the way for a possible ontological discourse in his own thought as well. Does Aristotle's contention that poetry's task lies in representing the possible really amount to a separation of art from every ontological source? Are not the possibilities of man, a kind of "being," to be imitated by the poet?

## The Ontology of the Beautiful as Existential Foundation

Such objection might seem captious, if it had not been raised by Perpeet in *Antike Aesthetik*, the last of the texts I shall examine here. For him, there is no opposition between the ontological foundation of the beautiful and the reference to man—they are one. Perpeet, too, starts with a critical attitude toward modern aesthetics, though less explicitly than Grassi, not so much because he sees in it the dissolution and fall into aestheticism; rather, he refuses to identify the question of the beautiful with that of art. Behind his attitude there is the same sensitivity for the ontological question of the beautiful, for which he seeks solutions in ancient aesthetics. Just as Grassi had marked out the theory of the beautiful from aesthetics (the last being necessarily condemned to aestheticism), so Perpeet sharply draws the line between aesthetics (i.e., the theory of the beautiful) and a theory of art. He focuses his attention only on aesthetics, thus overturning, almost therapeutically, the exclusivist focus upon art in modern aesthetics. This is why he devotes only one line to Aristotle (to the effect that he "is the founder of the theory of art, but not of aesthetics") throughout his otherwise detailed discussion of the subject.[14]

The question left open by Grassi's work—whether it is precisely in Aristotle that one should seek out the mediation between the technical and the ontological character of art—is not given an answer in Perpeet's work. However, he does provide an indication of the path one might follow to answer this question. In fact, in his own work, the ontological reference of the beautiful, which in Grassi remained only at the conceptual level, is made precise as a reference to the being of man.

Thus, Perpeet speaks of an existential and anthropological outcome of Platonic aesthetics.[15] This does not imply that Plato separated himself from the ontological-religious tradition of the beautiful as it was originally formulated by pre-Socratic poets and thinkers. On the contrary, this tradition acquires for the first time in his work the philosophical shape of a problem, accounting for the fact Plato, the first philosopher to arrange in an orderly manner the philosophical question of the beautiful, does not reach a complete systematization but rather formulates a series of hypotheses that are dialectically linked together.

The anthropological and existential outcome of Platonic aesthetics, which does not contradict but rather makes clear the ontological meaning of the tradition, can be grasped precisely with respect to this tradition. We should also keep in mind that what is in full view in the concept of the beautiful as luminosity—which is predominant in this tradition, and which remains the determinant element of aesthetics up to Plotinus—is the link among the beautiful, luminosity, and vitality. The luminosity of the beautiful is not the appearance of static being; rather, it is the imposition of the living being, well proportionate and adapted to live. It seems possible, for the author, to state in the conclusion of his inquiry that the ancients never shared the sense or idea of what we call natural beauty, in the sense in which this term was understood in the Christian tradition, with its belief in the divine creation of the cosmos.[16] *Policletus' Canon* is not a specific and isolatable fact, rather it acquires a meaning that is far broader than is usually assigned to it. It becomes a typical manifestation of the whole mindset of ancient aesthetics, for which the beautiful is understood only in relation to the living, and among the living to man in particular.[17] So if it is true that ancient aesthetics was entirely united in its identification of beauty with luminosity—hence the idea of the beautiful as an ontological predicate and self-manifestation of being—it is equally true that the being of which the beautiful is manifestation and splendor is nothing other than living being, that is, man.

Plato, who in the *Greater Hippias* defines once and for all the problematic sphere to which the philosophical theory of the beautiful would belong for many centuries, reached this conclusion by formulating a series of hypotheses that culminated with the attempt, in the *Timaeus*, to define the beautiful in terms of measure. This attempt can be correctly grasped only when seen in relation to the ethical meaning that the measure acquires in Plato. The beautiful is both proportion and measure, in a very dynamic sense: for the Greeks "music" is the unity of word, dance, melody, rhythm, and mimicry. Beauty is perceived as measure only when it is imitated, that is, when it is lived as a moral attitude, measured in all the aspects of life, rather than in the perceptions of art only. By virtue of this anthropological reference of the beautiful as measure, Plato took over and deepened the links between luminosity and vitality that was already pervasive within the ancient aesthetics of

Greece. The same conclusions—as Perpeet suggests—is reached by Plotinus, the other great representative of ancient aesthetics, though in a more explicit manner. Plotinus saw much more clearly than Plato that to enjoy the beautiful is to be assimilated to it, living it in an experience of ecstasy. Once again, the ontological reference that grounds the beautiful is inseparable from the anthropological reference.

Hence, it is more sharply in Perpeet's work than in Grassi's that ancient aesthetics constitutes a compact unity by virtue of its ontological and anthropological mark, quite distinct from that of subsequent aesthetics. This seems to be the sense of the final chapters of his book, which are devoted to the origins of Christian aesthetics and to its biblical foundations, which transform it into a completely new and relatively autonomous phenomenon. In regard to Grassi's view that modern aesthetics has an aestheticist and technical character, it would be interesting to explore to what extent precisely the novel element brought about by the biblical tradition has contributed to determine this process, in which case it would be no longer solely or principally referred back to Aristotle. Perhaps Aristotle belongs much more deeply to the Greek tradition than it might appear from this interpretation, whereas modern aesthetics, with all its technicity and subjectivism, belongs to the world that was inaugurated by Christianity. This seems to be, implicitly, the (romantic) thesis put forth by Perpeet. His conclusions, however, lead us back to our point of departure: if, in fact, the ontological foundation of the beautiful is nothing other than its anthropological and existential foundation for ancient aesthetics, it seems that the aestheticism and subjectivism that should have been exorcized or at least put in question have paradoxically returned in full force at the end of the process that instead should have led to the recovery of Being. It may well be possible that, despite the theoretical impetus of these two works, we are still in need of a broader discussion of what we mean when we speak of ontology.

# 2 Toward an Ontological Aesthetics

## Art, Aesthetics, and Ontology

Even though the following essays attempt to present an ontological approach to the question of art, or at the very least to shed light on its exigency from a variety of perspectives, it seems necessary to clarify preliminarily[1] how the links between poetry, and art more generally, and ontology are addressed in the following pages and how this inquiry stands in regard to contemporary aesthetics.

What does it mean, in general, to pose the question of art ontologically or to raise ontological demands in the realm of aesthetics? The question immediately implies a leap from the limited sphere of aesthetics (but, as we shall see, the very existence of this sphere is in question) to philosophy. At this level, the first possible answer is that an ontological formulation of the question of art or of any other philosophical problem has to do with elaborating a discourse that will not be oblivious to what Heidegger called the "ontological difference," a question that assumes first and foremost ontological difference as its central theme.[2] The ontological difference is the relation that joins and disjoins Being and beings. To illustrate the meaning of such difference, we can make recourse to another idea of Heidegger's, which has basically the same meaning, namely, the *epoché*. Its meaning should not be confused with the meaning it has in Husserl's phenomenology, even though it would be easy to show a relation, where Heidegger's *epoché* was revealed as a genuine foundation within Being of the necessity of the *epoché* (as a subjective attitude) of which phenomenologists speak.

Heidegger's *epoché* is the character by which Being reveals and conceals itself simultaneously in the appearing of beings, that is, things and persons that inhabit the world.[3] In fact, Being gives itself insofar as it is the light within which beings appear.[4] On the other hand, Being as such withdraws precisely so that beings can appear, subsisting in some way in the horizon it has itself instituted. Being *makes* and *lets* beings appear: one could say that Being makes place for them, giving to this expression all the ambiguous meaning to which it is susceptible. Being makes place for beings insofar as it provides the horizon within which they come forth; Being withdraws without calling attention upon itself and lets the horizon be free.

Such a formulation is always inadequate, because it conjures images of "a place" Being could occupy in lieu of beings and vice-versa, so that Being, thus understood, always remains a species of being, albeit the most supreme. By contrast, what is fundamental in Heidegger's theory of *epoché* is his emphasis on difference: the recognition that Being, by virtue of which beings are, can never be confused with beings. In other words, Being can never be conceived as an entity, not even as the maximum of all beings. This is clear, after all, if we consider that whenever we ask what the Being of beings is, we never seek a cause or an origin; the fact that beings derive or come from such and such a place does not in the least resolve the question of being; if what is shown to be the cause or origin is itself a being, then the question of being is posed once again in its entirety, even with respect to itself. According to Heidegger, it is characteristic of the history of Western metaphysics to have mistaken the question of being for the question of the "why," of the origin, as a result of which thought was put off track identifying Being with beings, thereby forgetting the ontological difference, that is, the fact that Being is irreducible to any specific being.[5]

Heidegger's notion of *epoché* has a very important corollary at the level of philosophy of history. In withdrawing (*epoché* also carries, literally, the meaning of retention and suspension), Being not only makes place for beings in the spatial sense of the term, but also and more importantly in a temporal sense. Being withdraws itself and lets beings distend themselves within time. So there is authentic history only insofar as Being is always yet to come. And the epochs of history are made possible by the epochal character of being. In other words, it is only because Being withdraws that there is authentic history, possibility, future, and so on.

From this summary description of the ontological difference we should retain the negative character of the relation that appears to be established between Being and beings. It would be quite problematic to see how knowledge and reflection on beings—for example, on the art world as a determinate region of beings—could be given at all without forgetting and pushing aside the ontological difference.

If the exigency not to forget the ontological difference (whether this exigency can be concretely met remains to be seen) gives us an indication of the meaning of the adjective in the expression "ontological aesthetic," there is still something to say about the meaning of the substantive in the same expression. The latter should become clear in the following pages as a result of the discussion of the ontological character of our inquiry.

Let me state provisionally that by aesthetic I mean what historically goes under this term, that is, a reflection on the structure and value for human life of the experiences that put us in touch with "works of art," or the beautiful. Thus understood, aesthetic discourse is very distinct from the discourse of the arts, of poetics, and of criticism, insofar as it concerns the structure and value of aesthetic experience *überhaupt*, without attempting to modify, evaluate, or produce this or that experience in particular.

In what follows, I shall argue that an aesthetic understood in this way is extremely problematic. It is not necessary, therefore, to defend any further the validity of my "definition," which is taken here merely as a point of departure delimiting the field of inquiry without any rigid determination. However, note that what has been stated here in very generic terms is a philosophical concept that has became broadly popular in modern philosophy from Kant onward. Since then (outside of Hegelianism), philosophers have generally thought that their task was to give a "transcendental" description of the structures of human experience, taking such a description as a foundation insofar as it highlighted the conditions of possibility of various kinds of experiences. This mindset has penetrated into aesthetics as well, since many contemporary aesthetics may be traced back to it; these are the same aesthetics with respect to which we defend the exigency of an ontological discourse on art. I shall begin then with a general examination of these aesthetic currents and of the extent to which they do or do not correspond to the exigency to speak of art, without forgetting the ontological difference or the epochal character of being.

## Aesthetics and the Foundational Metaphysical Mindset: The Ideal of Explanation

In this chapter I propose to clarify how the methods and outcomes of the principal currents of contemporary aesthetics are complicit with what in Heidegger's language is called metaphysics. That is a type of thought constructed on the forgetting of the ontological difference. These aesthetic trends, and above all the philosophies to which they more or less explicitly refer, still conceive knowledge in general and philosophy in particular in the language of metaphysical foundationalism.

As is well known, the foundational ideal of knowledge appeared for the first time in the philosophical canon, in a definitive and rigorous manner, with Aristotle, who took it over from earlier philosophers and gave it its definitive meaning: to know means knowing the causes. After all, Aristotle's polemics against Plato revolve around what exactly the proper conception of the foundation should be. In Plato, we can find a way of recollecting the ontological difference in his insistence that *ontos on* inhabits a region which is not identical with the region of sensible things. Instead, Aristotle massively defends the exigency for knowledge of grasping (i.e., encountering) being once and for all, since one cannot go back ad infinitum; why, then, should one concede that genuine being resides in other entities (i.e., ideas) rather than in sensible beings? By means of this Aristotelian reasoning the foundational mindset triumphed in European thought, thereby removing from the debate the ontological exigency that had remained alive in Platonic dialectics.[6]

This foundationalist spirit has survived throughout the entire course of Western philosophy, and appears once again in contemporary philosophy and the aesthetics that hark back to it. It is needless to say that the foundationalist spirit forgets the ontological difference, since if the Being of beings must be given in some way, it must be given, in turn, as a specific being. As Heidegger rightly observed, the thought that is inspired by the ideal of the foundation paradoxically culminates in the total lack of foundation, thereby justifying by way of its outcome the need of an ontological recovery of thought.[7]

In spite of my reservations about making any claims in regard to the completeness or historical accuracy of the scheme that I am outlining here to "situate" my argument, it seems possible to identify three main currents within contemporary philosophy, and therefore within aesthetics, often grouped together in different ways in common culture, in the critical currents as well as in philosophical aesthetics. What is striking in this landscape is the presence, often unconscious, of a substantively Hegelian mindset. This mindset, of course, must be sought out in those philosophers who refer explicitly to Hegel, above all Marxist philosophers. It is precisely Marxism that, having proposed to break definitively with any equivocal confusion with positivist determinism (though not with materialist determinism), has gradually recovered the very substance of Hegel's thought: dialectics and the idea of totality. This dialectical attitude is common to the authors who publicly declare themselves to be revisionists like Karl Korsch,[8] as well as authors who are more explicitly orthodox theorists like Georg Lukacs.[9] For all of them, rationality consists in understanding every aspect of reality in reference to a totality. It could be objected that here totality is not conceived in dogmatic fashion as fully given: but the fact remains that what is stated here is precisely a determined ideal of Reason and of thought. Lukacs's recent *Heidelberger Ästhetik*,[10] in which the outcomes of a decade-long reflection are brought together, is a massive effort to articulate an understanding of the phenomenon of art in its different aspects and in its historical determinations with the totality of the historical process.

But even above and beyond the philosophical currents that explicitly acknowledge their links to Hegel, the presence of a dominant Hegelian mindset seems testified to by the personal itinerary of philosophers like Sartre (who, having started out as an existentialist, has gradually returned to Hegel through his increasingly closer debate with Marxism) or by the ideal of knowledge as demythologized explanation that is largely dominant in our culture, criticism, and journalism, even where any explicit reference to the totality of the historical process that is constitutive of dialectics is recognized as a problem.[11]

Note that the larger part of contemporary culture, as testified to by the importance increasingly assumed by contemporary psychoanalysis, conceives of knowledge as comprehension of a particular phenomenon, with respect to a background that can disclose its true meaning. From this perspective, aesthetics always presents itself to a lesser or greater extent as a "dialecticizing" of art; in other words, aesthetics makes it its task to understand and explain art by placing art in relation with the general structure of spirit, history, society, the evolution of styles, language, and so on. We could speak in a broad sense of aesthetics having a "structuralist" mindset, in the sense that knowledge is viewed as the collocation of specific structures onto broader structures, into more complete organisms.

According to this mindset, the ideal of knowledge is that of the foundation, however one understands the ultimate authority to which totality has to be referred, even when there is no question of an ultimate authority at all. A specific being, or type of experience, is known when it is referred back to a totality in respect to which it is defined; the Being of a being is its dialectical link to the whole. The foundation is totally identified with explanation in the sense that dialectics always constitutes the coming to consciousness of the links. (In Hegel's thought the identification of foundation with explanation is complete and paradigmatic: self-consciousness is the end point of the dialectical-foundational process. And in this respect, too, much of the contemporary mindset reveals itself to be a watered down Hegelianism.)

This way of conceiving knowledge as dialectical process—whether it acknowledges an ultimate authority in the self-consciousness of Spirit or in praxis, or whether it is content with constructing units that are never definitive—reveals the specific character of foundationalist thought: namely, that it always culminates with the lack of foundation. If there is no totality, not even ideally so, with respect to which minor totalities could be explained and justified, the foundation is reduced to the founding act itself. However, if there is an end point of the spiritual process as in Hegel, this will be identical with spirituality itself; here, too, the will to foundation never encounters a true foundation but rather finds itself always and everywhere.

## Aesthetics and the Metaphysical Mindset of the Foundation: Neo-Kantianism and Phenomenology

In the perspective outlined so far, neo-Kantianism (which is the other attitude that has a distinctive place in contemporary aesthetics) does not present a valid alternative to the various forms of Hegelianism. By neo-Kantianism, I mean not only or principally the philosophical movement that goes historically under this name but also the general current of thought that is visible in different authors; nor should we forget the permanent influence exerted by Ernst Cassirer's neo-Kantianism in Germany and by his disciples in the United States.

In my view, neo-Kantianism is a philosophical attitude that conceives of philosophy above all as a philosophy of culture, that is, as a systematic presentation of the different activities of man, each of which is referred back to its own a priori, to the directions of consciousness. In this view, aesthetics is understood as a transcendental description of the structure of the experience of the beautiful and of art, its realm of possibility insofar as it is the identification of the dimension of consciousness in which it is actualized.[12] Here too we encounter a foundationalist attitude, with less metaphysical pretension, if you will—and this is the meaning of the recovery of Kant after Hegel. The foundation, understood in this way, is not ontological-metaphysical, but transcendental. It remains to be seen to what extent this way of conceiving and practicing philosophy is not an instance of scholarly philosophizing, an instance of the "technical" transformation of philosophy, which distracts it from the task of discussing the great systems of thought; and whether a philosophy that no longer responds to questions about the great systems of thought that are addressed by the world ends up objectively promoting irrationalism, handing these questions over to fideism or to the producers of the mythologies of mass culture to be resolved.

From my perspective, the outcome of neo-Kantianism is the same as that of the Hegelian mindset: philosophy is knowledge of the modes in which Spirit operates, so it is ultimately self-consciousness, totally closed to the possibility of truly encountering something other than Spirit itself.

A testimony to the living presence of the Kantian idea of foundation in contemporary philosophy may be found in the current fashion of phenomenology, which after all does present itself as transcendental phenomenology. *The Crisis of the European Sciences*[13] shows clearly that, for Husserl, phenomenology is simply a matter of taking up the Kantian program and "radicalizing" it; note that it is a kind of Kantianism that is not very different from that of the neo-Kantians, that is to say, deprived of any possible metaphysical openness, reduced only to the problem of the foundation for knowledge's validity. For the Husserl of *The Crisis of the European Sciences*, Kant had not been critical enough in formulating his critique, because he presupposed that he could develop a theory of the a priori that would ground science, without taking into account the life-world in which both the scientist and the philosopher lived. Philosophy "cannot fulfill its primal establishment as the universal and ultimately *grounding science*" (my emphasis) if it leaves this realm to its anonymity." It cannot admit any "presuppositions, no basic sphere of beings beneath itself of which none knows, which no one interrogates scientifically, which no one has mastered in a knowing way."[14]

In Husserl and in his followers, the plan to "radicalize" Kant by focusing the attention on the *Lebenswelt*—the pre-categorial and the way in which, in its midst, an experience is structured in clear and intelligible forms—ended up with the abandonment of the rigid transcendentalism of the neo-Kantian school, for the sake of a new metaphysical attempt, oriented more or less in the direction of naturalism or in conversation with Marxist historicism.[15]

In regard to the question of knowledge as foundation, phenomenology does not present a true alternative to neo-Kantianism insofar as it remains faithful to the Kantian program. To the extent that it opens itself to metaphysical developments, phenomenology manifests its vocation to take the foundation as a way of locating the rational activity of man in the midst of a nature that has become synonymous with being. Once again, the ontological difference is forgotten, the ground-foundation (*fondo-fondazione*) of beings is simply the undifferentiated totality of beings considered dynamically as life that supplies a basis to history and to cultural productions, as well as ground from which the definite forms of experience originate.[16]

The naturalist vocation of phenomenology is evident and more concretely spelled out in its reflection on art: this, for me, is illustrated by the latest developments in systematic aesthetics, like that of Mikel Dufrenne.[17]

In outlining by way of samples the contemporary philosophical and aesthetic landscape, or at least the methodological ideas that appear in it, I intended to show that given the persistence of a foundationalist and metaphysical mindset, in its various forms, none of the philosophical methods discussed so far satisfy the exigency of attending to and thematizing the ontological difference. From the point of view of this exigency, the foundationalist methods, albeit cursorily described, end up reducing thought to an activity of pure and tautological self-reflection of Spirit, or at most of "Life."

The metaphysical ideal of foundation is contradictory: insofar as it claims to have reached the foundation and "possess" it by leaving nothing unexplained, it removes any genuine possibility of grounding because it does not really encounter anything or anyone other than itself that is not reduced to the activity of Reason. One could speak here of a kind of natural dialectics in the sense that the exigency of a foundation is a genuine one; foundationalist thought arises in order to satisfy this exigency but betrays it instantly. The proof of such a betrayal is the groundlessness with which metaphysics culminates in its latest (and final) representatives, or more simply the incapacity to encounter an other, something other that would be maintained in its otherness. Indeed, the foundation that metaphysics discovers is valid only to the extent that it is recognized by the subject. The subject, then, is the true foundation: in the activity of grounding, the subject encounters nothing other than itself.

This, indeed, is the genuine exigency that remains concealed in the metaphysical instinct of grounding: the search for the *Grund*, dominating the entire Western philosophical speculation, stems from the somehow implicit certainty that the Being of beings is not identical with beings. What in the history of philosophy became the search for the ground in the sense of grounding was originally just consciousness, more or less obscure, of the fact that the Being of beings is not identical with beings; or, if you will, that the truth of beings consists in disclosing their openness to the relation with something that is not a being, one that can never be reduced to the ground-grounded chain.

## The Positive Meaning of the Epochality of Being

If, once we reach the idea of ontological difference, it is quite easy to emphasize the "ontic" or metaphysical character of the philosophies that have historically followed one another and that still share the field of contemporary philosophy, it is difficult to spell out the character that philosophy or aesthetics should possess in order not to miss from the outset the only authentic question, that is, the question of being. As aesthetics it should place at the center of its inquiry a consideration of the problem of art, but as a philosophical aesthetic—and precisely as philosophy—it should keep in mind the central philosophical question of the relation, and difference, between Being and beings.

The difficulty of elaborating an ontological aesthetics is far more radical than it might seem at first sight, and concerns not only aesthetics but every specific or "specialized" discourse of philosophy that wants to constitute itself in an ontological perspective.

The epochal character of Being—namely, its permanent difference from beings—also signifies that philosophy can in no way lay claim to having attained Being by way of deepening its knowledge of beings. This was the presupposition on which the great metaphysics of our tradition were established; they always assumed that the relationship between Being and beings was basically positive, that Being reveals itself, gives itself, manifests itself, spreads itself, realizes itself in Beings; so knowledge of beings, albeit by way of analogy, would supply knowledge of Being.

However, if, as we have seen in the case of Heidegger's ontology, the ontological difference and the epochal character of Being prevent us precisely from establishing such a positive relationship between Being and beings, what is the meaning of the specific philosophical investigations of the single philosophical disciplines? Here, paradoxically, ontology could be in agreement with those perspectives that deny the very possibility of a philosophical aesthetics on the basis of empirical, neopositivistic, and—in Italy—actualistic premises.[18] From the view of ontology, any specific philosophical discourse that takes a determined field of human experience as its object is to be condemned to the ontic realm. After all, Heidegger conducts a very explicit polemic against aesthetics, ethics, and logic in the name of the inexorable, and perhaps not merely historical, link that these disciplines maintain with metaphysics, that is to say, ontic thought.[19]

Put in these terms, the question that we are engaging here becomes decisive and full of developments. In fact, it is a matter of seeing whether or not, in a specific case, it is possible to embrace Heidegger's lesson without reducing philosophy to monosyllables, to *Winke*, to nostalgic and evocative discourses, as Heidegger seems to do in his latest writings. The very lack of a Heideggerian school of thought may be explained not so much with the obscure characteristic of his writings—which are not impossible to understand—nor with the "personal" feature of his own thought (which, on the contrary, blocks any recourse to personalism, intimacy, autobiography) as with the objective difficulty of elaborating a discourse once the epochality of Being has been acknowledged.

Now, is the epochality of Being to be conceived really as a negative relationship between Being and beings? What has been said above concerning the authentic meaning that is concealed in the demand for a foundation that is defended by metaphysics sheds light, in my view, on the fact that the ontological difference does not simply signify that Being is not a being, but also positively that the truth of a being consists in its relationship with the other, in being open to an other that is radically other than itself. The fact that this formulation of the ontological difference is, at least in a certain sense, positive means simply that if the truth of beings consists in the openness to the radically other, such an openness belongs in the end to beings themselves. Even though it remains substantially apophatic, the investigation of the structure of beings is no longer something irrelevant: the very structure of beings is not closed upon itself, so that the approach to Being would have nothing to do with the knowledge of these structures themselves; rather, the story of the metaphysical mindset reveals that beings manifest a breach, a discontinuity, an openness to the other.

It is clear, after all, that there is a positive meaning of the relationship between Being and beings, even if the epochality of Being is understood more radically than Heidegger intended: the self-concealing of Being cannot be conceived as "being present" somewhere outside of the world of beings, as if Being really were something or someone that is given somewhere, hiding itself. Actually, Being is not, except as *epoché*: if you will, Being is nothing but its history, its epoch. For example, the epochs cannot be compared to one another, as if they were different modes of manifesting and concealing a being that is not totally given, somehow "existing." Being is the illumination of the realm within which beings appear. It is of no interest here to follow all the general ramifications of this interpretation of epochality; instead, I should point out that if interpretation holds knowledge of the epoch, and therefore of beings, it is the only possible path of access to Being. And it is an authentic path of access to Being to the extent that Being, not reduced to beings, does not stand outside or above the epoch.

Only by focusing on the positivity of the epoch of Being can one find a path for developing authentically the discourse initiated by Heidegger, not only on the plane of aesthetics but also of philosophy in general. To do so, it is necessary to recognize that perhaps Heidegger, by pushing himself toward what is essentially an apophatic philosophy, at the very limit of silence, ended up conceiving the presence and absence of being in an ontic manner.[20] In other words, he did not clearly see that the epoch of Being constitutes its only mode of being, and therefore is a positive way of approaching it.

## Two Characteristics of Ontological Aesthetics

Let us see then what kind of indications emerge from the formulation of the positivity of the epoch of Being. First of all, for an ontology that does not consider Being as a completely actualized structure that could function as support and substance of beings, but rather considers Being as an event that remains always to come, an origin that is always originating. Philosophizing signifies acknowledging essence, in the originary sense in which Heidegger employs the word *Wesen* in German, not as a substantive but as a verbal infinitive. As a first approximation, this means that philosophical investigation on the essence of beings can never be an investigation into their permanent and rigid structure, beyond their particular and accidental modifications; rather, it is an effort to single out the actual modes of occurrence of beings within the horizon of Being. For example, what ontology can say in the case of man's essence is not that man is always and necessarily this or that, but rather that in the determined epoch of Being in which we are living man *west* (is, essentially becomes, or simply occurs) in this or that modality.

However, this is still just approximation. The ontological question about the essence of things cannot merely mean that characteristics of things as event has been recognized; rather, it means more consistently that things are the event of Being. To sum up: for classical, ancient, and medieval philosophy the question about the essence sought out the universal and necessary structure of particular beings, or even the most supreme being to which such a structure was bound; in modern philosophy to ask about the essence basically signifies seeking the foundation, the condition of possibility, the critical accounting for the specific being; in the perspective of ontology the question about the essence is transformed, once again, to ask "what is a being" means asking what is the business of such a being with Being.

Thus, two conditions are required so that there can be a philosophy of this or that experience, of this or that region of beings from the perspective of ontology: first, essence must be conceived as event; second, essence must be grasped as the event of Being.

One of the consequences of the first condition—insofar as aesthetics is concerned—is above all that ontology of art is not placed along with other aesthetics as an alternative proposal of a different description of aesthetic experience and of the world of art. The aesthetics that ontology enters into dialogue with, and which allow themselves to be led philosophically to the dimension of metaphysical consciousness and of its history—as I have attempted to do in a cursory manner in the preceding paragraph—constitute authentic modes of being of art itself in the present epoch of Being. In other words, they do not represent alternative, different descriptions of the phenomenon that the ontological philosopher could claim to have reached more authentically and more originally than others; rather, they basically grasp the same mode of being of art of our epoch. In other words, they are themselves part of the region of beings that is to be understood ontologically.

The obvious objection to this formulation is that here I am somehow repeating the same violence perpetuated by Hegel against all philosophies other than his own. They were reduced to particular aspects, symptomatic of the entire situation of history, which could be understood authentically only by Hegelian philosophy. Now, in spite of every declaration of the good will to dialogue, it is true that other perspectives change from being about a situation to becoming simple *elements* of the situation that has to be interpreted from my perspective, so that they always undergo a certain weakening (*depotenziamento*); this has to do with the recognition of the interpretative structure of knowledge. However, this phenomenon should not be confused with Hegelian dialectics, which always realizes itself from the perspective of the absolute, which always presupposes the full presence of the consciousness of totality. Here instead one moves on a plane where, even though one recognizes that the inevitable and constitutive feature of interpretation is the fact that it always becomes the object of an interpretation, the logic of interpretation cannot be dialecticized into a definitive schema with the situation, or closed off into a necessary frame, in order to draw from such a necessity the same persuasive force as the system.

In sum, it is not a matter of reading other aesthetics as necessary components of the history of Being that somehow would be known otherwise; however, since the epoch of Being is constituted by the concrete mode of the being of art as much as it is by reflection on art, it is necessary to elaborate the knowledge of the epoch of Being and of art in its midst, in light of the outcomes of aesthetic thought. Ontological aesthetic is, from this perspective, exactly the opposite of claiming to reach somehow the pure essence of the phenomenon, suspending in Cartesian fashion every cultural prejudice about its structure. In this, it is recognizable as a philosophy of culture or as a cultural philosophy: there is no authentic structure of the phenomenon covered, as it were, by cultural suprastructures;[21] the only mode of being pertaining to the phenomenon is its integral mode of being historical, which is embodied in the concreteness of our ways of relating to it. From this point of view, ontological discourse on art has not only the outcome of aesthetics, understood as concrete modes of the being of art in our present epoch, as its thematic content; it also takes up the data of poetics and, as we shall see, the very products of art. In fact, the production of determinate artworks, the invention of styles, or even the proposal at the level of criticism

of ways of reading certain artworks of the past is not merely within the purview of art and criticism; rather, it reaches deep into the very structure and
essence of art as long as one understands "*Wesen*" as event.

Once again, here one could refer to Hegel, who accomplished the greatest
attempt to integrate the whole history of art into aesthetics (just as he integrated the whole history of philosophy into philosophy). However, he did so
from the perspective of dialectics, which implied the actualized consciousness of totality, the point of view of the absolute.

The danger in formulating the problem in this manner is not so much a
return to Hegel as it is the confusion of "planes," which could erase with a
single stroke the entire work carried out by aesthetics in our century—above
all the work carried out by the Italian aesthetics that freed itself from Gentile's actualism and its unifying fury—thus reaching precise distinctions,
and rigorously locating the level of philosophical discourse, technical discourse, and so on. Now, without neglecting the importance of these distinctions, it is a matter of defending along with them the exigency of an
integral investigation of the phenomenon of art.[22] In this view, even the
philosophical reading of the work of a poet becomes aesthetic in its full
right, where by philosophical reading I understand the shelling out of the
frame of the human condition present in the work as well as the study of
how the poetic work concretely modifies the very meaning of poetry. In
other words, aesthetics has to do with everything that concerns the meanings of the phenomenon of art, from the transcendental description of aesthetic experience to the definition of the meaning a given artwork has for
our present epoch.

As always happens whenever an exigency is raised, it is possible that this
formulation sounds still too excessive, if not imprecise. The problem,
though, is clear: to recover the possibility of an integral reading of art, even
by putting provisionally the exigency of distinctions between parenthesis,
with a view to liquidating once and for all the concept of philosophy as pure
description of the structures of experience, where the exigency of foundation is met in a purely tautological manner.

So far, however, the exigency that has been defended is merely that of
considering the entire event of art as an event by refusing to isolate an aspect
within it that would be taken to be permanent and essential, and for this
reason assigned to philosophical reflection. But such an integral consideration of the art phenomenon would still be a pure and simple description of
structures, albeit considered as events, unless one understood a second mo-

ment, in which *Wesen* is not seen merely with respect to its being an event but to its openness to Being, also.[23]

If the genuine exigency present in the metaphysical mindset of the foundation is that of opening to the relation with an irreducibly wholly other, an ontology of art will have to show, at all the levels of description alluded to above, all the breaches through which the event of Being makes itself visible as the happening of Being. In this sense, ontology of art exerts pressure on the aesthetic systems, thereby putting in crisis their apparently close and systematic character. This pressure must be exerted not only on aesthetic systems but at all the levels of inquiry, that is, on the critical reading of the works of art. The ontological character of the event of Being is not revealed in a privileged manner at the level of what the tradition understood as philosophical discourse. Rather, in this view, genuine philosophical discourse is given always and only where the character of openness and ulteriority belonging to Being appears as such, whether in the transcendental descriptions of a certain field or experience or in the more specific discourse around a determinate work. This is why, strictly speaking, an ontology of art can be understood as general philosophical discourse as well as a specific reflection on a single work. The idea that the proper realm of ontology is philosophy, in the historical sense of the term, perhaps implies a hierarchical vision of beings and of science, like the Aristotelian one. Ontology is not "first philosophy" or "first science" in this hierarchical sense. It constitutes the question about what is the business with Being, how it reveals the opening to Being, a determinate being or region of beings; in other words, it is a question about its own essence, understood in its event character.

The description of the art phenomenon—which can be carried out at different levels of analysis using the most varying contributions, including those of the positive sciences applied to such phenomena—must have a preparatory role. It has to introduce the material on which ontological thought exerts itself.

In sum, if it were simply a matter of reaching maximum clarity and unity of vision of what we happen to experience (the foundation as an indication of the conditions of the possibility of experience; laying bare of the structures as a way of appropriating experience, and of enjoying it in a more integral manner), the role of philosophy would be reduced to the cultivation and satisfaction of a sophisticated narcissism of Spirit, which has an inclination to increasingly possess itself, to be pleased with itself, and to be fully present.

If, instead, the task of philosophy is to satisfy the exigency (which has been raised even by metaphysics) of truly encountering the other, where the "foundation" of philosophy can be found in this manner, philosophy has to come down to the level of description of experience. It must aim at the points of discontinuity of the breaches or openings through which something that is not a being or irreducible to a being comes forth, on the basis of which a being becomes "possible."[24]

For such an inquiry, art offers a vast field, perhaps even more so than other dimensions of experience, whether it is interrogated at the level of its transcendental structures, of poetics, of the programs or critical methods, or at the level of the content, meaning, and outcome of the works. Art appears to not only allow but also explicitly to request an ontological interpretation to lay bare the openings of ulteriority against every illusory attempt at systematically closing off the systems. Since ulteriority can never be fully attained, philosophy will retain an apophatic character. The fact remains, though, that considered from this perspective, human situations are revealed to be truly the paths of an access to Being. Art constitutes one of these paths of access, and it will be the task of ontological aesthetics to elaborate this character.

# 3 The Ontological Vocation of Twentieth-Century Poetics

## The Twentieth as the Century of Poetics

Surely, one of the more general definitions one can give of the twentieth century from art's perspective is that it is the century of poetics. The phenomenon of explicit poetics—of manifestos and art programs that are put forth, discussed, and fought over by the artists themselves not only by means of their artworks but also of essays, in which they take a stand on theoretical views—goes back after all to romanticism, and not by chance. Strictly speaking, the expression "the century of poetics" may describe a chronological period harkening back to the last decades of the nineteenth century. However, its remotest presuppositions are to be found in romantic poetics (it is sufficient to think of the "romantic school" or of authors who, like Hölderlin, were not members of the school in the literal sense of the term). Thus, the blossoming of explicit poetics that is particularly striking in our century has deep roots; this must be said as a preamble, to anticipate possible objections and to clarify that what will be said in regard to our century—for the convenience of our inquiry—applies to a period that is chronologically longer, and which in its ensemble may be called the "century of poetics."

The curious reference to our century has a very precise reason: never as today (although this too can be probably explained on the basis of our temporal proximity) has a programmatic enunciation prevailed over the production of works. So it is not so much a case of poetics serving us to better understand and evaluate the works as it is that the works are nothing but provisional examples and illustrations of "programs" that claim to be held and recognized as such. Therefore, although the phenomenon of explicitly enunciated poetic programs is quite old, the complete reversal of the traditional relationship between poetics and works—a reversal that is still at work—seems to me typical of our century (and of the last decades of it). While in past centuries it was legitimate for art to position itself in front of the work—whether or not it was possible to recover the explicitly stated program of which it was the realization—today the opposite attitude is the norm. While there are no legitimate realizations (i.e., consistent in and by themselves) of specific poetic programs, these programs pretend to be held as such. Having formulated the problem in this way, it is clear that the poetics of our century appear to constitute an aesthetic problem: they disclose themselves as actual theoretical-philosophical positions in regard to art and thus demand a philosophical reading and evaluation.

That it is a matter of taking a stand on philosophical positions, which are therefore relevant for aesthetics, is clear enough when we consider the questions to which the most significant poetics of the twentieth century—and those most full of developments—have chosen to respond. For these, it was not so much a matter of inventing certain styles, of assigning certain rules of production, as it was of determining (against a tradition that was perceived to be alien) more originally the meaning of art among the other activities of man—the artist's position in the world; the ways of approaching the work on the part of the spectator or reader. None of these themes, strictly speaking, are themes that philosophers would naturally leave to the "immanent" reflection of the poet or of the artist; for all three are distinctive philosophical problems. From the point of view of "content," then, it seems unquestionable that twentieth-century poetics are susceptible to "philosophical" discussion. However, these may constitute a problem for philosophy and for philosophical aesthetics from another point of view, too. Before taking into consideration their statements, philosophy of art can ask what in general is the meaning of the fact that various poetics have come to prevail over works (if it is true that certain works of the most recent avant-garde present themselves as provisional examples of specific programs). Above and beyond the content explicitly stated in art's programs, this phenomenon bestows a particular character on the experience of art, from which aesthetic experience lives and to which it must continually refer.

The philosophical problem of poetics has two features: first, it concerns the meaning of poetics as a general characterization of the art world in our century; second, it concerns the value and philosophical bearing of their content and statements. We are dealing with two distinctive questions for which a separate answer must be sought, even though the two solutions may ultimately converge.

## Different Ways of Approaching the Phenomenon of Poetics

To speak of "the death of art" in regard to the phenomenon of the emergence of poetics may be justified only if the Hegelian expression is taken in all its weight and therefore if the contemporary situation of art is placed into a historicist and idealist frame of interpretation. Outside of such an interpretive frame, the expression "death of art" has only a generic sociological meaning that might generate a lot of misunderstanding. Nevertheless, whether or not it is employed in a precise or appropriate sense, the expression indicates a possible interpretative hypothesis of the phenomenon, which can be verified not so much by demonstrating whether it is true or false as by considering it as one among other means for understanding the situation. True, the emergence of poetics as a phenomenon has its origin in the romantics, and it is precisely to this origin that Hegel was referring to when he spoke of the death of art. It is pointless to recall here the "poetry of poetry" of the romantic school: actually, the romantic concept of irony may well be considered, at all effects, as the first massive affirmation of a self-referential tendency in literature. The poetics of the romantics are never or not so much technical discussions about the ways of doing art or enunciations about productive programs; they are reflections on the meaning of art.

After all, it is generally assumed that the rejection of rules, of precepts, and therefore of any poetics understood as pure technical discourse is a phenomenon that has its origin in the romantics. Romanticism, at least in its major philosophical representatives and in its great poets had no poetics in the technical and programmatic sense of the word, and precisely insofar as it reflected on the meaning of art. The romantic origin of the phenomenon of poetics, which is called to mind by the expression "death of art," already contains an indication of what emerges from the reading of these programs; it is a matter of poetics sui generis, i.e., of actual philosophical stands on views about art. Even the most technical aspects of twentieth-century poetics— for example dodecaphony—do not constitute a technical perspective, since they do not concern the ways of producing but rather the position of art and of the artist in the human world.[1]

Nonetheless, the Hegelian expression "death of art" calls to mind, in addition to the romantic origin of most poetics—with all the qualifications that derive from such an origin—another possible interpretative hypothesis revolving around romanticism. The poetics are not above all or exclusively a sign of the "death of art" that Hegel theorized, as romantic poetics of irony could well be. Instead, they are an indication of the ways in which art has sought and still seeks to defend itself from that death. Here, too, we meet once again the ambiguity characteristic of all the key concepts of Hegel's philosophy and of the theoretical views that are inspired by him.[2] On the one hand, the emergence of poetics may be a phenomenon characteristic of the death of art, but, on the other hand, if art was condemned to death because it was not philosophy—because it was not reflection—the attempt to make art reflect on itself, to make it conscious of itself, is ultimately an effort to save it. From this point of view, post-Hegelian poetics would be radically different from romantic poetics, properly understood, which revolves around irony and self-contestation; here, instead, it would be a matter of claiming a "permanent" place for art in the life of spirit by tearing art away from the limbo of unconsciousness to which it had appeared to be condemned. Before the triumph of rationalistic philosophies and positivism, for which art is something inessential and provisional, artists were compelled to answer in a preliminary way the problem of their own "existence."

This hypothesis, too, which if taken in isolation cannot account for the phenomenon in its totality, has at least two aspects that must be emphasized and that might contribute positively to the overall interpretation. First of all, it is true that if a strong need for self-justification could have arisen in art and in the artists themselves, it is because Hegelian and post-Hegelian philosophy have not done justice to art. This will become clearer below when I examine the philosophical meaning of the substance of poetics. We can already say, however, that the artist's need of self-justification is diametrically opposed to the philosophical tendency of affirming the inessential character of art, its provisional status, and therefore, as Hegel put it, its "death."

If we see this hypothesis as an indication of the way in which, in their poetics, the artists defend their right to existence and preliminarily resolve the problem of their own existence, then it can be expanded to significations that are no longer strictly tied to the Hegelian death of art. Instead, the death of art refers to the constitution and modification of social structures and more specifically to the social conditions in which the artist lived throughout the nineteenth century. The poetics no longer present a way of defending the right to existence of art against the claims of rationalistic philosophies; rather, they are more concretely the ways in which artists, confronted as they are with a new social position that had never before been experienced, seek to give meaning to this situation and to give a meaning to themselves in it.

In the nineteenth century, more or less, artists begin to feel the first massive effects of the industrial revolution, that is, changes in the social and political structures and the advent of mass society. All this, for the artist, basically comes down to one meaning: the loss of direct contact with a restricted and well-known public and the acquisition of a much wider public, albeit unknown and far removed. Consider the contempt on the part of romantic and postromantic aesthetics for "occasional art," commissioned art, and so on. By contrast, the larger art of the preceding centuries, for example Bach's music, was exactly an art of this kind. The romantic artist already is an artist abandoned to himself, who generally has no commissioner in the traditional sense of the term; who has no specific, precise, or given demands to which he must respond; and who must seek solely within himself, in his own personality, the inspiration, the source, and rules of his own art. In sum, the artist has lost a clearly defined social condition and has not yet acquired a new one in turn. The horizon to which he is connected is far more extensive and more anonymous than that to which the parish maestro, the court poet, and the traditional artists were accustomed. As a social figure, that of the "integrated" (or complete) artist is replaced by the bohemian artist, who can well be seen as a typical phenomenon of this transitional stage of the first "industrialization" of art.

This hypothesis could be corroborated by the fact that today—when the process of industrialization has been largely fulfilled—the figure of the bohemian artist has gradually fallen out of fashion, while the figure of the integrated artist is becoming increasingly popular once again, though this time the artist is integrated in the culture industry as a functionary of the great institutions of mass communication: the press, cinema, radio, and television. With respect to the new integrated condition of the artist, the phenomenon of poetics seems to be lagging behind because—at least in the sociological interpretation that we are examining here—they bear witness precisely to the lack of integration of the artist, to his problematic condition in the world, whether in the world of concepts or in the social world. This does not conflict with the fact, which is visible in several European countries, that today many among the most activist writers of poetics, poets and avant-garde novelists, are for the most part integrated as functionaries of the culture industry, too; instead, it is precisely their integrated condition that accounts for a certain technical void in their programs, which can be observed in the works originating from them.

These kinds of interpretations, which are both philosophical and sociological at the same time, associate the phenomenon of poetics with the problem of the artist's condition in the world (or of art in the life of Spirit), and instead put into the background the more fundamental and constitutive relationship between the artist and his tools and materials. I am referring here to the perspective paradigmatically shown by Thomas Mann's *Doctor Faust*. Here, too, we face an interpretation with a sociological background in which sociology is present in a less "rough" and generic manner than in prior interpretations. What holds sway over the twentieth-century artist is not so much the problem of his own relationship to the world as it is that of his means of expression (or if anything the former mediated by the latter). These means of expression are not just "means." The consummation of strains of artistic languages is the actual phenomenon of crisis. What Nietzsche called the historical disease makes itself felt in the realm of art as an impossibility of still speaking in forms and linguistic structures wherein everything seems already to have been said. Languages are not merely means but also delimitations of the field of possible experience. From this perspective, the problem to which the poetics intend to respond is not that of the role of art or of the position of the artist in the world, but the question of whether and how art as original creation can still exist.

While this hypothesis justifies well the markedly technical feature of much twentieth-century poetics, it also supplies useful indications for interpretation: The fact that in the art of our century programs are increasingly prevailing over works may be indeed explained by saying that in the epoch of the trivializing consumption of languages, every artwork always starts from a zero degree because it has no tradition behind itself which would ground it and guarantee its structures and comprehension; so it must invent its own language from the ground up, remaining mostly at the embryonic stage of the level of programs. It is undeniable that in all the poetics of our century the *pars destruens*, that is, the polemic against tradition, clearly prevails against the *pars construens*, even though different explanations of this fact could be given.

## "Languages" of the Arts and Language-Word

This interpretative hypothesis centers on the consumption of the various languages of the arts without reducing everything to the level of technical problems; instead, it implicates the very existence of contemporary man in the question of language, drawing us closer to a clearer view of the problem. While the preceding hypothesis was in part verifiable, it had the defect of being too generic; instead, here I shall examine the artist in his immediate relationship to the materials that are formed in the radical concreteness and specificity of his own work. However, there may be a more direct way of addressing the question posed by poetics, that is, by reducing the phenomenon to its most immediate structure, one that is taken for granted at first. In fact, in the phenomenon of explicit poetics, of manifestos, we face a new specific relationship instituted between the "languages" of various nonlinguistic arts (understood as language-word) and the Word.[3] The condition—quite common to all the arts, and the subject of numerous ironic portrayals—of the passionate lover of contemporary music who goes to the concert and receives a printout explaining the composition he is about to listen to, shows at least that artists acknowledge the propedeutic or explanatory role of the word, whether spoken or written, with respect to linguistic or nonlinguistic works of art.

One way in which the problem raised by such events can be liquidated is to absorb them into criticism, referring the question concerning the roles and limits of art back to theory itself. However, this is just a way of postponing the question without resolving it: since one could ask why criticism has come to assume such a fundamental role in contemporary art that it did not have before. The answer to this question is linked to the rapid consumption of symbols in our society that I just examined. Such rapid consumption of symbols, which is conditioned by sociological factors like the power of mass communication, forces the art market to constantly introduce new products, symbols, and mythologies. But precisely because of their rapid succession, it is necessary to mediate these new symbols, so that they can be accepted and generally understood on the vast scale by common consciousness. The formulation of poetics—that is, criticism in its preliminary propedeutic or explicatory function—has the task of rapidly introducing into common consciousness symbols, which, taken in isolation (I am thinking of the visual arts), would assert themselves much more slowly.

Apart from the contradiction visible in this position—that is, language makes people accept symbols more rapidly and contributes to their rapid consumption at the same time, but such consumption would not have occurred without the mediating activity of language, which supposedly becomes necessary owing to consumption—such response leads to more interesting and broader sociological and journalistic arguments, which must become philosophical and metaphysical. Won't the affirmation of explicit poetics, which could be explained in part on the basis of the arguments examined so far, be an indication of something that is much more radical and much more worthy of attention, namely, that the specific relationship between language-word and the "languages" of the various arts has been disclosed clearly for the first time ever? Here the focus would be precisely on the phenomenon of the poetics in their characteristic immediacy, that is to say, on the relationship instituted between spoken or written word and the languages of the various arts. Today, if we no longer continue to consider understanding and communication accidental occurrences that are totally unnecessary for the artwork, these arts reveal as never before that they are radically in need of the Word.

Undoubtedly, criticism, too, taken in its traditional meaning and applied to art over the centuries, had the role of "mediating," that is, inserting a work into a common consciousness manifesting and realizing itself precisely as language. It appears then that with the affirmation of explicit poetics, the mediating role of language-word has been gradually heightened and shown in a clearer light. Today, none could approach contemporary art without taking account of the programs, the literary formulations, as it were, merely by acquiring familiarity with determinate worlds of forms, sounds, and so on. Or at least, in so doing one could train one's own sensibility for certain forms, but this is not what the artists themselves intended. Instead, for their works they demand an understanding that goes well beyond a merely formal enjoyment. And, after all, works offered with a view to the traditional mode of enjoyment are increasingly rare. Consider how one might be able to "contemplate"—understood in its more common and "intransitive" meaning—a work of Dada, a product of pop-art, and so on. These works do not attract upon themselves attention because they are accomplished works; rather, they demand to be inserted into a more general argument (i.e., ironic or destructive arguments against specific ways of living and thinking), which becomes comprehensible and fully meaningful only as word. After all, the nonevaluative, illustrative, and explicatory function of criticism that has always been its dominant feature and that was instead subordinated to evaluation in the preferences of aesthetics, may lead to the same conclusions, that is, the suspicion that language-word might have a grounding role for the languages of the arts. The same conclusion can be reached by examining our own personal psychological attitudes as consumers of art. The work is "understood" when it has de facto penetrated into our consciousness, when we are able to talk about it at least with ourselves, and when we assign to it (or recognize in it) a meaning.

This argument can and must be developed in many directions, for example, by taking account of why artworks or poetry—in contrast to "explanation" in words—always appear to be something transcendent and richer that do not allow themselves to be exhausted; and, since we have spoken of poetry, how the language-word of common consciousness stands with respect to poetic language, which is made of words, too. What I wanted to call attention to was that the phenomenon of explicit poetics may well present, once again, the general problem of language-word's relationship with the languages of the various arts. If what I said about the mediating role exerted by common consciousness holds—insofar as it inserts artworks into the consciousness and heritage of a culture— then here, too, we have an indication of the possible development of our argument. The artwork needs a realm of comprehensibility in order to be understood and enjoyed. In certain periods characteristic of the rapid transformation of society—and here I recover certain elements of the sociological interpretation—such realm of comprehensibility is no longer so peacefully established and obvious, so it needs to be continually reconstructed and regrounded. The grounding function of language-word, which could not appear as a theme in ordinary circumstances, bursts into view in this situation with poetics, criticism, and spoken and written language over other kinds of languages. So it is not so much that language did not possess a grounding function in preceding epochs when explicit poetics or manifestos were either rare or nonexistent, as it is that the grounding function carried out by language went unnoticed. It is indeed only in times, like the one we are living through now, of tension with the symbolic structures that this function comes to light in all its clarity.

Thus, a first possible conclusion of the examination of our century's poetics is that it is a matter of the thematic manifestation of the grounding function of language-word with respect to all other languages, and so to all the arts. So far, however, I have only given an indication of such a grounding function whose philosophical expression can be found in Heidegger's aesthetics. It is a question that requires further elaboration and for which significant data will be gathered in the second inquiry that shall I carry out below of the content and philosophical value of the statements of twentieth-century poetics.

## Post-Hegelian Aesthetics as Aesthetics of Play

If the most conclusive and complete hypothesis (insofar as it can be broadened to comprehend and ground the valid aspects of the other) concerning the phenomenon of poetics seems to be the hypothesis that language-word has manifested its grounding function, an inquiry of twentieth-century poetics will focus, one the one hand, on the fundamental contrast between the data supplied by the poetics and those supplied by the aesthetic doctrines of our century (which here are not examined with a view toward exhaustive account but rather in order to draw the general outline of a tendency, a direction, among them); on the other hand, it will show how twentieth-century poetics, taken together in what they have in common in spite of their profound differences, defend the value and ontological meaning of art that aesthetics has increasingly forgotten.

It maybe needless to repeat that the examination I intend to carry out is only preliminary and extremely general; its value lies merely in illustrating a hypothesis that does not pretend to be valid as demonstration or verification. Twentieth-century poetics will be the object of a very general and incomplete inquiry; such a preliminary examination seems necessary, though, to find an orientation for a more in-depth examination.

To understand the meaning of the hypothesis I am elaborating here, it is necessary to begin with an overview of European aesthetics during the second half of the nineteenth century and during the first part of the twentieth. These aesthetics appear to be dominated by the idea of art understood as "play," even though this term or its corresponding concept are not always explicitly used. The term obviously refers us back to the initial development of the Kantian outcomes at the end of the nineteenth century. The reference is justified, though, not only because of the importance that neo-Kantian themes and perspectives had in philosophy and in aesthetics in the nineteenth and twentieth centuries but also because all the aesthetics elaborated outside of neo-Kantianism, in spite of their differences, appeared to take as a stable point of departure the Kantian idea of disinterestedness and free play of the faculties characterizing aesthetic experience.

While the basic assertion that the European aesthetics of the nineteenth and twentieth centuries is an aesthetics of play may sound paradoxical, it is nevertheless understandable once we specify that the term "play" is intended to point to any vision that places art outside, above, or beyond any "serious" (i.e., moral or cognitive) activity with respect to the world or, more generally, to being. The reactions against Hegelian rationalism, on the one hand, and the affirmation of positivism and the parallel attempts of experimental, psychological, and sociological aesthetics, on the other, allied themselves to deprive art and the aesthetic sphere of their "ontological" value, thus confining art to the secondary, or at least the disengaged (i.e., disinterested) activities of the human being. Kirkegaard's category of aesthetic stage—an existential category characterized by immediacy, disengagement, and lack of historicity—seems to acquire a prophetic meaning with respect to the developments of nineteenth- and twentieth-century poetics. In fact, many of the features that neo-Kantianism, positivism, and vitalism assign to aesthetic experience could be easily traced back to Kierkegaard's concept of aesthetic stage.

There should be no doubt about the "ludic" meaning of art for positivism. Consider Spenser's idea that the excess of forces that are not employed in the struggle for life are discharged instead into art.[4] Also, the entire trend of positivistic criticism and aesthetics that constitutes the background of naturalism—as it is expressed in the works of Taine, for example—does not move out of this schema. That art is a "symptom" of a historical, social, and psychological situation does not change its basically ludic nature. It is not so much the value or ontological weight of art that changes as it is its cognitive usage, its usage made possible with a view to the knowledge of a given epoch, society, or individual.

All the aesthetics that appeal to the concept of *Einfühlung*, which is largely dominant in the philosophy of art in the nineteenth and the twentieth centuries, do not escape from the general characterization of art as play. Here the concept of play is not explicitly discussed, and yet the inessentiality of art is equally evident. It has been rightly observed that there is a close connection between the theories of Volkelt and Lipps, on the one hand, and Kant's *Critique of Judgment*, on the other, with its concept of the free play of the faculties.[5] But more generally, the so-called school of *Einfühlung* can be traced back to the concept of play because of the vitalist background that characterizes it. It is important to take note of this background because it appears in much nineteenth-century aesthetics, with a different origin and with a different approach, as in Dewey, for example. However the doctrine of *Einfühlung* is characterized, the fact remains that the meaning of art, within the framework delimited by this doctrine, is nothing but the heightening of vital feelings, which is not far removed from the play of which Spencer speaks.

The third general direction of nineteenth- and twentieth-century aesthetics to be recalled here in the list of examples of the hegemony of the concept of play is neo-Kantian aesthetics.[6] Here, art and aesthetic experience are the objects of philosophical reflection insofar as they are dimensions of consciousness: there is an art world and an aesthetic sphere because there is a specific way in which the human being relates to the world, which is defined always with reference to the Kantian play of the faculties, neither theoretically nor practically but rather aesthetically. It is well known that the neo-Kantianism, based on an approach that revolves around the possible directions of consciousness, was developed by Cassirer, its most famous representative, in the direction of a philosophy of culture that has had a great influence on American aesthetics. Art constitutes a dimension of culture, understood as the totality of the symbolic forms produced by consciousness. According to neo-Kantianism, "aesthetic consciousness" is the foundation of art. Here too one does not explicitly speak of "play," and yet when the aesthetic sphere is more precisely defined in relation to the other spheres, the idea of "play" (or disinterestedness, sentimental attitudes, and so on) is a determinant factor. The idea of art's inessentiality calls to mind the element of play as well as the idea that art is grounded in the possible directions of consciousness and of human action, which in final analysis is a de facto foundation: since there is aesthetic experience, this must be part of a philosophy of culture.

What has been said so far seems to be true above all for German aesthetics in the nineteenth and the twentieth centuries, and in part for French aesthetics, though not for Italian neo-idealist aesthetics. However, Croce's encapsulation of art into the dialectical couple "beautiful-ugly," at the exclusion of any reference to truth and falsity, good and evil, and so on, amounts precisely to reducing art to play, even in a context that intends to remain true, in its basic outline, to Hegel's teaching. It is true that art's "seriousness" is not contested here, but such seriousness belongs only to the first moment, which insofar as it is withdrawn from the alternatives that characterize the seriousness of existence, remains immersed in a limbo of disinterestedness and disengagement that basically falls within the limits of Kierkegaard's aesthetic stage. On the other hand, the idea of art's inessentiality lives on in many of the perspectives that find their origin in Hegel and that in Hegel are expressed with the thesis of the death of art. According to Hegel's thesis, the more art is considered a serious fact rather than pure play, the more it is resolved into philosophy and reflection. This seems to be testified to by the history of Marxist aesthetics—even though it cannot be properly identified as an aesthetic of play—that holds on to the thesis that the truth of art is recognized only by reflection, which by making art relative to its historical conditions and revealing in them the hidden economic and social infrastructures, abolishes its provisional form and makes it true by overcoming art. In these Hegel-derived perspectives, art's lack of seriousness and its ludic character return as inessentiality, in the literal sense that they "lack the essence," the substance. It can be said then—broadening somewhat what has been said about play—that art is play insofar as, albeit serious, it does not deserve to be "taken seriously." In other words, art reveals its own truth only by emptying itself of the specific characteristics that distinguish it from philosophy and reflection.

We could proceed with a more detailed examination of the positions of several aesthetic currents of the nineteenth and the twentieth centuries with respect to the question of the serious or ludic nature of art. However, the meaning of play as the dominant concept of nineteenth- and twentieth-century aesthetics should be sufficiently clear from the few examples that I have discussed so far while putting forth a hypothesis that does not want to be understood as demonstration.

The prophetic value of Kierkegaard's interpretation of the aesthetic stage is equally clear: although independently of Kierkegaard, post-Hegelian aesthetics moves within the common background of an aesthetic stage that has the same features that Kierkegaard ascribed to art at the level of ethical reflection. This holds, at least, for the larger part of post-Hegelian aesthetics: if one wants to indicate the direction of a thought that attempts to recover the ontological meaning of art, one can name immediately Nietzsche and Heidegger—especially Heidegger—who separate themselves from the general tendency to empty art of its ontological content and open new paths to recover the ontological bearing of art.

## Defense of the Ontological Meaning of Art in Avant-garde Poetics

If this is the situation—albeit outlined by examples only—of post-Hegelian aesthetics, what are the concrete aspects characterizing the defense of the ontological characteristic of art on the part of contemporary aesthetics? Here, too, as in the case of aesthetics, the picture is not a unitary one; when we speak of the ontological weight of art, such an expression has a different meaning for different poetics. In general, however, the expression has been sufficiently defined by way of negation, and precisely by opposing the concept of play and of art's inessentiality, which is characteristic of aesthetics, as we just saw. The poetics defend the ontological bearing of art, above all, to the extent that they refuse to see and practice art as a disinterested activity beyond true and false, good and evil, and so on, or as an activity that could appear to be true only once unmasked, demythologized, and relativized by reflection. Once we give this provisional meaning to the expression "ontological bearing of art," it becomes clear that the whole or most of twentieth-century poetics may be defined as ontological poetics. To corroborate opposition between aesthetics and poetics, the question can be examined from the angle of the disappearance or even of the polemical denial in contemporary poetics of feeling, which had dominated Kantian and post-Kantian aesthetics for a long time.

Now, it was precisely by virtue of its association with the concept of art as play that feeling took up the value of the definitive concept of the aesthetic sphere. It was a feeling totally emptied out of all the metaphysical bearing that the great romantic systems had attributed to it, which recaptured the spirit of Kant's system in its collocation with the theoretical and the practical as the ground of a third world or sphere of aesthetic experience, though no longer as problematically as it occurred in Kant. Now, the most conscious and significant poetics of our century have had the merit of doing justice against the aesthetic sentimentalism that maintained art within the sphere of disengagement and inessentiality.

What are, more specifically, the trajectories followed by twentieth-century poetics so as to recover and reaffirm the ontological bearing or more generally the seriousness of art?

All the poetics that defend the ontological bearing of art—insofar as they take it as a form of knowledge of reality, at times more adequate than others and more specifically adequate than discursive thought—remain close in many respects to a traditional conception of art that is fundamentally mimetic. In this domain fall numerous poetics from the nineteenth and the twentieth centuries that more or less explicitly conceive of art as a transcription of experience, which is grasped originally and radically or so is claimed. To speak more generally—as we cannot avoid doing in a context where we are trying to sketch a typology and an overall interpretive framework—we can understand among these still traditional poetics the program of impressionism, at least insofar as it regards painting, because it presents itself as an effort to grasp and represent experience at its embryonic and constitutive phase, not without some influence from the dominant scientific and scientist mindset of the epoch.[7] Along the same lines we can basically position the later poetics, like cubism[8] and futurism.[9]

For cubism it is a matter of finding languages capable of transcribing experience into intimate and elementary geometric structures rather than in the stereotypical and conventional forms of the entire pictorial tradition that have accustomed us to merely grasping the surface of things. For futurism, the point is equally to discover a language capable less of supplying us with the intimate structures of things than with describing and fixating by means of painting the new reality of technology and of the machinelike world as well as the dynamic of such a world.

It seems important for me to underline that in all these cases the revolution takes place exclusively at the level of language: a new language positions itself next to other traditional languages, the legitimacy of which is sometimes explicitly recognized, albeit on different planes.[10]

It is surely the case that impressionism and cubism, and futurism as well, put in question neither the artist's role in the world (which remains the same as in previous spiritual constellations, namely, representing reality), nor the general meaning of art among the activities of man, nor above all the position of the spectator or the reader in front of the work. It is understood that

to the extent that the work becomes a cognitive instrument for knowing reality, aesthetic enjoyment cannot be conceived in terms of a purely disinterested contemplation of the beautiful, as in the free play of the faculties. At
most one reaches the point of "recognition," of which Aristotle already
spoke: there is always a reality presupposed by the work (whether it is the
natural or the technical and mechanistic world) in reference to which the
work is defined, measured, evaluated, and finally enjoyed.

Instead, we should observe the motif in these poetics, of romantic (i.e.,
Schelling and Schopenhauer) and postromantic origin, that defend the originality and superiority of aesthetic knowledge of reality over intellectual and
discursive knowledge. This defense is quite meaningful, and we should take
notice of it because, on the one hand, it constitutes a prelude to the will of
autonomy from philosophical reflection and critique that will become dominant in the later poetics and on the other hand, it shows that the same poetics still move within the domain of the traditional opposition between
discursive and intuitive knowledge of things. For these poetics, art can become independent from reflection and liberate itself from the realm of inessentiality and of free play only by defending its superiority over rational and
reflective knowledge.

The "irrational" motive—that is, the affirmation of the superiority of intuitive over discursive knowledge—increasingly asserts itself with surrealism
and symbolism. These, however, present new elements that enable them to
clearly distance themselves from the other, far more traditional poetics. It is
this element that justifies the chronological arbitrariness with which we have
positioned symbolism on a par with surrealism, addressing them only after
the examination of cubism and futurism. Besides the fact that it is not so
much a matter of establishing historical priorities, origins, and genealogies
here as it is of putting forth a sufficiently abstract typological scheme that
would allow for chronological displacements of this kind, we can give a historical reason in support of this chronological displacement: the longstand-
ing and multiple ramifications of symbolic poetics are such that symbolism
cannot be taken exclusively as a phenomenon of the eighteenth century, as it
continued to live in and to act upon numerous poetics of the nineteenth,
even though conceptualized and transformed in various ways.

What is new and from our view worthy of notice in symbolism can be
summed up by bringing closer two polarities within this poetics that are apparently far removed from each other. On the one hand, there is the prominence of the physical aspect of sound and vision of the work of art (e.g., in

poetry), by virtue of which we observe in symbolism a significant technical impulse that is not at all negligible; on the other hand, the faith of symbolist poetics in the mystical bearing of such physical qualities of the work, words and images. So the logic of poetry and of art in general is increasingly and more sharply detached from the logic of common discourse. The relationship with the suprasensible or with the depths is not mediated by a series of dialectical (i.e., discursive) transitions but rather takes place in the wake of an immediate and essentially mysterious symbolic call that originates from the sign and from the isolated Word, resounding in all its weight. Even though it is still a matter of tapping into a reality much deeper than the everyday, the novelty lies entirely in the union of such an intuitive effort with the formal rigor and with the constructive will.[11] Paul Valéry may be considered the heir of these two trends, which are brought together without residues in his work, for his technicity is an actual mystical attitude.[12] Only superficially could one associate Valéry with an aesthetic of play and disengagement. While some of his explicit statements to this effect might lead one to think along these lines, it is equally true that he represents a decisive stage on the way to defending the ontological bearing of art. He frees the field from the ambiguous residuals of epistemology and puts at the center the structure of the work—the work in itself—its construction, no longer viewed as a means for knowing a reality that is given otherwise, and thus opens the way to the reconsideration of the ontological bearing of art outside of the Hegelian alternative between intuitive and reflective knowledge. It is possible to say that the various formal poetics of the nineteenth and twentieth centuries acquire a meaning in Valéry and free themselves from their philosophical origin. To the extent that they call attention to the work in itself, these poetics open the way to the realization that art is not a means for gaining access to a supposedly given reality of nature and history but a *founding of reality*.

By contrast, the contribution of surrealist poetics to the recovery of the ontological meaning of art lies in a different plane, which is less visible though no less meaningful or less determinant, where it is not distinguishable from Dadaism. If surrealism presents the traditional claim of supplying a path to a more valid authenticity than that of discursive knowledge—and this path is identified with automatic writing and with the coming into prominence of the unconscious as the true relevant element of art and of surrealist poetics, more substantially so of Dadaism—this is the irruption into the artwork of the trivial ordinary object, the vulgar or obscene word, the *ready-made*. Both surrealism and Dadaism explicitly posit for the first time a question that is highly relevant for contemporary aesthetics: whether and to what extent the idea of aesthetic contemplation—which in the larger part of the history of aesthetics retained an intransitive and static character—is valid and still applicable to much of contemporary art.[13] This is the question to be addressed to anyone who, taking for granted that the only way of approaching artworks lies in the aestheticist satisfaction with the perfection and harmony of a work—an attitude that always corresponds to the "free play" of the cognitive faculties—finds avant-garde poetics essentially scandalous if not demonic.[14] Now, several surrealists and Dadaists,[15] above and beyond the generic destructive attitudes that struck the middle culture at the time, were clearly conscious of this more specifically and more precisely polemical function against the aestheticist consciousness of the time. If one of the ways in which art was emptied of ontology took place by confining the enjoyment of the artwork to the level of the free play of the faculties (no matter how the concept was translated: disinterestedness, instant of intuition-expression, intransitive contemplation), the most scandalous aspects of Dadaism and surrealism (followed in this by the later poetics, including pop-art) decisively contributed to putting the aestheticist consciousness of the nineteenth century in crisis.

Too often, art criticism, entrapped as it is into far too rigid conceptual frameworks, has reduced the avant-garde to its technical or linguistic aspects, so that in its view understanding a specific avant-garde basically means learning a new language, getting accustomed to an unusual world of symbols, colors, and forms. Of course, a new language also brings new content, though this always occurs at the level of "worldviews." Traditional figurative painting represented a certain world; abstract, expressionist, and cubist painting, by virtue of their employment of new tools, also represent new things (inner realities, the in-depth structure of things). But the relationship to the work remains substantially unaltered because enjoyment remains dominated by the idea of perfection and the corresponding pleasure of aesthetic satisfaction, and so of play. Indeed, with the gradual affirmation of abstract painting, formalist sensibility celebrated new triumphs both in aesthetics and criticism because it became clear that the abstract work could not be enjoyed apart from structural rhythms and the play of colors, moving in the opposite direction of the "ontological" ambitions of the first theorists. All this is quite comprehensible as soon as we observe that what has been denied and discarded is precisely the fundamental message of such art, of the avant-garde, that is to say, the appeal to reexamine the very concept of aesthetic enjoyment. Abstract art produced a great renewal of formalism with respect to the enjoyment and reading of traditional art, too: think of the taste for primitivism, whose artistic products are analyzed in purely geometric perspective and structural terms and seen as precursors of cubist sensibilities.

On the contrary, the attack on aestheticist concept of enjoyment by twentieth-century poetics should have stimulated an ontological reading of traditional art, too. In other words, it is not only in regard to surrealist and Dadaist works of art that aesthetic enjoyment is revealed as unrealizable. It is inadequate even for traditional works of art. It will suffice to remember the most celebrated and famous example of the *Divina Commedia* and what has been a "purely" disinterested, exclusively aesthetic reading of Dante's masterpiece. It is not only that avant-garde art requires a new attitude; it calls attention on the insufficiency of an aestheticist reading for all times and for every type of art.

In my view, the most ripe and complete indications of the recovery of the ontological bearing of art are found within a domain of the expressionist movement that is not easily circumscribable. It is precisely on account of the difficulty of circumscribing this movement that I must commit an act of oversimplification in speaking of an "expressionist logic," an indispensable act for a work that has to circumscribe an interpretative hypothesis, to be elaborated and further discussed at a later time.[16] The simplification consists above all in isolating a few motives that are without doubt present in the various statements of the expressionists (even though they are not characteristic of all the members belonging to this movement), which appear as the most salient features, and most fecund in their possible development, from a general aesthetic viewpoint.

I can single out three among the most salient features of expressionism in accordance with its historical definition and above all in light of the inventory of its cultural meaning and heritage. First of all, there is within expressionism a strong impulse for revolutionary *engagement*, whatever reservations about the clarity of its social and political awareness one might have, at least to the extent that in it more than in any other contemporary avant-garde, art's renewal is viewed only as an aspect of a broader program for the renewal of morality and society.[17]

The presence of *engagement* has been widely corroborated by other elements of the expressionist movement, such as the polemic against the sentimentalism and egocentrism of traditional art and poetry; consider Kurt Hillel's passages on lyric, for example—which inevitably call to mind songs and subjective attitudes—where he prefers to speak of poetry rather than of lyric because of its etymological links with *poiein*, to more emphatically underscore its productive and actualizing character; or the statement by Frantz Clement, who juxtaposes symbolist egocentrism to the cosmocentrism of the new art;[18] or more generally, much of great expressionist poetry, for example, Benn's great lyric, which radically formulates a poetic creed that has completely left behind the idea that poetry is the expression of feelings, autobiography, and impressions.[19]

The aspect of *engagement* appears to be understood and summed up in a second and broader character typical of expressionist poetics that we could call the "cosmic" nature of poetry, clarifying right away that it is not the same cosmic nature of romanticism that implies the presence of the "cosmic feeling"; on the contrary, the cosmic nature is an allusion to the construction of objective worlds that the expressionist poet takes as his task in lieu of the sentimental autobiography and the expressions of emotions. It is certain that poetry frees itself once and for all from its exclusive links with the sphere of feelings and emotions, which was an essential aspect of its lack of ontological bearing, both in the case of revolutionary engagement, whether more or less politically concrete, as well as in the case of poetry as construction of worlds, which cannot be reduced to the level of pure symbolization of emotional and sentimental states but rather lead to more and more growth of being.

A third element can be linked to the cosmic will and engagement, which seems to be present in expressionist poetics though only fully documented in one of the members of the movement—Kandinsky—and especially in some of the essays that cannot be chronologically arranged under the period of expressionism. The deep links between the third element and expressionism seem to me unquestionable because of its meaning, and historically because Kandinsky remained an expressionist till the very end, at least insofar as his poetic conceptions are concerned. Indeed, it is Kandinsky who speaks of an explicitly *prophetic character* of art, thus interpreting and giving rigorous form to a widespread mood in the whole expressionist movement and in the whole avant-garde of the nineteenth century.

However, in other expressionists and in the avant-garde, the prophetic element is generally reduced to an immanent tension toward a world that is different from the world against which they inveigh, a different world that art announces or intends to construct. By contrast, Kandinsky theorizes the prophetic character of art in an explicit and rigorous manner as to give decisive indications of the type of enjoyment that is appropriate for prophetic art. In this way, Kandinsky and the expressionism in which his poetics has its roots truly make the most important contribution to twentieth-century poetics on the way to its recovery of the ontological bearing and meaning of art. Kandinsky's position is construed once and for all outside of the alternative between the intuitive knowledge proper to art and the discursive knowledge proper to reflection, where most of the poetics that protest the ontological evacuation of art are situated, and to which they are condemned by the aesthetics of play and disengagement.

It is true that to a certain respect Kandinsky's justification of abstractionism is still in part bound up with the opposition between the surface and the deep structure of things (which would be attained by abstractionism). However, next to such a still traditional—that is, mimetic—argument there is another, more fundamental justification, which defends abstract art in the name of concrete art[20] and which "renounces the objects and creates its own means of expression, placing along with a 'real' world a new world, which has nothing to do with reality."[21] Nonetheless, this separation from reality is relative: the artwork configures a de facto reality, not yet real or actualized. So the word reality, set off by quotatiopn marks in the extract above, has a retrospective meaning. It is real in the sense that we call real whatever takes place, whatever is experienced and becomes habitual. But the reality configured in the abstract work of art is the reality of a future world, not yet present or fully given. The decision over the artistic value of a work—over the aesthetic enjoyment of a work of art—amounts to a decision about whether or not it represents a new world; whether it is truly concrete; whether in this prophetic sense it has an object.[22] "Every spiritual epoch expresses its particular content in a form that corresponds exactly to that content. In this way, every epoch assumes its true 'physiognomy,' full of expressive power, and thus 'yesterday' is transformed into 'today' in every spiritual realm. But apart from this, art possesses another capacity, unique to itself, that of sensing 'tomorrow' in 'today'—a creative and prophetic force."[23]

It seems to me that in these few lines of Kandinsky we have a clear indication of how the ontological bearing of art and an ontological approach to the art work can be understood apart from the old polemics between discursive and intuitive knowledge. To evaluate or enjoy a work of art, says Kandinsky—and here I am translating his words in Heidegger's language—means nothing else than encountering a new world and attempting "to inhabit it." The meaning of art does not lie in expressing or representing a determinate mode of looking at things as they are in themselves (such an expressive function belongs to other forms of spirit), nor in allowing certain faculties to be employed more freely. Instead, art constitutes the occurrence of a radical novelty at the level of being-in-the-world in that it founds being-in-the-world. Kandinsky's statement to the effect that the occurrence of novelty is entrusted to the intuition of the artist should not enclose us within the limits of epistemological discussions.[24] His reference to intuition expresses only the demand that the original and underivable character of the artistic event be retained. After all, Kandinsky's entire work bears witness to his distance from any form of irrationalism, even in regard to the concrete production of the work, for his effort—just like that of Klee—is directed precisely to withdraw art from the *arbitrium* of inspiration and instead to supply it with a grammatical structure that is as rigorous as possible. The prophetic force of art is not exhibited in practical jokes or arbitrary constructions but in concrete projection of works that constitute worlds, the human world in all its physical structures included.

From this view it is not an accident that Kandinsky was, like Klee, a teacher at Gropius's Bauhaus. The Bauhaus constitutes precisely a possibly valid dimension for developing a prophetic poetics like that of Kandinsky. In fact, in Gropius's school, the prophetic force became a concrete effort to project a world.[25] This effort loses the initial mystical impetus and reduces its original disclosure and breadth to the extent that it becomes concrete.

However, one cannot say that the ideology of the Bauhaus is the only outcome of Kandinsky's prophetic poetics (which, after all, was explicitly stated only after the experience at the Bauhaus had ended). It is true that here, owing to the recovery of the ideal of the *Gesamtkunstwerk*—albeit completely transfigured insofar as it is ruled by the category of the future—art's ontological character is affirmed in the forms of high ornamentalism (understood in the best possible sense of the term) so that art is called upon the task of founding the environment in which the human being lives, that is, the world of human experience. Such a vocation can be realized at different levels of tension and totality: it can be actualized in epic as the summa of the spiritual values and substance of a world in which successive generations recognize one another and which they inhabit; or it can descend to the level of industrial *design*, where the cosmic nature of art is still present, though merely as capacity to inhabit the world that is already fully given. It is important to underscore the extent to which art remains faithful to its prophetic vocation, its ontological engagement completely oriented toward the future. To be sure, this is one of the most precious data that aesthetics has encountered in reflecting on contemporary aesthetics.

## Aesthetic Enjoyment as Dialogue

Just as what I have illustrated in the preceding pages was presented as an interpretative hypothesis concerning twentieth-century poetics, the concluding argument will be equally a schematic representation of the same hypothesis, though not without the addition of clarifications and examples. The order in which I have arranged the various poetics already constitutes an implicit proposal to classify these poetics with respect to their philosophical meaning and to their minor or major bearing of the question of the ontological status of the artwork.

The schema I have outlined so far does not put forth an absolute value judgment of the "meaning of art," strictly speaking. In regard to that question, this framework can be subdivided more or less in three groups: First, the poetics that are still fundamentally mimetic in the sense that they do not question that the task of art is to represent reality; instead, they invent new languages and new forms of representation. These poetics obviously do not raise the question of the artist's existence in the world, nor that of aesthetic enjoyment, thus confirming my view of their traditional character. A second group comprises the poetics that already begin to recover the ontological bearing of art or to underscore its institutive and nonmimetic character or to defend a privileged cognitive function of art over against discursive knowledge—remaining faithful to the original romantic and Hegelian polemic—or, as in the case of Dada and surrealism, to vehemently attack traditional aesthetic enjoyment and reading of the work. The third group, constituted mainly by expressionism, comprises those poetics in which the cosmic character of art is clearly asserted in the form of engagement and prophecy.

An important corollary of my hypothesis—and it is something to which I want to call attention and that becomes clear upon examining the expressionist movement—is that the artist's revolutionary political engagement arises as a specific phenomenon only in the midst of the more extensive movement of poetics oriented toward the recovery of the ontological bearing of art. While this is the main thread of twentieth-century poetics, it is only a particular case—as Kandinsky's essays demonstrate—of a broader, deeper, and more metaphysically committed movement that raises the general question of the artist's relationship to reality. After all, only such an "ontological" hypothesis could account for the poetics—like Dada and surrealism—that, from the point of view of those who privilege exclusively or mainly the revolutionary engagement, end up losing any real positive meaning and are relegated to appear more or less as aberrant manifestations or at most as forms of engagement that have deviated from their true aims.

In addition to proposing to arrange the poetics of our century, my hypothesis makes a more precise indication of the philosophical character of aesthetics. In opposition to the larger part of nineteenth-century aesthetics that continue to elaborate motives derived from Kantian, idealist, and positivist aesthetics, which remain tied to the aesthetics of play and disengagement in different ways, twentieth-century poetics supplies very concrete indications for recovering the ontological bearing of art.

These indications can be summed up in two points. From the point of view of the production and of the work, the ontological bearing of art signifies its cosmic character or, more deeply, in the Kantian sense of the word, its prophetic character. Here, in my view, the poetics encounter the results of Heidegger's ontological speculation. After all, the protest of poetics against the aesthetics of play and disengagement took place also at the level of the enjoyment and reading of the art work. Here the first outcome is polemical and negative: in regard to the programs and artistic productions of the avant-garde, the theories of enjoyment and reading elaborated by aesthetics appear to be insufficient and thus demand to be revised, especially with respect to their aestheticist aspects (contemplation understood as intransitiveness, delight in the beautiful structure). A precious, positive indication of the trajectory to be followed in order to develop a theory of reading and interpreting that would do justice to the ontological character of art is given by Kandinsky in the essay *Der Wert eines Werkes der Konkreten Kunst* (1938): the evaluation of an artwork signifies deciding whether it projects a world, and whether or not it contains a prophetic dimension.

The conclusions of the second part of my inquiry about the indications of poetics concur with those of the first part, which examined the phenomenon and meaning of poetics. There I argued that the most complete hypothesis (i.e., more adequate to the facts themselves) was the one that showed the affirmation of the founding character or at least of the privileged character of language-word over the languages of the various arts. Now, if we ask how we can concretely elaborate the aesthetic enjoyment formulated by Kandinsky, we encounter language-word, once again. To establish whether a work of art has a prophetic character can only be a discourse not on the work but *with* the work, *starting from* the work. Perhaps, a way of inhabiting a work of art concretely is to enter into dialogue with it—since our consciousness is consciousness of spiritual contents, it is always realized in discourse, and therefore has a linguistic character—that is to say, to grasp and to be grasped by the work at the same time. If the world—and here I am referring to the outcomes of Heidegger's existential analytics—is basically a system of meanings into which we are always already thrown, the artwork founds a world insofar as it founds a new system of meanings: to encounter the work is like encountering a person; the former cannot be merely set into the world as it is. Rather, it represents a new perspective, a new proposal to arrange the world in a different manner, and as such it constitutes a *Weltanschaaung*. However, since the world does not independently stand as an object of *Anschauungen*, but is instead reduced to, is entirely the system of meanings, the work is tout court a world.

The essentiality of language-word consists in the following: the discourse on the work (or to put it better, discourse with the work starting from the work) is no longer a contingent or superfluous addition to aesthetic enjoyment, which would always happen as an immediate encounter, as a visual and sonorous perception of the work's perfection. Instead, discourse becomes the fundamental way in which the work of art can be encountered and enjoyed, and all the other acts constituting an approach are merely preparatory. Similarly, criticism, understood in its most general meaning, as a discourse on the work that starts from the work itself, is an essential mode of enjoying the work, insofar as it is not an accidental addition, grounded, as it were, on an encounter that would happen at the level prior to discourse, that of the nonlinguistic. The work comes to be enjoyed (i.e., actualized) and thus lives again concretely not only or mainly insofar as it is performed, that is to say, made present in its physical structures: sonorized if it is a musical work or visualized if it is a pictorial or plastic work. The performance (as a way reliving the work in its concrete physical nature, which constitutes already the outcome of an interpretative process) is the preliminary condition for an ulterior discourse with the work. This is a discourse in the literal sense of the term inasmuch as it is a dialogue that we eventually carry on with ourselves on what the work means and is for us. For the work can be introduced into our consciousness only if it becomes an object of discourse or better a partner in dialogue.

An important consequence of this problematic argument is that aesthetic enjoyment becomes essentially interpretation and dialogue, while the moment of evaluation as the static recognition of the work's perfection is subordinated to a secondary level.

If there are stages and arrival points of interpretation-enjoyment, then, it is in the sense that the dialogue with a work reaches a moment in which it is summed up and crystallized so that we can say "we have understood"—as always happens in the course of a real dialogue—not in the sense that a dialogue is just a preparatory stage for an "aesthetic pleasure," which would be considered its essential aim. On the contrary, what appears to be a moment of accomplished contemplation is only a provisional summation of the state of an argument.

It is not at this level, then, that we could connect the judgment that would be expressed in the statement "the work is beautiful or accomplished."

This is reinforced by the difficulty encountered by all the aesthetics that intend to avoid the canonization of poetic rules as general rules for the beautiful and art in an effort to describe the evaluative judgment upon the work, especially in the case of failed works. As is well known, this occurred in the aesthetics of Croce, who associated evaluation with an abstract dialectical distinction that still dominated the idea of art's disengagement. The solution to this question is indicated by the theories that emphasize in enjoyment the interpretive and dialogical moment to the extent that they pay attention to the work as a living form. For the theory of formativity, the value of the artwork can be measured not so much when the work is said to be beautiful and successful as it is when the work, taken concretely and historically, stirs and gives rise to an infinite process of interpretation, to an infinity of arguments in the sense mentioned above. This is why the evaluation of a failed work can never be expressed with judgment like "such and such a work is ugly"; in fact, a failed work is not even an object of discourse, since it does not give rise to or open onto a dialogue.[26] We are not far away from Kandinsky's idea that the value of a work consists in its prophesy of a new world. If, as mentioned above, our world is above all a system of meanings, the cosmic nature of the work is actualized and grasped in discourse—and I don't mean this just in a metaphorical sense—in words through which

we "explain" the work to ourselves or take possession of it, thus truly entering and inhabiting the world opened by the work.

In this way, the salient outcome of twentieth-century poetics would be a
re-ontologization of art through the affirmation of the originally ontological, founding function of language. It is clear that as a possible objection we
could immediately indicate a danger in this theoretical position. It is the
danger of a massive return to Hegelian aesthetics, and so to the death of art.
If, indeed, the best way of enjoying every work of art is to "translate" it in
words—but I am speaking of translation only for the sake of understanding;
in actuality, we are dealing with a dialogue with the work—won't translation be purely and simply a Hegelian *Aufhebung*, of which we find eloquent
examples in all those reductive and demythologizing critical methods, be
they sociological, psychological, or structural, that tend to speak of the work
in the sense of explaining it, telling us why it is what it is and so rationalizing
it, so that in the end aesthetic experience in its specificity evaporates?

It is true that the danger is not an imaginary one, as testified to by the
Hegelianism that lingers in (reductive) contemporary criticism. Once again,
it is a matter of observing that in these cases the work is not an interlocutor
that participates in a dialogue but rather an "object" of discourse. The quo-
tation from Kandinsky anticipates this possibility; since the various forms
and types of spiritual production are expressions of their own epoch, the
*Aufhebend* and reductive reading is true in regard to them, but the work of
art is prophetic. The point is, then, to read the artwork as prophecy, as a
point of departure rather than a point of arrival. The critical discourse that
in the face of the structures of the work seeks to reconstruct the reasons for
its genesis cannot be dialogue-enjoyment. Indeed, the point of arrival of this
reconstructive process is precisely a transfigured contemplation (of an aestheticist type) of the purely formal perfection of the object. If the prophetic
character of the work is to be taken seriously, we have to ask not what it
means or what it refers to or what reality it should be referred to in order to
be explained (or demythologized, which is the same thing); instead, we
should ask literally what it wants to say.

The only example of this kind of reading that I can provide is the relationship of the Western tradition to the Bible (here, too, we should make a few
clarifications because the rationalist exegesis that stands at the root of the
[reductive] literary reading that we know and practice has replaced prophetic
reading in the modern epoch). Although the Bible is an example of huge
proportions, not easily translatable to the level of the concrete reading of

artworks, it nevertheless bears witness to the possibility of a hermeneutic reading that would be no longer thought on the basis of the Hegelian *Aufhebung*; it would be a reading that does not pretend to make the object its own but rather accepts its fate to move within it, allowing itself to be transcended. This would mean taking seriously the artworks in their moral, philosophical, and existential meaning instead of reducing them to data concerning the biography of the artist or of evaluating them only in the measure by which they serve the structure of the work. It is a long inquiry in need of concrete experiments of the ontological reading of poets and artists. After all, such an "ontological" reading has been practiced more than one might be led to believe within traditional critical schemes, which, however, obscure and mystify it. Nonetheless, the acknowledgment of the aestheticist prejudice predominant in much of contemporary aesthetics and the initials signs of its revision in the light of the concrete experiences of our century's avant-garde are a step in this direction.

# 4 Art, Feeling, and Originality in Heidegger's Aesthetics

## Poetic Language in *Being and Time*

If we read the few lines Heidegger devotes to poetic language in *Being and Time* after scanning the sections that Heidegger dedicates to art and poetry in his more recent works (i.e., *Holzwege* [*Off the Beaten Track*] and *Unterwegs zur Sprach* [*On the Way to Language*]), we may well get the impression we have found the evidence for the "turning" (*Kehre*) in Heidegger's thought. There is indeed a turning in Heidegger's philosophy, the importance of which has been greatly exaggerated by a lot of interpreters, which nonetheless does not undermine the fundamental unity of his speculative path of thinking.[1]

While, from his essays on Hölderlin to the poetic readings of *Unterwegs zur Sprache*, Heidegger remained faithful to the stated aim of recognizing the "objectivity" of poetry (by objectivity I mean the event character of Being belonging to poetry and more generally to art, in contrast with a vision of the poetic event as pure "fact" of consciousness), the allusion to poetry in

*Being and Time* (paragraph 34) seems to be entirely encapsulated within the limits of what I might call an emotive view of art, or at least within a perspective that is not radically distinguished from the neo-Kantian views that are diffuse in the aesthetics of many German authors of his time, including the first aesthetic thinkers of the phenomenological movement.[2]

Indeed, Heidegger writes:

All discourse . . . which communicates what it says has at the same time the character of expressing itself. In talking, Da-sein expresses itself not because it has been initially cut off as "something internal" from something outside, when it understands. What is expressed is precisely this being outside, that is, the actual mode of attunement (of mood) which we showed to pertain to the full disclosedness of being-in. Being-in and its attunement are made known in discourse and indicated in language by intonation, modulation, in the tempo of talk, "in the way of speaking." The communication of the existential possibilities of attunement, that is, the disclosing of existence, can become the true aim of "poetic speech."[3]

According to a first reading of this text, poetic language is entrusted with the task of disclosing, in a very specific manner, the affective dimension of existence (i.e., what Heidegger calls *Befindlichkeit*, "attunement"), which is never thematically in the foreground in ordinary discourse. This dimension is found not at the level of what one says but of *how* one says: the intonation, modulation, and "tempo" of discourse are the ways in which ordinary discourse lets one see or know attunement, that is, the specific emotional disposition of the speaker. Hence it is not fortuitous that musicality and rhythm play such an important part in poetry. For far from being purely "formal" facts, musicality and rhythm are bound up with the essence of poetry itself, understood as discourse that thematically manifests an attunement, an emotional disposition.

Put in these terms, this view does not go beyond a generic version of neo-Kantianism: poetry, or more generally art, has to do neither with knowledge nor with action but is rather relegated to the world of feelings. An aesthetic aspect, namely, the presence of an emotional element, is found in every situation, but in art it becomes thematic as the object of a specific communication. As a result, one cannot evade the impression that poetry isolates, and chooses for itself, an aspect of existence that is quite marginal, after all, since it has to do only with subjective reactions to situations; it is never a constitutive or determinant feature of discourse but is confined to its intonation, modulation, and tempo. If this really were the meaning of the passage previously cited, it would be difficult not to see an insurmountable gap between the theory of *Being and Time* and the successive statements regarding poetry as the event of being.

Upon closer inspection, such a banalizing interpretation is not entirely without reason when compared to Heidegger's oeuvre developed after *Being and Time*. The hint—and it is much more than a hint inasmuch as it indicates, clearly and forcefully, the direction and development of his thought—to an ontology of feeling in *Being and Time* is almost never taken up or elaborated in the later writings (other than in the discussion of anxiety in *What Is Metaphysics?*), leaving the impression that Heidegger's notion of emotion does not really go beyond what is found in the larger part of the philosophy of his epoch. It is necessary to put the brief reference to poetic language in *Being and Time* in the context of the embryonic ontology of affectivity that Heidegger did not fully develop in all its possible consequences, in order to recover the unity of Heidegger's thought in this element, too (in spite of the obvious contradictions), and above all to draw some useful indications for my argument on art.

## Affectivity in the Existential Analytic

It would not be difficult to give a purely intellectualistic reading of *Being and Time* that would confine itself to the plane of understanding: an inquiry into worldliness as the totality of things-tools, presenting the concept of the sign-tool as the tool that brings the worldliness of the world into the foreground—both in the sense that every sign inherently reveals the referential structure of all tools and in the sense that every sign is a tool of the tools, that is, it makes the world understood as a system of tools concretely available in its inner, universal connectedness. Even the concept of care, understood in its fundamental structure as project: this complex phenomenological discussion of the being of being-there (i.e., man) could remain at the level of knowledge without any regard for affectivity.

So far, affects and feelings could remain marginal aspects, "subjective" connotations of our way of being-in-the-world, reduced to accompanying being without touching its fundamental structure. Moreover, the notion of "thrown project" from which the discourse on attunement starts could be seen as a pure indication of the finitude of our cognitive projects, that is, as the recognition of all the prejudice that is always already there, namely, the pre-understanding of the world beyond which we cannot move, and which we must explicitly assume as the circle of our understanding-interpretation. This circle appears vicious only to an abstract and rationalistic mindset. Thus, I would offer an exposition of the first five chapters of the first section of *Being and Time*, excluding only paragraphs 29 and 30, which, strictly speaking, would not reveal any gap or inconsistencies, even with more analytical precision. Nothing would be missing at first sight. Heidegger's thought would appear as a kind of rationalism tempered with the recognition of the finitude of the project, its "thrown-ness." However, thrown-ness (*Geworfenheit*), understood in this way, would not only be assumed as the de facto insurmountable condition that it is, it would not be susceptible to meaning, to interpretation.

It seems to me that we should insist on this (hypothetical) possibility (which seeks to demonstrate a point by showing its absurdity) of giving a consistent reading of the first section of *Being and Time* without taking into account the notion of attunement. Such a paradoxical reading would show precisely the importance of affectivity in determining the ontological disclosure of the existential analytic and would exhibit the structure of attunement as such. The fact that one could give a reading of the existential analytic in which attunement could be suspended shows that it has a "fortuitous" character, one on which the rationalistic perspectives dwell whenever they reduce affectivity to the meaning of a purely subjective fact, in the narrowest and most intimate sense of the term. In other words, it is true that attunement is not a character of existence, to be placed next to the others in a systematic description of it; however, this is only because, in addition to constituting a systematic unity with the other existential structures, as Heidegger calls them, attunement is the background or a kind of common source of which they are the modifications and determinations. Here we can consistently move on to describing these determinations. But in doing so the possibility of attending to their genuine meaning is lost, even though the consistency of the argument is safeguarded.

All this becomes clear if we keep in mind that attunement is connected to *Geworfenheit*—that is, the thrown-ness of Dasein. Moreover, it is nothing other than the resonance for us of our thrown-ness, that is, the way in which *Geworfenheit* is manifested to us and becomes fully present in all our attitudes as the totality of the world-project that constitutes our existence. Heidegger calls *Befindlichkeit* (attunement) what I have translated as affectivity. Etymologically, and in accord with one of its literal meanings, *Befindlichkeit* simply means the fact of finding oneself positioned or how one finds oneself positioned in the same sense in which in Italian people say "*mi trovo bene o male*" (literally: I find myself well or not well) to indicate that one is comfortable or uncomfortable with a certain situation. *Befindlichkeit* is the very situation in which we find ourselves situated, in its meaning for us, where meaning does not indicate an intellectual fact but a global and confused (attuned) perception.

Nevertheless, it is necessary here to make a clarification, because the habit of reasoning in terms of subjective and objective is so natural for us that it asserts itself even when we explicitly decide to place ourselves beyond this or that side of the distinction. The attuned valence of the situation is not an accidental modification, which would be added to a structure that already subsists in itself, only in reference to us. In fact, I shall recall that it is precisely when Heidegger formulates the definition of things as tools that he emphatically stresses that being-tool is the very essence of things: the thing as such is a tool. The essence of the thing is nothing other than its belonging to a web of referential significations that has man at its center.

The whole unfolding of Heidegger's speculation demonstrates that this conception of the being of things as tools is not an idealist position, that is, a reduction of the being-in-itself of things to what they are for us. The point is that Heidegger, consistently with his position toward metaphysics and toward its aporias, no longer conceives of being as fully present objectivity, imposed upon us the revelation of the stable ground of all becoming.[4] On the contrary, things are inasmuch as they come to being, inasmuch as they enter into the lighting, where Dasein (i.e., man) has a central function. The human being does not have the lighting at its disposal; he is not its master; he is only the care-taker and shepherd of being.[5] The fact that things belong to the world—that is, to the system of tools that has man at its center—does not concern only us, or things to the extent that they are related to us; it constitutes the being of things and our being: in other words, Being in its event character, in its happening.

## Affectivity and Being-in-the-World

To understand the ontological implications of Heidegger's theory of attunement, it is necessary to keep in mind that what is said about things as tools is
true with respect to their attuned valence as well. Only a remnant of intel-
lectualism prevented Heidegger from developing this opening toward an
ontology of affects, at least to the extent that it would have been possible. In
his latest work, the event of being always principally constitutes an event of
meaning, the instituting of an intellectual web of significations, more intellectual than emotional. Heidegger gives a positive indication of affect when
underscoring that the disclosure of the world of meaning always occurs in
poetry and in art. It is in poetry that language is born, and the world in it.
Above all, things come to being in the language of poetry. Heidegger, however, will no longer thematically discuss the relation between poetry and
attunement alluded to in *Being and Time*, from which my argument set off,
as if he wished to concur with those who see his early theoretical characterization of poetry as being later abandoned once and for all.

   And yet it is clear that for *Being and Time* the worldliness of the world—
that is, the world of referrals and meanings—is an attunement rather than an
intellectual fact connected to comprehension. Among the three existential
structures—attunement, understanding, and discourse—attunement comes
first insofar as it has a grounding position with respect to the others. Attunement (*Stimmung*) determines (*be-stimmt*) our being-in-the-world. Dasein is
never in the world as before a spectacle of meanings, namely, as the bearer of
universal reason that reaches the truth inasmuch as it is capable of a universal
exercise independently of the specific determinations of singular individuals.
Dasein is always existentially involved with this order (or disorder) of meanings because things, in addition to having a function, possess an attuned
valence. This is not placed alongside intellectual meanings, as if it were just
another aspect of the thing. Rather, the *Stimmung* determines (giving it its
tonality) our being-in-the-world and therefore our understanding of the
world, that is, the manifestation of the world as a totality of referrals; the
coming to being on the part of things. It is possible to say, as for Heidegger,
that all understanding and interpretation of the world are founded on a pre-
understanding that is identical with the fact of existing, pre-understanding
is more originally rooted in *Stimmung*, attunement. It would be absurd to
object that pre-understanding and attunement are situated on different planes,

precisely in light of the spirit and method of Heidegger's inquiry, which never proceeds by adding on new elements. As is typical of genuine phenomenology, Heidegger proceeds by means of a global apprehension of phenomena and by delving deeper into the argument by way of concentric circles. In other words: before being inside a web of meanings, being-in-the-world is inside attunement, an affective valence. The coming to light and becoming precise of meaning is already a sort of inner articulation and explanation of the original attunement (*Stimmung*). If it is true that the world is not "there" independently of the meaning it has for us but rather comes to being inasmuch as it comes to meaning, it will be equally true that its coming to being is first and foremost the presentation of an attunement, a *Stimmung*, before it comes to meaning.

This argument, which is fully justified by *Being and Time*, corresponds faithfully to the aim of Heidegger's later thought, which constitutes what I have elsewhere called an ontological repetition of the existential analytic or the happening of the existential structures.[6] In fact, the so-called turning in Heidegger's thought is nothing other than the repetition of what should have been carried out in the third section of *Being and Time*, according to the original plan, but was never accomplished. Just as the second section of *Being and Time* "repeats" the analysis of "being-there" (Dasein) that was carried out in the first from the point of view of temporality, to discover once again the same elements as the first section, the third section as originally sketched was intended to repeat the analysis of being-there from the specific point of view of Being as such. When considering *Being and Time* we may still have the doubt that it is a matter of defining the essence of man, in the most traditional meaning of the term "essence"; the successive works—above all the *Letter on Humanism*—make clear that what in *Being and Time* might have been construed as characteristics of man's nature are actually events, facts, occurrences of Being, that is, the mode in which Being is, occurs, and gives itself.

The same ontological repetition that Heidegger developed principally with respect to the circle of understanding-interpretation, thus reaching the positions of an ontology of language in the essays published in *Unterwegs zur Sprache*, should be applied to the first existential structure, attunement. Besides, a vaster and more consistent elaboration of the ontological meaning of attunement in the sense disclosed by *Being and Time* would have anticipated and resolved at the ontological level a whole set of problems that has increasingly engaged phenomenology, with its appeal to the life-world, the world of affects and emotions. However, while phenomenology ended up developing the argument in the direction of an implicit naturalism and vitalism (thus confusing originality with primitiveness of the datum), Heidegger clearly possessed principles for an ontological transcription of the entire problematic.[7]

## Affectivity as Ontological Fact

Acknowledging the ontological character of *Stimmung* as a global apprehension of the world, in which understanding appears as its internal articulation, is nonetheless the first step toward applying to *Befindlichkeit* (attunement) the ontological repetition of the existential analytic. What seems to come to light is not only that attunement has an ontological bearing (it is an event of Being rather than a "characteristic" of Dasein); it is precisely *Befindlichkeit* that opens the way to the ontological understanding of the other existential structures, fully cohering with its grounding position with respect to them.

Indeed, if the recognition of Dasein's ontological character is linked to the recognition of *Geworfenheit* (thrown-ness), *Befindlichkeit* is the existential structure in which the fact of being-thrown is more clearly and more directly made present. Understanding-interpretation, and discourse as its articulation and clarification, is always in the end sites of mediation. It is true that interpretation and discourse are internal articulations of a pre-understanding that is always already given and precisely "thrown." However, to a certain extent the circularity of the hermeneutic circle holds true for the pre-understanding, too. It is true that understanding always supposes a pre-understanding and therefore never possesses itself completely; on the other hand, it is equally true that the original and always given pre-understanding does present itself only in understanding, precisely insofar as it is understanding. In a certain sense, then, understanding truly consummates its own presuppositions, to the extent that it articulates and discloses itself. It is ultimately only for this reason that it is possible to recognize, from Heidegger's view, how Hegel or the truth of Hegelianism was possible.

This operation of "consummation of the presuppositions"—insofar as it is possible—as a thesis concerning the circle of understanding-interpretation and the two existential structures, *Verstehen* (understanding) and *Rede* (discourse), is unthinkable without *Befindlichkeit*. In *Befindlichkeit*, the finitude and thrown-ness become present in a manner that withdraws any mediation. For Heidegger, affective *Stimmungen* are the true sign of the finitude of Dasein, that is, of the fact that Dasein does not dispose of, has no power over its own principle, over its whence. To find oneself in such and such a emotional disposition—sympathy, antipathy, love, fear, mistrust, and so on—cannot be modified or commanded, even if one were to assign or deny them an intellectual ground. More than finding myself positioned in a specific prejudice, in determined possibilities of knowing that have to do with the language I employ or the culture in which I happened to be born—all "facts" ultimately open to mediation and resolution insofar as they take place at the level of discourse—*Stimmung* evades completely any form of control and therefore is the most visible sign of finitude.

In this way, the ontological meaning of feelings emerges precisely from the character that are most striking in them, that is, their complete groundlessness. What comes forth in the groundlessness of feeling is the same groundlessness that is constitutive of existence: the fact that existence cannot be grounded, to the extent that it evades any schemes in which we might put it in relation to a ground-reason that would account for it to us (i.e., ultimately delivering it to us as our own possession, insofar as we possess reason). Our existence in the world, prior to becoming a center within an order of meaning, of a pre-understanding, is "a fact," a "that," and it is precisely this facticity (*Faktizität*) that we encounter in our affectivity, attunement.

Thus considered, affectivity is not the ensemble of specific affects but rather more generally the coming forth of our being-in-the-world as such. Indeed, as an application of Heidegger's method, we could say that the single affects, understood as the specific determinations of the affective sphere, are possible only because they are rooted in affectivity as being-thrown. Pain, love, joy, hope, and so on are not private or subjective states, accidents that leave untouched our deepest metaphysical situation of being-there; on the contrary, they are the modes in which this finite condition of being-in-the-world is made present in a radical way.

From our cursory examination of *Befindlichkeit* as an existential structure, there have emerged two distinctive elements that will remain constitutive of Heidegger's theory of poetry up to his recent works. One the one hand, the affective situation has a grounding function with respect to the other existential structures: the world that is given only in understanding and interpretation arises originally as a more global, affectively determined (*bestimmt*), fact. If, in fact, things come to being—that is, the world constitutes itself as such—only in the light projected by Dasein over things, and if this light is the understanding-interpretation articulated in discourse, the affective situation that precedes, comprises, and grounds understanding stands at the very origin of the constitution of the world.

In this way, *Bifindlichkeit* already acquires a precise ontological physiognomy, where the term "ontological" has a specific meaning; it indicates what regards Being rather than beings or the totality of beings. The affective situation, inasmuch as it constitutes the opening moment of the world (things come to being in the light of Dasein, but this light is illuminated as affectivity before it is understanding) does not concern this or that entity but the very fact of coming to being (to the world) of every entity belonging to a certain world. To put it in Heidegger's language: affectivity concerns the instituting of an epoch of Being, of a global configuration in which beings set themselves at a given historical moment. In this sense, the affective situation has the ontological meaning of an event that takes place at the level of Being, rather than at the level of the existent.

This explicit ontological view of the affective situation is corroborated by the other element that has emerged from the description mentioned earlier. It is affectivity that allows the fact of existence and finitude to come to light in all its groundlessness. Once more, then, from the perspective of the existential analytic, what matters is the fact of being-there and of existing in the world, and not the fact that the world is defined emotionally. In affectivity the fact of existing comes forth, even before putting in question the "how" of its being-there. Now, I call ontological what does not touch the how, the where, and the when of existing (one could list here the entire table of Aristotelian accidents) but the *that* of existence (that existence be). It does not concern the entity, or a determinate situation of the entity, but being as such, the happening of whatever arrangement of beings, that is, of the world.

Starting with the essays "The Origin of the Work of Art" and "Hölderlin and the Essence of Poetry," Heidegger increasingly assigned to poetry the character of instituting and founding the world.[8] By developing the presuppositions already present in *Being and Time*, Heidegger increasingly made clear that things come to being inasmuch as they come to language. Language is not a tool that the human being makes use of in order to indicate, to describe, and to come to understanding with others in regard to a fully given world, independent of the discourse that speaks about it. Instead, there is world, for man, only to the extent that there is a language that speaks of it, that arranges, organizes, makes it comprehensible, penetrable, and inhabitable.

Language may also be a simple tool of communication in the ordinary usage of everyday discourse. In that case, it is only an explicit repetition of a system of conventions and of acquired significations. But there is a type of discourse that is radically new and that does not allow itself to be reduced to what already exists. It is the discourse of poetry or, more generally, the language of art as setting-to-work of truth. In the genuine work of art a language is born that was never spoken before, heralding a general reordering of the world. If the artwork is genuine—and we experience this all the time—it does not install itself peacefully into the world but rather reorganizes it and puts it in question. In this sense, a new language and a new world are born by virtue of poetry.

## The Work as Setting-to-Work of Truth: *Stoss* and Anxiety

Now that we have seen affectivity in all the breadth of its ontological opening, the opposition I noted earlier between the aesthetics of Heidegger's recent works and his statements on poetry in *Being and Time* no longer subsists. The fact that poetry assumes the task of thematically communicating the manners in which the affective situation unfolds signifies that poetry concerns the genesis of a world in the sense explained above of giving birth to language and to a new total and systematic reorganization of beings.

Far from isolating poetry and art to the level of the emotions, understood as purely subjective facts, this definition opens poetry to an ontological event of enormous implications. Indeed, conceived in this way, poetry is the ontological event itself, the site where Being happens. Furthermore: the recognition of the nexus between poetry and affectivity contributes to the clarification and further specification of the meaning of affectivity for the existential analytic and Heidegger's ontology as a whole. It is, in fact, only by keeping in mind the links between poetry and affectivity that one can retrace in Heidegger's mature work (from the essays in *Holzwege* onward) the development of the ontology of feeling anticipated by *Being and Time*. With the emphatic shift from being-there (Dasein) to Being as such, sanctioned by the turning in the *Letter on Humanism*, affectivity and other ideas of the existential analytics seem to disappear entirely from Heidegger. On the contrary, affectivity is still present in Heidegger's mature work, though with a different terminology (in my view, this other terminology is meant to avoid any equivocally "emotional" interpretation of art) by virtue of its link with poetry and with its opening function, as *Being and Time* had already anticipated.

One of the elements on which Heidegger insists more forcefully in his analysis of the artwork in the essays published in *Holzwege* is the idea of the novelty and underivability of the work. Here he takes over and makes more radical one of the characters of the artwork that had been increasingly affirmed in aesthetics from Kant onward; the novelty and underivability of the work, which Kant had traced back to nature in his theory of the genius, was gradually deprived of any ontological meaning and reduced to the gratuitousness of play and disengagement in the aesthetics of the nineteenth and twentieth centuries, or became a provisional character of the aesthetics that acknowledged the ontological meaning of art only to enclose it in dialectical schemes.

Based on the conception of truth and of being as event gradually elaborated in the light of *Being and Time*, Heidegger recovered the notion of art's novelty in its entirety and grounded it on more solid grounds than Kant. The absolute novelty of the work, for Heidegger, is that it is the setting to work of truth. In other words, the work does not install itself as an entity among other entities, within an already open horizon. Rather, it institutes the horizon inside which the totality of beings places and arranges itself. We have already seen in what sense it is possible to call this an ontological event. The equivalent of this event for readers or consumers of works of art is a phenomenon that must be thought above all at the level of affectivity. It is what in the essay "The Origin of the Work of Art" Heidegger calls the *Stoss*, the shock produced by the work. What is it that produces the shock in art? It is important to clarify this, in order not to confuse Heidegger with the theorists of the "marvelous" (or wonder) understood as the end of all poetry. What produces the shock in art is not a specific mode of being of the work (a marvelous character of the work), but the fact that there is a work of art at all.

This is not something that strikes us only as a "sheer fact." As is well known, for Heidegger, things are basically tools destined for some use and are generally inserted into a framework of necessities and significations that is already given and in force. By virtue of its refusal to be peacefully installed into an already open horizon, the artwork is nevertheless not outside the world. The work opens and founds around itself its own world and imposes a general rearrangement of things. In this sense, its novelty and gratuitousness coincide with the very fact of founding and opening a world; while novelty is irreducible to this or that original character of the work, it is not empty but full of instituting force.

Since the work's novelty constitutes the foundation of a world, it never has an arbitrary character; it is new, underivable, though rigorously held by the lawfulness of things. The shock produced by the work is linked to law: in the work a world is encountered as it is being born. While with respect to things belonging to the world nothing is more normal than the fact "that the entity be," the fact that in the work there is entity at all becomes strange and is encountered in all its radical underivability. We are accustomed to considering the world as always already given: we are interested in what stands inside the world, but we miss it because we take for granted *that* there be world. Instead, the work brings into the foreground "that" there be world inasmuch as, by refusing to situate itself in the world as it is, it opens a new world and shows it to us in the moment of its disclosure.

Although it seems sufficiently clear from the analysis carried out so far, that the shock has to do with affectivity is corroborated by its analogy to, if not identity with, the affective situation of angst. At first approximation, it may seem that the two situations stand at the opposite polarities: the shock is the feeling of someone who sees the world in its nascent act, whereas dread is generally linked to the representation of an entity's annihilation in its totality. In actuality, the *Stoss* of the artwork and angst are the two sides, if you will, the positive and the negative, of the same affective situation. By placing me in front of a nascent world the artwork makes strange and unfamiliar the world that up to then had seemed obvious. For Heidegger, it is in fact without question that in our concrete experience the encounter with an artwork is always the beginning of a general revision of our relationship to the world: the work puts in question our way of seeing and standing in the world.

Now, the becoming strange of what, up to a certain moment, had seemed obvious and familiar is constitutive of the affective situation of angst as described in paragraph 40 of *Being and Time*. There is a feeling, says Heidegger, that looks like fear but is not so. This is always the fear of something. The other "fear," instead, has no cause that could be pointed to. On the contrary, in order not to feel it, Dasein does not escape from the entities but rather seeks them out and takes refuge in them. Angst, analyzed in the light of fear, is "fear of nothing." This is essentially what angst reveals in its depth. What angst is afraid of is nothing, because it is not an entity, it is the nothing of the entity. Yet what is not an entity, what cannot be described as an entity (i.e., as a "thing") is precisely being-in-the-world, Dasein (i.e., man) inasmuch as it opens and founds the realm within which beings appear. Dasein, as it is the opening of the horizon in which beings are, is the nothing of the entity. What someone who has angst runs away from is precisely being-there (*Da-sein*), to the extent that it is being-in-the-world.

In angst, the world loses its meaning. Heidegger thinks of meaning as the referral of one entity to another, which is consistent with his definition of things as tools and of the world as the totality of the tools connected by means of functional relationships. Now, in angst the ensemble of tools appears strange: it is not enough for someone experiencing angst to point to a "why" that would account for an entity by means of another entity, since it is precisely the totality of this system of referrals that in its sheer fact of existing (its *that*) appears enigmatic. In this situation, things become unfamiliar, so that Dasein finds itself in a condition of homelessness. Whereas in the everyday consideration (i.e., what Heidegger calls the realm of the inauthentic) Dasein always thinks of itself, at bottom, as a being among beings, and from such nearness to things draws a sort of reassurance of safety (i.e., the wealthy man thinks of his own existence as an economic and biological fact and only thus can he be reassured by the fact that he owns money), angst exposes it to the sheer nakedness of its being-there. In other words, dread exposes Dasein to the fact that it is a being that opens the realm within which any system of meanings and therefore any reassurance and familiarity become possible.

All this happens because, in the experience of angst, Dasein does not encounter another entity or the totality of beings, but rather the very fact of being this totality. The annihilating aspect of angst (which is predominant in *Being and Time*) is manifested only by virtue of its link with a positive element: angst encounters the nothing of being inasmuch as it encounters, positively, the fact of being the very horizon, the light that makes beings possible, rather than being itself an entity inside the opening.

As we have seen, this is precisely the *Stoss* (shock) of the artwork: in encountering a great artwork, the world I was accustomed to seeing becomes strange, is put into crisis in its totality, because the work proposes a new general reorganization of the world, a new historical epoch.

## Feeling and the Experience of Art

The introduction of the notion of shock and the analogy or identity it reveals with angst enable us to see how Heidegger's notion of affectivity, understood as a way of encountering the world in its nascent act (thus the relation between affectivity and originality), is constantly and consistently developed, thus laying bare the essential role of feeling in Heidegger's aesthetics.

Clearly, this recognition of the role of feeling is not linked with any of the ways in which traditional aesthetics have conceived of it. In fact, for this tradition the nexus art-feeling always had the meaning of taking art back to the most private and subjective realm of emotions, which were ultimately incommunicable or the object of art's sympathetic or allusive transmission; or of entrapping art into a sphere that was rigorously distinct from that of knowing and of acting, keeping it at bay from being and from the world, which were still thought as objects of knowledge and of the field of action. These two facts are basically reduced to one: art, to the extent that it is linked with feeling, is cut off from being (conceived metaphysically as fully present objectivity). Instead, in Heidegger the connection art-feeling is found precisely within an aesthetics that is resolutely ontological. To be sure, this is possible only because the way of conceiving being has been renewed. If Being were really fully present, that is, identical with the factual givenness of things, feeling could represent nothing other (as metaphysics wishes) than a way of reacting subjectively to what is fully given, having no meaning for what is already given, and given its private character, with very narrow possibilities of being communicated to other subjects. Now, it is true that the *Stoss* is a "subjective reaction" to the encounter with an artwork. However, since in the work the event of being is at work, feeling acquires a more markedly ontological coloring and is not reducible to a spectator of the event of being. For being is not an immutable datum entirely established and constituted before I might encounter it; rather, being is an event in which I participate, indeed it has its privileged site in happening in me insofar as I am a Dasein.

The impression that feeling is still a matter of "reacting" in the face of the event of being may be emphasized by the fact that Heidegger, like all the aesthetic thinkers coming from the phenomenological school, focused his attention on the completed work as well as on enjoyment rather than on the becoming of the work and on the act of production. Nonetheless, it would be easy to show that the *Stoss* is a reaction not only on the part of the reader but also on the part of the author inasmuch as the work is a gift for the author as well, that is, an event that happens in his work that can never be reduced to the author's will.

If all this constitutes a more certain and more meaningful basis for reproposing the question regarding the relationship between art and feeling in an ontological perspective, it still leaves unanswered the question concerning what art has to do with feelings, with the specific modes in which the affective life presents itself. This question is pointedly raised by concrete experience, above all, since the suspicion for any emotive vision of art that has increasingly crept into aesthetic philosophy is rooted in the mode of being of today's art, which banishes any substantial reference to feeling. Now, it seems out of the question that Heidegger's thought on this matter, as I have reconstructed it, in no way privileges expressive art,[9] the art that more or less programmatically expresses feelings, identifiable modes of the affective life. The nexus art-feeling, as Heidegger conceived it, is much more radical; it invests art with the nature of an event that is absolutely new. Art has to do with feeling not to the extent that it expresses this or that determinate and individual feeling, but only inasmuch as it is a work, namely, an ontological event. Feeling, in turn, must not be thought in opposition to knowledge, reason, or moral deliberation: feeling is solely and above all the way in which Dasein encounters the origin, that is to say, the act in which Being happens and illuminates a certain order of beings, a certain world. There is a *Stoss* before abstract art, be it the most cerebral and the most coldly removed from any reference to specific modes of the affective life.

This offers a few indications for resolving the more general question: if art is linked to feeling in this manner, how is its relation to feeling, to the individual modes of the affective life to be specified? It seems that if even abstract art represents for Dasein an event on the plane of the affective life, at least to the extent that it presents itself programmatically without expressing feelings and emotions, one might want to resolve the problem by means of a logical game, that is, by changing the meaning of the term "feeling." There would be feelings in art, even though they would have nothing to do with what we customarily call feelings, so that feeling would be nothing other than the *Stoss* of radical novelty, the ontological event. On the contrary, we should resolve the question in another way: what we are accustomed to calling feelings (i.e., love, joy, melancholy, and so on) are to be considered from an ontological perspective only as "special cases" of the structure of feeling that is fully realized in the experience of *Stoss* and dread.

As we have seen above, what constitutes feeling or affectivity in *Being and Time* is already *Befindlichkeit* (attunement), the fact of finding oneself situated or disposed. This view illuminates the very opposition between feeling and reason. Reason holds as the faculty of reasons, the faculty of the "why": something is rationally known only when it is grounded. Feeling, instead, is the faculty of groundlessness, the way of encountering the *that* that does not allow itself to be entirely consummated in the *why*. It is not fortuitous that the fundamental structure of feeling realizes itself as an archetype in angst and in *Stoss*, that is, in those modes of the affective situation where the fact *that* the world is appears in its totality as such without mediation or covering.

Art fulfills the structure of emotional event inasmuch as it is work, namely, an event of being. This is why so often in the past art was envisioned as the specific site for expressing feelings, that is to say, for the specific and concrete modifications of the emotional situation, as something that was especially addressed to the sphere of the emotions at the "level" of accomplished work. Feelings, of which aesthetics so often speaks as the substance or nature of art, are modifications of the fundamental affective structure that is connected with originality.

It seems possible, then, to ground the art-feeling nexus on the ontological rather than on the psychological plane, though no longer asserting that feelings, as specific modes of the affective life, must always be present in art, and with the awareness that the links between these specific modes and the archetypical structure of *Befindlichkeit* (the structure of angst and *Stoss*) still remain to be clarified. Nonetheless, from the viewpoint of the concrete reading and understanding of expressive art and poetry of the past centuries, it seems a positive outcome to have clarified that the phenomenon of expressiveness is not exclusively linked to the specific poetics that are by now more or less far from our taste; but on the contrary, that expressiveness is the mode in which the affective character that belongs to art is realized, to the extent that it is viewed as a fundamental event of being, as the happening of the origin.

# II *Hermeneutics*

# 5 Pareyson
## From Aesthetics to Ontology

If contemporary hermeneutics is to continue to develop its vocation for ontology, the importance of Pareyson's thought for the philosophy of interpretation is destined to have an increasingly central role.[1] The
following remarks intend to show: that the ontological implications of
Pareyson's hermeneutics above all spring from his reflection on the experience of art not only in its interpretative moment but also in the moment of
artistic "producing"; the ontology of the inexhaustible elaborated in the
last period of Pareyson's philosophical speculation, which he also formulated in terms of "tragic thought," is much more deeply bound with the
theory of interpretation he elaborated in his *Estetica* than it is generally assumed.[2] It is often the case that readers of the late Pareyson implicitly or
explicitly connect his last work with his reading of existentialist philosophy and Schelling, thereby completely neglecting his works on aesthetics.
I intend to show, instead, that reflecting on aesthetics is not a marginal or
specialized current within Pareyson's thought; rather, it is key to understanding his specific view on hermeneutics and the decisive role that his

thought is increasingly and more distinctively destined to play in this domain.

To be sure, the point of departure can only be a hypothesis regarding the specific meaning Pareyson's thought may take in contemporary hermeneutics, which is on its way to becoming more and more explicitly hermeneutic ontology. Now, it is precisely this meaning that appears to be summed up in his affirmation of tragic thought. If it can be shown that the radical consideration of the hermeneutic character of human existence as a whole—which for Pareyson appears emblematically in the experience of art—necessarily leads to tragic thought or in any case to an ontology of the inexhaustible (since there is no absolute identity between these two theoretical outcomes), then some significant progress will have been made in making clear the ontological outcomes of hermeneutics and the possible contents of such an ontology. In fact, there cannot be any philosophy of interpretation without radically revising the metaphysical conception of being.

Pareyson's tragic thought has a decisive importance for contemporary hermeneutics, especially if we think of the objections that are not without some reason often raised against hermeneutics: that it is a "philosophy of culture" fatally destined to collapse into relativism or in any case confined to apology for the plurality of paradigms, the metaphorical systems that describe the world, tolerance, and so on. If, above and beyond the specific views of the singular authors, hermeneutics were really characterized by this general humanist orientation (and this would raise the question of whether its appeal to Heidegger would still be legitimate), Pareyson could not be considered a hermeneutic thinker at all. Surely, though, nothing appears to be less popular than tragic thought among the theorists of hermeneutics, from Gadamer to Rorty. So much so that as a result it would seem legitimate to distinguish within Pareyson's thought between a hermeneutic trajectory (which revolves around interpretation theory and is elaborated in the direction of an ontology of the inexhaustible in the *Estetica*) and an existentialist trajectory that culminates with the proposal of tragic thought. However, if these two trajectories can be connected other than in a purely biographical way that pertains to the history of the thinker, it is possible that it will have a much broader significance: it will put in question several of the theoretical outcomes of the thinkers mentioned in my previous chapters, and consequently may well free hermeneutics from the limits for which it is often blamed because as it has been viewed exclusively in the light of those works.

Is there, then, a nexus that is not merely fortuitous between the existentialist Pareyson of *Studi sull'esistenzialismo* (1941), *Jaspers* (1940), and *Esistenza e Persona* (1950), and the more "naturalist" and almost Brunian (i.e., Giordano Bruno) Pareyson of the *Estetica* of 1954?

Let me clarify this nexus and the overall meaning of Pareyson's theory for contemporary hermeneutics by starting with an elementary observation. Pareyson, among the theorists of hermeneutics (excluding Heidegger), is perhaps the one who has given the most complete and accurate analysis of the interpretative act as such. This may be surprising, but outside of his work, in the classical works of contemporary hermeneutics it is difficult to find a definition or even an in-depth description of interpretation. Gadamer, too, seems to be more or less satisfied with continuing the German tradition of *Verstehen* in opposition to *Erklären*. In fact, his interpretation theory is marked out only because it adds a more specific accentuation of the hermeneutic circle to the prevailingly empathetic features pointed out by Dilthey. Unlike Dilthey, though, Gadamer does not consider the hermeneutic circle in its vital meaning (i.e., that interpreter and text ultimately belong to living life) but rather in its more specifically historical meaning. The interpreter belongs to a history that has been shaped by the text itself. Furthermore: the interpreter belongs to objective spirit, broadly understood in a Hegelian sense. It is possible that the vagueness of hermeneutics results from its minor attentiveness, at the level of knowledge, to the problem of an in-depth inquiry into the interpretative act. It is this vagueness, for many critics, that makes hermeneutics suspicious of cultural relativism, of a purely apologetic emphasis on the plurality of paradigms, a sort of "hurdy-gurdy song" that Nietzsche saw in the superficial interpretation his animals give of the terrifying doctrine of the eternal return.[3]

By contrast, it is precisely in the analysis of the interpretative character of human knowledge that Pareyson brings to bear his familiarity with existentialism and with Kierkegaard. Before developing the multiple implications of existentialism in the *Estetica*, in an essay written in 1950 Pareyson had laid down the basis for his own personal overcoming of the metaphysical conception of truth as correspondence.[4] To be sure, this did not occur independently of his reading of *Being and Time* and existentialist thinkers, though it was probably inspired by the study of German idealism in its Fichtian version. In that essay, interpretation—understood as the never purely passive character of knowledge—is shown to be already at work in sensible intuition. Sensible knowledge intuits things by actively configuring them by means of an image, both the image of the thing and the expression of the subject and of his feelings. Since it has its origin in sensations, "knowledge does not grasp something without expressing the knower, and . . . expression does not express feelings without grasping a known together with it." From this reflection on the interpretative character of sensible knowledge, Pareyson draws the first and most complete definition of interpretation he has ever given, one that shapes the meaning of his entire philosophy for the problem of hermeneutics: "Interpretation is a form of knowing in which receptivity and activity are inseparable, and where the known is a form and the knower a person." The two parts of this definition say the same thing from different viewpoints, and this is necessary in order to see the nexus between the existentialist heritage and Pareyson's own notion of interpretation. Since everything characterizing Pareyson's hermeneutics depends on the notion of interpretation as knowledge of forms on the part of persons, it is important to observe here (since we are seeking out the nexus between this definition of interpretation and Pareyson's existentialism) that such a definition would not have been possible without having established the impossibility of disjoining the receptivity and activity that is constitutive of the finitude of interpretation. In Pareyson's language, form and person are terms referring to finitude: they are both the outcomes of a formative process that generates a finality (*definitività*) starting from conditions that are always given and that orient it, while determining and delimiting the boundary of its possibilities. It is precisely insofar as it is knowledge of forms on the part of persons that interpretation has the character of infinitude, of being always open to further interpretative acts—and this brings Pareyson into proximity with the slightly vague and generic "optimism" of a hermeneutics according to which "everything goes," for which the multiplicity of interpretation can only be an indefinite mode of growth. However, precisely insofar as it is knowledge of forms on the part of persons, interpretation involves risk and the possibility of setbacks, too. His infinitude is not a peaceful openness to a destiny of limitless growth; rather, it is an indication of an ontology characterized by the feature of inexhaustibility, which is also deeply marked by a specifically tragic character.

To put it differently: if we do not confine ourselves to a slightly vague conception of interpretation in terms of *Verstehen* and of the hermeneutic circle in terms of *Erlebnis* but rather analyze it more deeply as Pareyson does, we will probably reach the same ontological conclusions as Pareyson, summed up in an ontology of the inexhaustible and in the formulation of tragic thought.

Two questions should be clarified now: What cogency has Pareyson's definition of interpretation? How is its origin disclosed in the reflection on aesthetic experience?

In regard to the first question, let us consider the central idea of hermeneutic circle. What is gained by defining it in terms of the inseparability of activity and receptivity and of knowledge of forms on the part of persons? The gain seems to consists above all in avoiding (mis)understanding the circle as the relativizing limitation of interpretation only, so that interpretation can still be conceived as a form of knowing that has the defect of not being a truly objective mirror of how things really are. There is a residue of this prejudice also in Dilthey, especially in his effort to legitimize the scientific character of historical knowledge.

Neither in Dilthey nor, perhaps, in Gadamer are the infinite openness of interpretation and its characteristic finitude brought back to the same source: on the contrary, they are two different aspects, not entirely reconciled, often in conflict with each other. Instead, in Pareyson these two aspects are inseparable. They ground each other reciprocally in a positive way. It is not only the person but also the form that is an infinity enclosed within a finality. Infinity is not at all theorized in terms of the metaphysical view of the person having infinite value as the bearer of freedom or of the form as the work of the person, of nature, or of God. The infinity of person and form is bound up with the outcome of a process, which precisely because it is determined and delimited by conditions that are always anterior to it, is open to indeterminate possibilities (its own origin always already escapes it, since all the possibilities disclosed by the origin are not entirely at its disposal) that remain effectively in the margins, constituting its precariousness and richness, even when they are excluded from the choice of a certain course of development. Person and form are therefore finalities that bear in themselves, as the trace of their formative process, an infinity that opens onto interpretation. Insofar as they are the outcomes of a formative process, they can be grasped only by a processional understanding. This process, in turn, has its own infinite possibility at play in the interpretation and reconstruction of the original process, which can bestow the characters of inventiveness and growth upon interpretation. However, as in the case of the formative process, the infinity of the interpretative act involves the risk of a setback. This possibility seems to fade

away in Gadamer's hermeneutics, because he has not made clear the ontological roots of the infinity of interpretation. Instead, he seems to entrust
it to the indeterminate multiplicity of generations of interpreters (from
Heidegger's viewpoint, this is not without its own logic: perhaps death is
"the coffer of being," as Heidegger writes, inasmuch as the enriching interpretation of being arises out the interpreter's mortality). The thing-form
(text, event, work) is situated in history, and the wealth of its effective
history (*Wirkungsgeschichte*) seems to arise from the fact that an infinite
number of interpreters approach it. Even though Gadamer refutes the hermeneutic nihilism expressed in Valéry's statement, "mes vers ont le sens
qu'on leur prête," the recurring questions regarding the limits, methodological rigor, and validity of interpretation that are constantly addressed
to him seem to indicate that this problem is present in his work. However,
if, as occurs in Pareyson, the infinity of interpretation is grounded on the
infinity of person and form, understood not as pure qualitative opening
and indefinite growth of meaning, but rather as a result of openness and
risk that is constitutive of the formative process, *Wirkungsgeschicte* appears
to be more clearly explicated and justified, and the characters of engagement and risk belonging to the interpretative act less vaguely theorized.

Hence, knowledge of forms on the part of persons signifies that interpretation is distinguished by its own specific infinity, both as an indefinite
opening to the growth of the work on the part of interpreters and to the risk
of a setback. Such a risk, which constitutes the specifically existentialist aspect of Pareyson's hermeneutics, is inseparable from the nature of interpretation, unless its infinite openness is understood merely in terms of
"subjectivism," resulting from the infinite succession of interpreters that
come into contact with the form. Indeed, the infinity of interpretation is
grounded on the infinity of the process that characterizes the genesis of the
form and constitution of the person. Infinity is the source of risk in a horizon of indeterminate possibilities, which by virtue of its success leaves its
traces on the form and on the person well after the process of formation has
come to closure and keeps them open for further developments as well as for
potential setbacks.

The aesthetic roots of this view of interpretation and its ontological implications are plainly visible. In Pareyson, even though interpretation is already at work in sensible intuition, the articulation of its moments and of its
characteristic infinity are worked out in the analysis of aesthetic experience,
especially in the instance of fruition and formation. Perhaps it is not neces-

sary to underline that in its totality the interpretative character of human experience is not separable from its formative character. Formativity (producing by inventing a mode of production, as well as art's law of producing) is the name for the initiated initiative that man is. If we consider the identity of the interpretative nature of the whole of experience and formativity understood as initiated initiative, then it is clear how deeply hermeneutics is bound up with the heritage of existentialism in Pareyson more than in other theories. Although he was quite familiar with Dilthey's problematic,[5] Pareyson did not draw his interest in interpretation from the reflection on the questions of the human sciences. In this, he is more akin to the framework of the existential analytic of *Being and Time*, where the question of hermeneutics results from the finitude of existence and from its formative character, the specific structures that come to the fore in the analysis of aesthetic experience. The existentialist roots, on the one hand, and the reference to aesthetic experience, on the other, lay the basis for the explicitly ontological turn of interpretation theory in his work.

The ontological elements shaping the whole subsequent development of Pareyson's hermeneutics come to the fore in the analysis of the formative process, first, and of the interpretation of the work of art, later. The formation of the work of art is an act not of creation but of interpretation: of a cue, of the materials (which, of course, are not only given but chosen), of the spirituality of an artist bent on the act of forming. All these elements converge to generate a "forming form," the intimate law of the productive process, which, albeit only completely "given" at the end of the work, must already somehow exist in the course of the process in which the "formed form" constituting the work is revealed; otherwise it would not be a process of inquiry in which one considered errors, corrections, adaptations, and remaking. The success of the work lies in reaching a point of convergence between the law and the work produced, the forming form and the formed form. Just as production already constitutes an interpretation (of the materials, one's spirituality, the situation, and the cues) on the part of the artist, so is the interpretative act above all a formative act. The interpreter forms an image of the work expressing his spirituality and at the same time grasping the work's form; it somehow retraces, albeit not chronologically, the entire process by which the work was formed. Interpretation succeeds when the image, reconstructed by the interpreter under the guidance of the forming form that speaks to him through the work, coincides with the effective physical nature of the work set before him.

As is well known, these are the main features of the two fundamental moments of aesthetic experience: the production and fruition of the work of art. A more detailed analysis—which is not possible here—could show that all the aspects of the hermeneutic problem take up a different meaning (which would make hermeneutics less open to vague and superficial readings) if situated in the background of Pareyson's definition of interpretation as knowledge of forms on the part of persons, especially when seen in light of the two fundamental stages of aesthetics: the analyses of the formative process and of the interpretative process. I will touch upon only a few of them: the question of the hermeneutic circle, interpretation as an act for which "everything goes," and the aesthetic model of the hermeneutic conception of truth.

According to the hermeneutic vulgate, the hermeneutic circle is conceived almost exclusively as the belonging of the interpreter to the historical context from which the text (work, form, event) to be interpreted comes from or at the limit (in Gadamer) of the historical-natural language in which the interpreter is always thrown. For Pareyson, instead, the hermeneutic circle is linked to the theory of congeniality, which is the condition for the success of interpretation, understood as the expression of the interpreter's personality and revelation of the form in its truth. The elements of openness and risk we observed in the definition of interpretation are involved in this central point of interpretation theory. First of all, the concept of risk: in its more generic version, the text is given to the interpreter in a situation to which they both belong as the very condition of understanding; here it does not seem possible to conceive of the failure of interpretation. In Gadamer, for example, we could conceive of the failure of interpretation only in the sense of an inaccurate recognition of the *Wirkungsgeschichte*, in addition to the unconscious prejudices that tend to appear in every pretense of an absence of prejudice. (Is there a trace of Cartesianism in this aspect of Gadamer? If the analysis, synthesis, and enumeration is complete, the errors should not be possible.) Pareyson places two conditions on the success of interpretation that cannot be clearly separated: the involvement of the interpreter and the congeniality that may or may not subsist between the interpreter and the text-work. Involvement produces no results without congeniality; or better, it does not even arise, because congeniality is the underlying condition for the work to address the interpreter to stimulate his interest, and ultimately his engagement. On the other hand, as always happens in the structure of formativity as initiated initiative, congeniality is never given as an entirely external or preliminary condition: it is there inasmuch as it is always already interpreted and actively taken up. The point here is that this "naturalistic" element (congeniality is an always already given spiritual affinity with which the interpreter starts but does not create) enforces a limitation against the radically historicist framework in which the play of interpretation appears to unfold in Gadamer, such that he cannot easily account for the possible failure of interpretation. In Pareyson, the hermeneutic circle loses the trait of tranquilizing completeness that it appears to possess (and perhaps really does) in Gadamer's historicist humanism. To be sure, the price of all this is a naturalistic type of ontological disclosure, which remains a characteristic of the last Pareyson's tragic thought, around which both the achievements and the problematic aspect of his thought are crystallized.

Whenever the hermeneutic circle is conceived in more existentialist terms, the act of interpretation is dramatized, and rightly so. The possibility of a setback is brought back to its horizon, together with the whole involvement of the interpreter who plays with his own destiny. Here, too, it is perhaps just a matter of nuances, which in the end assign a different ontological meaning to hermeneutics. True, in Gadamer's hermeneutical notion of truth as genuine modification of the interpreter's world, which is brought about by the encounter with the text-work and by the fusion of their horizons, the interpretative act is not conceived as an operation among others that could happen to an indifferent subject. Even though in its purview it has mainly the experience of the human sciences, hence a specific epistemic performance that must be liberated from the hegemony of the objectivist model of positivistic scientism, Gadamer opens the epistemological significance of his premises in the direction of a more global and more existential view of the interpretative act. Nevertheless, it is always a kind of shock, for those of us who are accustomed to viewing hermeneutics almost exclusively in the light of *Truth and Method*, to read once again the passages in *Being and Time* where Heidegger argues that interpretation is grounded in the understanding in which Dasein always already appropriates its own being.[6] The shock is probably motivated by the fading away of the element of destiny, of the person's total engagement, in the present version of hermeneutics, though not without betraying or reductively reading Gadamer's text.

If we consider hermeneutics in the version proposed by Rorty, the impression of disorientation is even more sharply marked. As is well known, for Rorty everything that has to do with arguments regarding the solution to problems that arise within accepted and shared (Kuhnian) paradigms falls into the realm of the epistemological. By contrast, Rorty calls hermeneutical every encounter with, or invention of, new paradigms, namely, new ways of describing the world, unheard-of systems of metaphor (as the Nietzsche of the fragment on "Truth and lies in an extra-moral sense" would say), which are presented as novel ways of reorganizing experience. It is difficult to say whether here the interpretative act or the invention of new metaphors involves the possibility of a dramatic outcome, since the failure of interpretation could still be conceived as a kind of invention. It is even more difficult to decide whether someone encountering a new system of metaphors "understands" it or goes on to invent a newer system (Wittgenstein: someone who calculates differently than me makes a mistake or plays a different game?). It is difficult to say what has become here of the "projection of one's own foremost possibility," of which *Being and Time* speaks as the very condition of interpretation. It is true that the inventor/interpreter's spirituality is engaged and expressed both in invention and in the interpretation of new systems of metaphors. However, every drama linked to the possibility of a setback seems to be excluded, so that in a certain sense "everything goes"; at best one may experience a shock on account of the metaphors' novelty.

Is this the meaning of the aesthetic model that seems to be at work in the hermeneutic conception of truth?[7] Once again, if we think of Gadamer and Rorty (the two extreme versions of hermeneutics today: the classic founder versus the "urbanizing" successor), it is plain enough that an aesthetic model is at work in contemporary hermeneutics, one that is not always recognized but still extremely powerful. To be sure, Rorty would deny such a statement insofar as he refuses to put forth any theory of truth, which he sees merely as an abstract noun that is no longer useful. Whatever one might call it, the truth of experience is still conceived on the model of an aesthetic or, better, aestheticist experience. It was already evident in the distinction between epistemology and hermeneutics Rorty put forth in *Philosophy and the Mirror of Nature* that the latter term was privileged over the former, a point that is underlined even more in *Contingency, Irony, and Solidarity*. Rorty has neither chosen for himself nor enthusiastically recommended to others the task of resolving the questions that arise within accepted paradigms. Both in the way in which he emphatically connects pragmatism to Nietzsche and Sartre in *Philosophy and the Mirror of Nature* and in his admiration for poets and writers expressed in the other book, there is an extremely mitigated and yet audible echo of Heidegger's notion of authenticity, of the existential involvement of which *Being and Time* speaks, albeit conceived in terms of pure poetic creativity. Ethics, too, is worked out in these terms in Rorty. Here, however, the aesthetic model intends to say more than the aestheticist model: the truth—or whatever one might call it—of experience coincides with the creation of forms of life that are proposed solely to the extent that they are "successful" forms of redescription of the self and of its experience. Nonetheless, it seems hard to conceive how once this is formulated in a work one could judge such forms to be unsuccessful. Once again, then, here the aesthetic model signifies that "everything goes."

Equally aestheticist, though in a more subtle way, seems to be the outcome of Gadamer's description of hermeneutics that is modeled on the experience of the truth of art. As is well known, *Truth and Method* begins its defense of the extra-methodological truth of the human sciences precisely with the recognition that there is an experience of truth in art, insofar as the encounter with the work of art truly transforms the interpreter. It is a fusion of horizons in which neither the one nor the other term of the relation remain what they were at the outset, since the work, too, is loaded with the traces of interpretation left by that particular encounter, which constitute its *Wirkungsgeschichte* and from which it cannot isolate itself. Nonetheless, as I have argued elsewhere,[8] the adoption of this aesthetic model to think the truth of hermeneutics enables Gadamer to articulate the experience of truth as the an experience of integration into a reconstructed totality rather than as the metaphysical evidence of a content of consciousness to be clearly and distinctly seen in Cartesian fashion. As a result, the outcomes of Gadamer's hermeneutics are deeply in contrast with Heidegger's critique of truth as correspondence, since a reconstructed totality, like Hegel's self-returning of Spirit, is deeply akin to the metaphysical notion of truth. Furthermore, his conception of truth seems to exclude once again any drama and any authentic possibility of a setback, thus giving reason to the objections that oppose this optimistic and peaceful outcome of hermeneutics to its Heideggerian and more generally existentialist origins (which should not be denied).

As I have already mentioned, in Pareyson and in the other hermeneutic thinkers the experience of art remains the fundamental point of reference for conceiving the notion of truth. However, it is precisely in its constitutive aspect of risk, which appears more visibly in art, where the formative character of the whole of human existence comes to light in all its specified purity (for Pareyson, art is a "specified formativity"),[9] that interpretation, actualizing itself in the production and interpretation of the work, is shown to be open to success or failure, according to a destiny that is never delivered into the hands of the artist or the interpreter but in which the unpredictable element of congeniality is involved. The success of the productive and interpretative process is then the model of the happening of truth, the coincidence of forming form and formed form, or image and thing. But the specific feature that characterizes these events specifically as truth is neither the attainment of a quiet integration to which Gadamer refers (Hegel's statement that "the whole is the true" still holds true), nor the pure and simple recognition of an original system of redescription of the world (as in Rorty's case). Instead, it is a matter of opening to an ulterior character—the rising of new formative and interpretative acts—which in the form and in the person are derived from the trace of infinity that has been stamped on them by virtue of the process whose outcome they are. To corroborate it, let me remind you that in the essays in *Verità e interpretazione*, where Pareyson elaborates the contrast between revelatory and expressive thought, the only possible criterion for distinguishing the latter (i.e., a pure ideology) from the former is precisely the claim to ultimacy characteristic of it. (In other words, we could say that every foundationalist thought that pretends to possess and enunciate the first principles is purely ideological and therefore not revelatory of truth.)

I have put forth only a few indications for a more detailed comparison between key concepts of contemporary hermeneutics (as they are found above all in Gadamer and in the theorists who refer to him) and the specific declination they undergo in Pareyson's work; I have attempted to provide a more in-depth and accurate analysis of the interpretative act, in its varied dimensions, while at the same time remaining faithful to the existentialist origins of Pareyson's theoretical approach. The ontology of the inexhaustible and tragic thought, two formulations summing up the philosophy of the last Pareyson, clearly spring from the premises of interpretation theory that Pareyson elaborated with a specific view to aesthetic experience, in the light of the existentialist heritage. His radical theory of interpretation has led to the recognition that the ontology of inexhaustibility is the unavoidable background of interpretation. In other words, it is not enough to stop with the observation that the mere succession of generations of interpreters naturally generates the multiplicity of interpretations that produce the text's infinity. The different interpretations put forth by various interpreters stand in need of an ontological justification, too. However, to confine oneself to the sheer affirmation of interpreting subjects would make it impossible to recognize the difficulties and possibility of specific setbacks, which in fact do occur in every event of interpretation. It is not only the world of interpretive subjects that is inexhaustible, but also that of the forms that are offered to interpretation. However, if the only argument for infinity (of person and form) is the concrete difficulty of the interpretative process, the ontology of the inexhaustible (which, in its varied forms, is only implicitly shared by a number of hermeneutic thinkers) is open to further development in tragic thought. Tragic thought links the inexhaustibility of Being (hence the fundamental hermeneutic character of Being) to a vision of being that is characterized by essential conflict. If Being is no longer to be thought under the category of necessity, as a metaphysical foundation that is fully actualized (making freedom unthinkable and generating all the figures of metaphysics described by Nietzsche and Heidegger, all the way up to the total technologically organized and administered world), Being will have to be thought under the category of "reality," as an affirmation that holds its own by triumphing over a negative possibility, which carries in itself the indelible trace of an originary conflict. There is nothing to be surprised that in his last works Pareyson makes recourse to the language of the Old and the New Testaments in order to reflect on these topics, especially when considering that the philosophical thematic of hermeneutics is linked to, and perhaps is unthinkable without, the Judeo-Christian tradition.[10] Pareyson's work was interrupted precisely while he was engaging these crucial issues, which have to do not only with his own specific thought but with the whole of contemporary hermeneutics. Hence, it will be a matter of further tapping into his work (the unpublished writings) to develop as best as we can the indications he has left us, with the conviction that only an ontology capable of rediscovering its links to the religious tradition of the West will enable contemporary hermeneutics to find a line of development that will eventually remove it from the reassuring tautologies of a "philosophy of culture."

# 6 From Phenomenological Aesthetics to Ontology of Art

What follows could be easily entitled "variations on the ontological perspective opened to aesthetics by existential philosophy." The horizon within which we are moving here is more or less defined by the questions and conclusions that were elaborated by ontological existentialism. By existentialism, I mean Heidegger's philosophy as well as the philosophy that more or less explicitly finds its inspiration in him. By virtue of this opening horizon, I argue, it is possible to satisfy the exigency of an ontological foundation of art that increasingly rises not only from aesthetics but also from contemporary poetics.

## The Problem of Art's Ontological Foundation

To speak of the ontological foundation of art involves, sketching out the theoretical as well as historical horizon within which we move. Accordingly, it is necessary to situate this argument with respect to the contemporary situation of aesthetics and to the history of philosophical investigations of art. To make the argument more productive and more comprehensible, we will have to reconstruct a preliminary understanding of the global interpretation of the history of modern aesthetics, which by force of circumstances will be inevitably generic. I shall briefly outline, then, such global interpretation to introduce the actual discussion of the problem.

As with all philosophical questions—though here perhaps in a more particularly sharp manner—aesthetics does not emerge as a question about the constitution and structure of the peculiar world of art, the world of production and artistic enjoyment. Instead, it emerges as a question of the very *fact* of art. What constitutes an element for reflection and above all gives food for thought is the general fact that there are works of art at all, objects that do not satisfy any advisable needs, whose existence is not required by any identifiable motive that might justify them. This is how Aristotle already posed the question, which he solved by elaborating the well-known doctrine of imitation, according to which art exists because it causes pleasure in us inasmuch as it is an imitation; such pleasure is connected to our natural tendency to know. Imitation, then, constitutes precisely a way of knowing.[1]

By means of this theory Aristotle's position became the foundation for the mimetic tradition of art (or at least his position became canonical in a very specific form, which has remained unaltered throughout the history of Western intellectual thought), and anticipated a series of answers to the question of art produced by modernity. These are based on the fact that art should be led back to a more fundamental and more constitutive attitude of consciousness, which could be summarized more or less as follows: there is art insofar as there is, in human consciousness, an attitude, a way of relating that is aesthetic rather than practical or cognitive.

In any case, Aristotle's answer, unquestionably accepted for centuries, was responsible for the degradation of aesthetics to the level of poetics. After Aristotle, it was no longer a matter of posing the question of art with respect to its roots as it was of discovering a way of producing good works of art, of encoding and handing them over by means of handbooks. In comparison with this tradition, the novelty of Kantian aesthetics seems to consist in its having taking seriously, once again, the question of art as an event that cannot be derived or explained by recourse to preexistent laws or needs. The Kantian doctrine of the genius, which brings the work of art back to nature, elevates the underivability of art to the level of theory. In fact, the nature that gives art its law through the genius is almost exclusively a negative term: the work comes from nature (i.e., from genius) inasmuch as it cannot be led back to a principle or concept that could be formulated intellectually. The fact that art's underivability leads to the grounding of the artwork upon nature only means that while Kant wanted to take seriously the enigmatic nature of art—the radical novelty of the work—he was also conscious of the need to provide a foundation for this novelty. Kant's recourse to nature, whose definition is left unspecified (this is the terrain in which idealist philosophies will carry out their investigations), only bears witness to his attempt to give an ontological foundation to art.

While Kant's doctrine of genius comprises the two essential elements—the novelty of the work and the ontological rooting of art—with which every aesthetics must reckon, it is also true that these two elements are precariously synthesized in the overall formulation of his aesthetics. Indeed, in post-Kantian philosophy throughout the eighteenth century, these two elements of aesthetics will be separated, motivating two diametrically opposed directions for the development of aesthetics.

To illustrate this separation, I shall refer to two examples that should be sufficiently familiar. On the one hand, the positivistic aesthetics of play as it is formulated and carried to the limit of its extreme banality by Spencer;[2] on the other hand, Hegel's aesthetics. In the first case, art consists in the activation of surplus energies that are not necessary for the life struggle; art is play in the fullest sense of the term, an unnecessary and gratuitous activity that has nothing to do with the seriousness of existence. In this case, the novelty and originality of the work is guaranteed by its own gratuity: the work does not respond to any need, nor has it any meaning in addition to the exercise of the faculties that it puts in motion and that otherwise would remain inactive. Here, the maximum freedom and gratuity of art is accompanied by the maximum ontological meaninglessness. By contrast, Hegel's aesthetics recognizes the irreplaceable and peculiar position of art within the life of Spirit, and yet precisely to the extent that it assigns such an important position to art, this theory takes away any true originality from it and from all the spiritual activities of man. The ontological bearing of art is recognized and guaranteed only within a dialectical scheme that grounds its "necessity," that is to say, its derivability, wiping out its novelty.

This alternative between an aesthetic of play and an aesthetic of derivability of art, which here is merely schematized for the sake of clarity and brevity, is present in different shades and forms in all of eighteenth-century aesthetics. The revival of Kantianism, too, which in Europe accompanied the twilight of the great philosophical systems (idealism and positivism) during the first half of the twentieth century, does not substantially escape from this alternative. It merely reproposes Kant's solution, emptied out of the ontological opening that somehow it still possessed in Kant. In fact, neo-Kantianism absorbs every exigency of ontological foundation by reducing art to the dimension of consciousness. While for Kant, once the aesthetic attitude has been identified as the transcendental possibility of the beautiful and of art, there still remains the problem of giving an ontological rooting to the genius, for neo-Kantianism such a problem no longer exists. The whole philosophy of art is reduced to the identification of its transcendental possibility, to the exhibition of the aesthetic dimension of consciousness.

Nevertheless, it is not only that in neo-Kantianism and in the many perspectives that are more or less connected with it the foundation of art amounts to a reduction to an attitude of consciousness. The whole dimension of consciousness is cognated on the model of knowledge and theory; therefore, both the moral sphere and, above all, aesthetics are defined only negatively on the basis of the model of knowledge. Neo-Kantianism dilutes the meaning of Kantian philosophy to its more strictly rationalist aspect of the enlightenment. The fundamental relation to Being remains that of knowledge; at the same time, Being continues to be thought above all as fully present "spectacle" (even though it is ordered by the a priori forms). In this framework, it is difficult to think *positively* of art's relation to being, that is to say, to resolve the problem of art's ontological foundation that Kant had indicated and left open in his doctrine of the genius.

In this framework, it seems to me that precisely the philosophy of existence, by virtue of its clearest ontological trajectory, offers the means for reproposing the question of art's ontological foundation on a radically new ground. If these means are indeed available in Heidegger's philosophy—as I believe they are—it is because he has revised from the ground up the question of truth and Being, which had remained largely unquestioned in neo-Kantianism and in all implicitly neo-Kantian attitudes, in spite of the Copernican revolution.

The necessity of recovering philosophically the ontological bearing of art, that is to say, its relation to Being, without at the same time sacrificing the originality and novelty of the work, did not grow in the realm of philosophy only. This is also the philosophical meaning that can be drawn from the manifestos and artistic revolutions of the avant-garde of the twentieth century. All the great artistic revolutions of the nineteenth century, ranging from expressionism to surrealism, from Dada to the poetics of *engagement*, arose to defend the fundamental meaning and importance of art for history and human existence. While philosophers believed they had resolved the problem of art by assigning to it an a priori structure that legitimated it, thus determining its position of subordination among the forms of the life of Spirit, poets and the artists rebelled against this very violence of reason and refused to be resolved, classified, accounted for, and pigeonholed in it. In this sense, they more or less explicitly defended the right to recognize the deeper relation between art and existence, history and Being.

If we consider that every grounding of art reduces it to the aesthetic dimension of consciousness, opposing it to knowledge insofar as it has nothing to do with the distinction between true and false, and to morality insofar as it has nothing to do with the distinction between good and evil, we realize that the characteristics of aesthetics ultimately coincide with those that Kierkegaard attributed to the aesthetic stage of existence. In other words, the aesthetic condition becomes synonymous with disengagement, so that it is possible to say that the artistic revolutions of our century rebelled against the aestheticism that was latent in every theory that has foregone the need to address the question of art's ontological foundation.

## Novelty and Lawfulness of the Work of Art as Basis for an Ontological Foundation

In this framework, the need for an ontological foundation of art grew up not only in philosophy but also in the concrete experiences of the artists. The expression "ontological foundation," which I have left undefined so far, signifies every attempt to recognize art's relation to being; that is to say, art's relationship not only to man but to what transcends consciousness and the human being, whose possibility it authentically grounds.

This attempt to raise the question of art's relation to being necessarily presupposes as given a description of art and aesthetic experience, so that one may generally know what has to be recognized as having a relationship with Being. I call such a description phenomenological aesthetics.

The "phenomenological aesthetic" to which I shall refer—even though it cannot by any means be reduced to a phenomenological description of the "fact" of art, insofar as it contains ontological disclosures that can be understood fully only at the level of ontology, at least in the interpretation of that I am proposing—is the theory of formativity that Luigi Pareyson worked out in his *Aesthetics*, published in 1954, and further elaborated in other essays in the following years.[3]

Two reasons justify my choice: Pareyson's specific sensibility for the most lively exigencies present in contemporary aesthetics, to which he intends to give a systematic response, makes these exigencies his own in his aesthetics, so that by starting out with his aesthetics we have to take account of the exigencies of contemporary aesthetics. Furthermore, Pareyson's aesthetic reflection, which took shape in the context of ontological existentialism, presents the maximum openness for the argument I am elaborating here.

The theory of formativity takes the question of art back to its roots. It poses once again the question of the artwork with respect to the enigmatic *fact* of its existence. The failure of all the attempts to find a canon of the beautiful, to which the whole history of art bears witness, signifies that the artwork is so precisely insofar as it does not allow itself to be reduced to laws that precede or transcend it, on the basis of which it could be evaluated, accounted for, or condemned. The inexplicability of art as a *fact* is, therefore, truly inexplicable. It is not a provisional character as numerous theories have argued; inexplicability is the definitive and constitutive aspect of works of art as such.

Nevertheless, although the work of art is radically new, it is not arbitrary. In other words, in the subjective experience of art we experience, combined with its novelty, a rigorous lawfulness (*legalità*). What drives us to say that a work is beautiful is not only or principally the fact that it is original but more radically that, in its wholeness, it is rigorously governed by a law. In particular, we assume we have truly "appropriated" the work once we have grasped the law giving order to its structure, so that each part appears in its necessary links to the whole and the whole is revealed in each of its parts. After all, this is the characteristic of aesthetic experience to which the formalist school, whose influence is large in the aesthetics of the twentieth century, has made us particularly sensitive.

Pareyson draws the fundamental concept of his aesthetics, that is, the theory of formativity, from his reflection on the novelty and underivability of the work of art and on its rigorous lawful character. To the extent it is radically new, and insofar as it rigorously responds to an intimate and constitutive law, the artwork reveals itself as the outcome of a formative process. Pareyson defines the act of forming as a doing that, in doing, invents a new way of doing. There is forming in all human activities. Even when it is a matter of applying the law to a specific situation, it is necessary to invent the *mode* of such an application, that is to say, the individual rule for the operation to be carried out. In the case of artistic production, however, invention has a much more radical meaning. Here it is not only a matter of inventing the specific mode of applying a general law that is always already given; with the specific rule of operation one must invent the law, too. In fact, the law is nothing other than the single rule of operation. All this amounts to saying that the artwork is truly new and does not respond to any pregiven laws. The exigency, to which the work responds, and which it satisfies, is instituted by the work.

The radical novelty of the work of art seems to be sufficiently broad and universally accepted to form the basis of the argument (at least as a fact: the problem arises when one has to put an artwork in relation to its law and when one has to disclose the meaning of this relation) to the extent that as aesthetics and criticism successfully liberate themselves from the residues of the Hegelian mindset, the absolute novelty of the work remains a fundamental aspect. Indeed, even where the critics give a less radical interpretation of the work, the absolute novelty of the work remains a fundamental feature. Consider, for example, Roland Barthes—the representative of the *nouvelle critique*—for whom the work is "retirée de toute situation."[4] We can recognize this situation, according to Barthes, thanks to the polyvalent language of the work, which does not allow itself to be overcome by or reduced to contingent situations, to which the work would refer as its own world and its own explanation. Whatever Barthes's use of the idea of the novel character of the work, note here is that the *nouvelle critique* has once again discovered the *fact* of art's radical novelty above and beyond the facile historicist schemes. This is precisely what philosophy has to account for and take as seriously as possible.

Once we acknowledge that the work is radically new and that it is rigorously ruled by a law, which becomes visible in the concrete experiences of the artists who make corrections, changes, adaptations, and remaking under the guidance of the principle of judgment, it remains to be seen how a law that is born with the work could be held to be the true criterion for judging the same work. If, in fact, the law identifies itself completely with the work, it responds to its own law precisely insofar as there is work. Hence, it is declared to be beautiful and valid. Now, to explain how the law of the work can serve as a guide and criterion for discriminating between what is good and what has failed in the course of the process of production, we need to concede that somehow the law transcends the process. It is possible to say that the law is invented insofar as it is created, but it is also invented in the other sense of the word, insofar as it is discovered as such. In other words, it imposes itself not only on the reader once the work is accomplished, but also over the author while he is producing the work. Only in this sense can it be rightly called a law. Pareyson's theory illustrates this transcendence by distinguishing within the work the forming form, that is, the law that guides the process and transcends it, and the formed form, that is, the work once it has been produced concretely. Only if one acknowledges this distinction is it possible to explain why the work, once it is made, can be judged without referring to preexistent needs or laws. Even in the work that is made and presented to the reader there remains a certain transcendence of the forming form over the formed form. The reader will judge the work as successful—that is, beautiful—if, after comparing these two terms, he sees that the work is truly what it wanted to be and what it should have been. The work is, then, the bearer of a law that is born with it; at the same time, this law transcends and judges the work.

In my view, the most noteworthy contribution of Pareyson's theory of formativity to the philosophical clarification of the meaning of the work of art and art's ontological foundation lies precisely in his idea that the law of the work transcends the process of production, the conscious will of the artist and the work insofar as it is formed. None of the numerous theories of the objectivity of art has ever given such a radical description of this phenomenon, without at the same time taking leave of the concrete terrain of artistic experience. Heidegger's theory of poetry as gift (*Dichtung* as *Geschenk*), elaborated in the final pages of the essay "The Origin of the Work of Art," suspends in a mythical aura the relationship between freedom and law. Poetry, says Heidegger, is *Stiftung*, foundation of the framework of man's historical experience insofar as it also *Gründung*, the collocation of the world on its own foundation, a foundation it does not create but finds and merely announces to men. It is the poet's gift to humanity because, more radically, it is the gift that the poet himself receives.

The distinction between forming form and formed form, which took shape in a thought that was attentive to the concrete elements of artistic experience, may well be taken as a less mythical and more phenomenologically faithful formulation of the idea of poetry as gift.

## Aesthetic Condition and Originality

However, aesthetic discourse cannot stop here once it has identified the phenomenon of art and the basic structures of this type of experience. The transcendence of the law over the work is an indication that in the work of art there is something more at work than the simple activity of the artist. Only in a neo-Kantian perspective could one argue that the novelty and absolute legality of the work are grounded once one has discovered a human activity that has the characteristic of producing something new. Instead, as Pareyson underscores in his *Aesthetics* and more generally in other philosophical works,[5] the dialectic of receptivity and activity explicitly excludes that what is born into art might be reduced to the artist's activity. Let me now briefly attempt to work out this argument in order to point in the direction of an explicit ontology of art.

If among the human activities there is one whose characteristic it is to produce radical novelties like works of art, we need to raise the following questions: How is the absolute novelty of which aesthetics speaks possible? In regard to the question thus formulated, the larger part of aesthetics has chosen either the way of transcendental justification (reducing art to an aesthetic dimension or direction of consciousness) or a way that I would call demystification; in other words, this school of thought has ultimately conceded that the novelty of the work is not truly as absolute as it appeared at first, for it can and should be explained with respect to the historical conditions, psychological structures, and intimate history of the language to which it belongs.

There is a third way that is neither satisfied with the—ultimately tautological—transcendental justification nor ready to liquidate the existence of the problem by conceding that the novelty is not truly so. The third way lies in deepening the idea of the work's novelty.

First of all, the genuine novelty of the work of art becomes visible insofar as it does not allow itself to be set into the world as it is. Nowadays, there is an exponential growth of expedients in contemporary figurative art—as in op-art, for example—which are new only in the sense in which an expedient can be new; these can be easily positioned in the existing order things, immediately becoming fashionable insofar as they respond to the specific needs of the market and of public sensibility. It is certainly not these works that present themselves as "retirée de toute situation"; their novelty is nothing other than a variation that is internal to the situation and that can be easily led back to it.

If we want a more radical description of the work's absolute novelty, we shall have to seek it in some of the decisive pages of Heidegger's essay "The Origin of the Work of Art," which I mentioned earlier. In that essay, the work's novelty is linked to the force by which it suspends our habitual relationships with the world or with the matter-of-fact-ness of the world in which we are accustomed to live. It is not only that the work does not allow itself to be situated as an object next to other objects of our experience; by virtue of its refusal, the work somehow puts our own world into crisis. If you will, by refusing to be situated into our world, the work reveals its insubstantiality and demands to be renewed. The encounter with works of art is never the encounter with another thing in the world; what one encounters is another perspective on the world entering into dialogue with our own. The work, as Mikel Dufrenne beautifully puts it, is a *"quasi-sujet"* (almost a subject).[6] To put it better: insofar as art is a perspective on the world in its totality, the work has a decisively personal character.

Nonetheless, it is necessary not to misunderstand the idea of the work as having a perspective on the world as a *Weltanschauung*. The concepts of perspective and *Weltanschauung* generally presuppose the idea of our world as the massive totality of the given, around which *Weltanschauungen* come and go just as Aristotelian accidents change the world without changing its substance. Now, when we speak of the work as a radically new disclosure on the world, we cannot reduce it to the purely accidental appearance of a new "world-vision." The fact is that the world is not the totality of the given, as Heidegger's analytic of *Being and Time* has shown once and for all. The world constitutes itself only in the openness instituted by Dasein, that is, by man. In their fluctuations these perspectives, which are the historically variable openings of Dasein, have to do with the very substantiality of the world, for the world *is* only in the perspectives. So the foundation of a new perspective on the world constitutes the real foundation of a new world, of a new comprehensive order within which things become visible, coming into being—and within which they are. So in employing this radical concept of world, we see that the work of art really constitutes the foundation of a new world; it cannot be set into the world because in its comprehensive totality it consists in a different perspective on the world.

In this sense, the novelty of the work of art may be called originality. The aesthetic discourse that wants to take seriously the work's novelty, in its underivability from the world as it is, and that wants to remain faithful to this premise, ultimately discovers that the aesthetic condition by virtue of which art is reduced completely to originality. In other words, the work of art is truly a work of art—beautiful and aesthetically valid—only to the extent that it constitutes an origin, an opening of a world. There is no other idea of the beautiful except that which reduces the beautiful to the originating and founding force of the work.

Having formulated this thesis so radically, we have to deal with a number of issues that follow from it and that may lead to an ontological foundation of art. Such a foundation would show how all the characteristics of aesthetic experience ascertained by phenomenological inquiry must be led back to the fact that the work of art is the origin of a world. Hence, it is really a matter of translating more radically aesthetics into phenomenology of art.

Here I shall discuss only the point of departure and the general principle for a more extensive argument, which should link beauty to the originality of the work. According to the theory of formativity I have discussed, the beautiful is resolved in the idea of success (*riuscita*). In other words, the work is declared beautiful when one discovers that it corresponds to its own law: it has succeeded in being what it wanted to be. According to this view, even excluding canons that are external to the work, the beautiful may be recognized on the basis of a rigorous judgment that has its criterion in the work. Now, what has the beautiful (as success) to do with originality? This point is especially important because all the specific features of aesthetics revolve around the concept of the beautiful.

The links between beauty as success and beauty as originality become visible only if the idea of success is not abstractly given a formal, geometric meaning. If the work truly succeeds to the extent that it corresponds perfectly to its own law, then this law is not an abstract prescription regarding its own purely physical structure. On the contrary, as Pareyson rightly shows, the law that rules the work arises out of the concreteness of the spiritual process, involving the whole personality of the artist. This personality constitutes the true *content* of the artwork. If the law of the work is such a spiritually rich and profound principle, it may truly found a world, rather than exclusively explaining the abstract perfection of the object. If the correspondence of the work to its own law is understood as a pure and simple perfection of the object, it is not clear how aesthetics could evade the view of art as play, hence the aestheticism of those who take art to be the production of perfect but useless machines. Conversely, if the transcendence of the law over the work is genuine—in the sense that insofar as it is a product, the work makes itself adequate to the law without ever exhausting it and therefore consti-tutes the first realization of such a law—the law has founding force with re-spect to the work and to the world. The work corresponds to its own law—that is, it is a success—not so much because, by virtue of its mere physical existence, it realizes and exhausts it completely in itself; rather, it represents, as it were, the first entity of the new world founded by the work, the entity around which all other beings in the world will be eventually situ-ated, in accordance with the law instituted by the work. The instituting force (*forza istituente*) of the work may be explained by assuming that the work as product does not exhaust the law that it bears in itself and lets hap-pen in the world.

It seems clear that the success cannot be conceived in terms of an exhaus-tive realization of the law by work, otherwise the work would be defini-tively closed; it would no longer open itself to reading and interpretation. The theory of formativity has shown how the distinction between forming form and formed form is necessary to justify the historicity and multiplicity of interpretation. This means, translated ontologically, that only the radical transcendence of the law over the work as product makes work an origin rather than a final point, an opening of history rather than its definitive closure.

The success of the work should be understood, then, as correspondence with a law that the work institutes but does not exhaust. It succeeds to the extent that it has a substantiality; that is to say, it truly announces itself as the bearer of a law that will reorganize the structures of the world. Accord-ing to this view of the work as instituting event, the beautiful is to be mea-sured not so much on the basis of an internal conflict between the work as product and its law but by its demonstrative capacity to found a history.

By resolving beauty into the founding force of the event, we deny the "aestheticist" temptation that accompanies all the aesthetics of our century in their efforts to identify and delimit the field of art, to mark its differences from the other spiritual activities. In this view, the meaning of enjoyment of the work of art changes as well. To encounter a work of art, to enjoy it as such no longer means statically contemplating it in its perfect correspon-dence with itself. The whole Western philosophical tradition has accustomed us to conceiving contemplation on the model of visual experience—as im-mediacy, simple presence—and the pleasure procured by contemplation as a state of tranquillity that has reached a point of repose and accomplished satisfaction from which no ulterior desire or curiosity to know may distract one any longer.[7] According to the view I am proposing here, such characterization of aesthetic contemplation should be denied. We truly encounter a successful-perfect object, its beauty, if the object is capable of generating movement rather than a place of repose and stillness. The work of art is beautiful insofar as it is a success. However, since the transcendence of the law remains at work in the work, its success can be ascertained only by moving away from the work toward the world that it has instituted. This is the sense in which I understand Heidegger's statement to the effect that it is a matter of dwelling in (*verweilen*) the truth opened by the work,[8] or as I would put it, of inhabiting the world founded by the work.

The only way in which the work of art can be genuinely evaluated is to see whether it really spurs a reconfiguration of our being-in-the-world. he criteria are that, at first, the work is successful in itself and then, in a second moment, it is also capable of reconfiguring our being-in-the-world because of its success. Its success depends entirely and exclusively on the work's instituting and originating force, as Kandinsky suggestively stated in the essay "Der Wert eines Werkes der Koncreten Kunst":[9] to evaluate a work ultimately signifies measuring its prophetic dimension, its capacity to exhibit a world.

While this perspective leaves any aestheticist temptation behind, it may lead for the same reason to the resurgence of the question of the specificity of aesthetic experience, of its difference from other forms of experience. It is clear that the encounter with a work of art, thus understood, does not exclude but involves the intervention of the intellect or the will. In other words, to speak Kantian language against Kant, this encounter is neither atheoretical nor apractical. The world opened up by the work is a world of concepts and ways of looking at things that has to be recognized conceptually, before which regard we must take an ethical position. From the perspective of ontology, if we were to seek out a definition of aesthetic experience in terms of the faculties or, as in neo-Kantianism, of the different directions or dimensions of consciousness, this path would not lead to any viable outcome.

Nevertheless, based on the concept of originality it may be possible to distinguish between aesthetic condition and art, on the one hand, and the other forms of experience, on the other. Accordingly, any experience may be called aesthetic, which does not confine itself to articulating, developing, and changing our belonging to a given world but rather radically puts this world in its totality in question. To move within a world signifies elaborating theories that are always grounded on an initial evidence, that is to say, on the recognition of certain presuppositions that are the same ones on which the world is founded; this movement also consists in acting to satisfy certain needs that have become visible in a specific situation. In sum, it remains true that aesthetic experience is not "committed" to things, though this must be understood in a completely different sense than in the past. Every commitment, be it cognitive or practical, already involves moving within a specific historical opening, assuming its fundamental substantiality rather than putting it into question, developing, changing, improving, or worsening it from the inside out of the situation. Insofar as it is an encounter with an entirely other world, aesthetic experience has nothing, immediately, to say that would change or otherwise articulate the world to which we belong. Instead, it confines itself to a denial of this world in its totality by refusing to let itself be situated in it.

The links among art, aesthetic condition, and feeling, which have been ascertained at all times, are radically justified in this perspective. In fact, if feeling and, more generally, the sphere of affectivity is not merely a contingent connotation of our being-in the-world but rather determines (*be-stimmt*) being in its fundamental roots, it makes sense to say that aesthetic experience concerns the sphere of affectivity as initial opening onto the world.

## Conclusion: Ontological Aesthetics and the Concrete Experience of Art

Finally, I should tackle at least three more questions, above and beyond the developments that this approach may provide for addressing various aesthetic problems ranging from the process of production to interpretation, from criticism to the "naturally beautiful," which here seems to acquire a greater meaning. First, what does reducing art to originality have to do with ontology, namely, with Being? Second, is this way of considering art truly adequate to the concrete experience of those who, like us, read and enjoy artistic products? Third, is it not the case that the theory I am putting forth here is merely a mythologizing of art, which assigns to art boundaries that are far too extensive, and whose bearing is too radical with respect to man's historical experience?

Insofar as the links between the work as opening of a world and ontology are concerned, I shall refer to Heidegger's notion of world: things exist to the extent that they come into the world; however, they come into the world only insofar as they arrange themselves within Dasein's open perspective. Such perspective is not accidental in things but constitutive of their being. Being is never fully given as a presence that could be seen in different ways; on the contrary, being is the lighting of horizons, the realm in which things acquire their meaning, that is, receive Being. Now, any fact that concerns not only beings taken as fully present but the opening in which they come to visibility—that is, the world in its totality—is original and ontological. A new opening of the world, the birth of a new world as a new order within which beings acquire new meanings and relationships, is not an event that regards beings only; it regards the lighting itself, that is, Being. Inasmuch as it is the origin of the world, art is the happening of Being, an ontological event.

It is only in light of this idea of being that we can fully justify the novelty of art. If being were fully given as the metaphysical tradition always thought, the novelty of art would not be genuine. It would always be an accidental change within a situation that could never substantially change. Lavoisier's law, according to which "nothing is created and nothing is destroyed," is the rigorous formulation of the vision of being as simple presence, full of metaphysical meaning.

As the event of being, the art work re-presents the instituting moment of historical epochs, the inauguration of a certain order of things within which humanity lives and makes its choices. A second question arises at this point: Is it possible to apply this vision of art to our experience as readers and consumers of artistic products? In other words, it seems that the idea of the work as origin could be valid for the great, epochal masterpieces, such as the Bible and the *Divine Comedy,* rather than for the short compositions of chamber music, for paintings hanging on the hall of a house, or for short lyrics. In other words, it does not seem to hold for many of the things that we are accustomed to consider artworks.

This question can be solved only if we acknowledge that the aesthetic characters of what we might call minor artworks are analogues of true originality, which belongs instead to great art. This means that true aesthetic experience—the encounter with an event that founds a world and a history—is far more rare than we are accustomed to think. What we commonly take as aesthetic experience—the enjoyment of works that are not unquestionably epoch making or foundational like the examples just mentioned—retains, albeit transformed and decreased, the character of an encounter with the origin that constitutes the essence of the enjoyment of art.

An example of this can be seen precisely in the type of aesthetic experience that might seem also the farthest removed from authenticity, the experience of the "mass arts" of the mass media. I would say that the belongingness of the reader to the work, a belongingness that in its authentic form is typical of the experience of encountering great works of art, can be found also in the mass media, albeit mystified. A mystified form of aesthetic belongingness to the work is found also in the attitude of the public to James Bond, which takes him as the model for its own behavior, ranging from the manner of dressing to that of treating women to the more general way of relating toward life. Even though we can concede that it is a mystified form (but we should ascertain to what extent and why this is the case), an encounter with the movie character James Bond and its public represents an encounter with a world in which one must inhabit, attempting to live up to it in one's experience.

Now, just as in the case of James Bond, we have an example of aesthetic experience as the experience of the origin in the form of the maximum distance away from authenticity, so all our aesthetic experiences can be arranged on a kind of scale of maximum or minimal nearness to authentic originality. What I wanted to highlight here was precisely the principle behind the solution to the problem: even though the aesthetic experience we habitually have never or rarely involves encountering originality in the sense described above, it is only by taking such an encounter as the model that we can explain it, even in its less genuine forms, because it always realizes this model more or less completely and faithfully.

The last question, not in terms of importance, is: Is the theory I am putting forth here an ontology of art or a mythology? In fact, one could think that my having assigned to art the character of opening and founding history is purely and simply a return to the idea of the poet possessed by the muse or inspired by the gods. On the contrary, it is clear that if the work truly has the meaning of founding a world, insofar as it is the event of being, it is necessary that the work not depend exclusively on the arbitrariness of the artist. It is not Being that is for man, rather man is available for Being. Indeed, the phenomenology from which we started off explicitly recognized that the law of the work is transcendent over the will and consciousness of the artist. The law of the work is both invented and discovered, created and found as mentioned above. The whole discourse I have developed so far has led us increasingly to highlight that the novelty of the work itself is inconceivable apart from its own lawfulness; the work is new only as the bearer of a law giving a new order to the world. Without the presence of this law, the novelty of the work is reduced to pure expediency, fortuitousness. The work founds inasmuch as it is, in turn, grounded; it is not the consciousness or will of the artist that is at work in art, even less the consciousness or historical situation of an epoch that might be expressed through the artist, but rather Being. Being as opening force institutes the realms and horizons within which a historical humanity unfolds its experience.

If you will, this is truly a mythology of art in the sense that in the light of it art no longer appears to be a "historical" fact that could be reduced and explained on the bases of the situation, the world, the same psychological structures from which it originates. However, this is precisely the point of departure, namely, the fact that the work is not in a situation, does not allow itself to be positioned and reduced to what it was beforehand. Now, if the recognition of the novelty of the work has any meaning, we must concede that something else is operating in the work apart from the artist and the historical world. To be sure, attributing the work's novelty to the pure arbitrariness of the artist, besides the fact that it does not explain the character of the productive process (the very obedience of art to the law of the work), does not in any way guarantee such novelty; psychology teaches us that it is precisely what appears to be arbitrary that conceals a rigorous and well-defined determination. In sum, in order to authentically guarantee the novelty of the work it is necessary to recognize in the same lawfulness that is present within it, which transcends the work, the artist and the interpreters, the very presence of Being. Any other way of conceiving the novelty of the work "reduces" it in the sense that it leads it back to preexisting conditions, making of the work something derivable from what it already was.

It is here that aesthetics as ontology of art becomes philosophy of history. Having established the equivalence of aesthetic condition and originality, to pose the question of art signifies, more generally, to inquire into the possibility of novelty within history or, more simply, into the very possibility of history. Based on what I have argued so far, it may well be that the only way of guaranteeing this possibility is to recognize in human activity and in art in particular what I would call the "ontological dimension," which means that in whatever he does, the human being expresses, that is, reveals and re-arranges in always different ways, not only the world as it is, namely, the totality of inner and external conditions of human activity, but also, somehow, being present as an originating force.

# 7 Critical Methods and Hermeneutic Philosophy

## The Death of Art in Criticism

It is possible that if Hegel can be said to sum up the whole tradition of modern philosophy (at least that part of tradition that Hegelian philosophy, in its historical self-awareness, recognizes as its own) and to be the prophet of our epoch, it is because he recognized and theorized as the center of his philosophy the *Aufhebung*, the mediation, that is, the overcoming and abolition of what is "mediated."[1] The *Aufheben*, the essence and power of thought, at least in the sense in which it is generally understood, is today critical as never before. Sartre's theme of nothingness, which has drawn so much attention—not fortuitously, inasmuch as it is the expression of a spirituality of an epoch (and perhaps only as such) is nothing other than an alteration of the Hegelian theme. The annihilating power of thought is the impossibility for thought to let something subsist outside of itself, that is to say, its implacably assimilating force.

Here, too, lies the reason for the quite common experience of reading and interpreting works of art. It is an inescapable impression when delving into an author or a work that the critic is always more knowledgeable than the poet, that the critic reveals the poet to himself for the first time, specifying what he "wanted" to say obscurely behind the numinous cloud of inspiration. The death of art, which not fortuitously was theorized by Hegel, and around which today there is a variety of discussions, seems to happen above all in the activity of criticism, though it is largely unnoticed, when the work becomes the focus of analysis, of an inquiry that aims to uncover its psychological subtexts, i.e. the social and historical references, the technical meaning of its innovation, conservation or regression with respect to its certain situation in the history of art or of poetics. In other words, it is the demythologizing character of the contemporary situation of thought (where thought unfurls as the annihilating and *Aufhebende* essence theorized by Hegel), which is associated with literary and artistic criticism, and in general with all hermeneutic methods, which in making their object conceivable and "transparent" dissolve and render it somehow superfluous.

It may be objected that no critic ever puts forth his own interpretation as a definitive thesis but rather allows the work to subsist as the objective possibility of other different readings. This mode of thinking is basically correct in that it seems to overcome the annihilating power of thought. However, upon closer inspection it is always driven by inauthentic reasons. The critic who wants to be rigorous (who conceives of reading and interpretation neither as purely personal impressions, which are always new owing to the variety of interpreters, nor as reinventions of the work—as in Gentile's idealism) always accounts for this reserve, which lets the work subsist as a field of ever-new interpretations, by referring either to the vastness and complexity of the references of which the work is product or testimony or to the determinateness and limitedness of the instrument employed (a reason that is reducible to the first). In short, the ideal is always that of a comprehensive, total demythologization in the sense of highlighting the rational structures of a phenomenon, its explanation, that is, showing its sufficient reason, its *Grund*.

## Demythification and the Rationalist Mindset

The impression that this is the case within the larger part of contemporary criticism is testified to by the lively presence in it of two trends, which in their own specifications and nuances tend to apply sociological or psychological models of explanation, or a synthesis of both, to literature. No matter how the basically Marxist conception of art (and of the Hegelian forms of Spirit) as substructure is inflected or specified, reading artworks under this thought will always amount to a sort of "abolition" of the work. To regard the work of art as a document of a historical situation or as its product, or in the best of all hypotheses as a way of acting in history at the service of a new social world whose guiding ideals are not established by or "invented" with the work of art, is always an activity of demythification and overcoming. The work is never taken seriously for what it says it is and how it presents itself, so its appearance requires unmasking. The question is whether after such an activity of demythologizing there is anything left of the work itself or whether unmasking is a way of grasping the work for what it is rather than a way of falsifying it by way of reading it with instruments that the work itself refuses. True, there is a possible reply to this objection, and it takes the form of the lack of respect that the rationalist mindset has toward the products of Spirit and "reason." What matters is not the subsistence of the work as such, but the self-growth of Spirit or, if you will, of "progress," that is, the incessant activity of thinking thought. This response is rigorously consistent with the spirit of Hegelianism. It shows to what an extent every perspective of thought understood as *Aufhebung*, namely, as a demythologizing activity, is connected with a vision of history and culture that is deeply historicist and humanist.

The same rationalist background of the Enlightenment can be observed in the criticism that is inspired by models of thought shaped by psychoanalysis and psychology. Here, too, we are confronted by a structure, the interpretation-comprehension, that consists in highlighting the reasons that account for it, to show syllogistically the premises on the basis of which it reveals its rigorous necessity and conceivability. Even though here the schemes of the sociological explanation are replaced by psychological ones (and perhaps this is not really a progress), we should pose once more the following question: What remains of the work once it has been psychologically and sociologically "explained"? Is what remains of it only what has not yet been explained or what has been incorrectly explained, implying that it is still definable and explainable based on given methodological criteria? Or is this way of explaining the work only a way of regarding the work from a specifically positive points of view, like a chemical examination of the colors of a famous canvas that leaves intact and untouched the very structure and substance of the artwork because it ignores them?

The point is not to argue that the studies of works of art that are based on sociological and psychological models are useless or that they should be rejected. On the contrary—and precisely to respond to the ideal of self-awareness that moves these critical trends—it is necessary to see to what an extent these methods of reading belong to or exhaust the way of reading according to which the work of art wants to be read. In other words, whether such methods take seriously the work for what it says it is and wants to be.

It seems beyond doubt, even obvious if we think of the example of philosophy of religion, that every attitude of demythification from its outset implies a lack of respect for its subject matter. For example, to claim that philosophy should provide the ground for religion by virtue of its identifying what is true in it, that is, what is justifiable from the point of view and with the instruments of philosophy—which is the desire of every rationalism—signifies destroying or "overcoming" religion in the sense explained above. Something similar appears to take place in every demythifying critique.

Given that the rationalist background of the Enlightenment is the domain in which the demythifying critique arises and develops, is there anything that could be referred to phenomenologically as constitutive of such an attitude? Here, it seems to me, we can refer to Heidegger, the contemporary thinker in whom we can find, by connecting freely the two opposite ends of his speculative path, some indications of a non-demythifying hermeneutics in *Being and Time*, at the beginning of the speculative path that brought him to this philosophical view, which regards the future as the fundamental and founding category of time. We shall not explore the possible links between Heidegger's interest in a nonrationalist type of hermeneutics and Dasein's constitutive openness to the future as theorized in *Being and Time*. It is possible to say that the essence of the demythifying attitude lies in its turning toward the past, in its historicist outlook not only in the sense that it reduces everything to history but also in the sense carried by the German term *Historismus*, which is connected with modern rationalist and technical thought, and refers to the will to systematize, historiographically, all the constitutive links with a given situation. In other words, the claim that a work can be explained on the basis of sociological or psychological models of explanation always signifies regarding the work as a final point, a product, therefore as a fact of the past. In this way, the de-mythologizing critique shows that, rather than an authentic historical atti-tude, it is a sort of archeology.

If the demythifying methods of reading are valid or are taken more or less explicitly as exhaustive, the only mode of being of the work of art is that of bearing witness to a past event. Understanding it signifies, then, recon-structing this event (observe that Croce's doctrine of reading leads basically to this attitude). It is clear that something of the sort—confronting a work with the intention of evoking an event of the past—may have meaning only for those who consider the incessant and narcissist operation of self-return as the activity of spirit: namely, history as the progressive grasp of conscious-ness. But, as Nietzsche had already shown in the splendid pages of the sec-ond of his inactual essays ("On the Utility and Damage on Life of Historical Studies"), an epoch that has reached this mode of thinking will no longer produce anything original: rather than producing art, it pursues criticism. This becomes the essential activity, at least for those of us who have reached historical awareness.

This position of Spirit is not simply a paradoxical hypothesis. It may well be that by virtue of this situation we can interpret one of the most widely debated themes in the European literature of the nineteenth century, namely, the awareness of the "self-consummation" of languages, the impossibility of still saying something with the historically laden structures of the grammars of the single arts inherited from tradition. Furthermore, even the tendency common to the literary and artistic trends of the nineteenth century to for-mulate themselves at first by means of poetics and manifestos and at other times by creating authentic works of art is a phenomenon that can be linked to "the death of art" in the sense that reflection and self-justification ulti-mately prevail over the creative spirit.

The fact that it is constitutive of demythifying critique to freeze the work of art into the category of the past, thus conceiving of interpretation, read-ing, and criticism as archeological attitudes, serves to show how such a cri-tique can be extended to criticism, which, with good reason, refuses to read the work of art with a schematic emphasis on content and aims instead to read it by attending to the stylistic structures of the work: the work is above all a linguistic structure that must be approached *juxta propria principia*.

Now, even though this way of approaching the literary work is beyond doubt more respectful of what becomes visible (the phenomenon of the work) in experience, it retains in the background the same prejudice that lies at the root of the demythifying critique. In other words, here, too, the work is a final point, since it is a matter of highlighting the antecedents behind the event, which are technical and linguistic rather than historical, social, economical, or psychological. True, what we generally call stylistic criticism can subtract itself from this critique by replying that the stylistic structures elucidated in the work are not "antecedents" inasmuch as they are born with the work.

It seems to me that this response, analyzed more in depth, can point to a viable path for solving the problem of the demythifying critique. In fact, to the extent that referentiality remains an essential instrument of stylistic analysis, that is, inserting a specific linguistic event into a domain (whether it is the work as a whole or language) from which it isolates itself but only within which domain it is definable, stylistic criticism, too (at least insofar as it realizes these characteristics), seems to aim at the ideal of *Erklären*, or at most of *Erläutern*, and therefore to a sort of historiographical sorting out of determinate structures. Stylistic criticism wants to make a literary work clear once and for all, at least tendentially; if not demythifying in the sense of unmasking, it certainly intends to "sort it out" (*sistemarla*), rendering it out of date, once again, and rigorously defining it as an event of the past.

## The Problem of a Non-demythifying Hermeneutic

It may seem, at this point, that through this form of the critique of critique (at most generally outlined as a sort of preliminary sketch), I might be arguing in favor of the necessity of returning to a naïve, immediate, and, as such, aestheticist approach to the work of art. On the contrary, it should be clear that this is not the case. If there is value in the heritage of Hegelian aesthetics that somehow is visible in what I have called the demythifying critique, and which is often lost in stylistic criticism, it is precisely that of seeking out in the work of art not only the validity of a successful form but also the vitality of moral and political motives, namely, the presence of truth. In the work of art—and this is testified to by the experience of any reader—there is an appeal to truth, to value (or its lack) that cannot be ignored.

It is not a question, then, of recovering an immediate attitude in aesthetic experience—an immediacy that in the tradition often served to define the so-called aesthetic sphere—rather, the problem is far more extensive. If we acknowledge that the question of thought as *Aufhebung*, or explanatory thought as we can now more clearly say, is a crucial question or the key question for contemporary consciousness, the problem of finding a way of reading works of art and a critique that would abstain from the explanatory tendency is the problem of realizing a type of thought that no longer destroys its object, hence its own ground of existence, via instantiation. The problem of criticism—and the possibility (or impossibility) of its letting the artwork as such subsist in front of itself without dissolving it into a document or expression of the past, of which one could only take stock, is significant at the general level of philosophy because it is a privileged and obvious case of a more general question: whether it is possible to conceive of a non-rationalist and nonhistoricist thought that would truly place itself at the disposal of a call without having to conclude (in order to make it more conceivable) that such a call comes from inside rather than outside (demythification as grasp of consciousness and self-consciousness), thereby reducing the life of Spirit to an absurdity encountering only itself, albeit disguised in its different forms.

Hermeneutics here broadens from special methodology to a principal question of philosophy; and it is the merit of Heidegger and his school to have highlighted this. Heidegger's *Satz vom Grund* (Pfullingen: Neske, 1957), which presents itself as an inquiry into the meaning of Leibniz's enunciation of the principle of sufficient reason as *principium reddendae rationis*, is a fundamental document for understanding the hermeneutic problem. The critic's impression of being more knowledgeable than the poet; the difficulty of thinking about the possible life of the work once it has been "explained" by means of separate or joint use of various critical methods, be they sociological, psychological, or stylistic; the general affirmation of the force and annihilating essence of thought, as we at least have conceived of it within the domain of rationalist philosophy—all this amounts to one and the same problem: Is a hermeneutic possible (since thought is always interpretative insofar as it responds to what positivist language calls a stimulus or, even better, an appeal) that would really place itself at the disposal of its object instead of reducing it completely to itself?

Once it has become conscious of the metaphysical, epochal background of interpretation, literary criticism can make a decisive contribution toward the foundation of this type of thought. However, if the negative and annihilating implications of demythifying hermeneutics, of *Erklärung*, are known at least in the form of an outline, how can we define the hermeneutic path that we seek? Heidegger, the thinker who has expressed the clearest and most decisive statements in regard to the deconstructing part of this topic, specifically his critique of explanatory thought, also gives positive, albeit obscure, indications in regard to finding the path of a new hermeneutic. In his correspondence with Emil Staiger, Heidegger discusses the interpretation of a poem by Mörike and provides a definition of reading that should be kept in mind inasmuch as it sums up his attempt to formulate the problem of interpretation in a new way: "What else is reading if not gathering: gathering in self-gathering of what in the said remains unsaid?"[2]

Here, as it is customary for him, and for very precise reasons, Heidegger plays with the etymology of *legere*. But what is striking in these few lines is the model, the inspiring metaphor, if you will (which can be called metaphor only as an approximation, since we should not employ models of thought that Heidegger himself rejects), that he adopts for rendering the spirit of reading. This inspiring metaphor shows approximately the reader's belongingness to the work, a sort of "dwelling inside the work"; much of recent Heideggerian hermeneutics, and more generally his conception of thought, finds its inspiration in this model. It is only on the basis of this "metaphor" (which is far more than a metaphor) that we can understand the other decisive aspect of the statement cited above, the relationship in the work between the said and the unsaid. Gathering and belonging constitutes a sort of dwelling inside and belonging to the work; however, in a deeper sense, it also constitutes a belonging together with the work (rather than *by means of the work*) to a more extensive domain that is made present by the work.

To understand the relation of metaphor to Heidegger's words on reading, it is necessary to refer to his essay *Der Ursprung des Kunstwerkes* ("The Origin of the Work of Art") of 1935. This essay inaugurates the so-called second phase of Heidegger's thought, which is seen by some interpreters in radical contrast with the first phase, represented by *Being and Time*, and which precisely because of its most salient aspects is nothing other than the consistent development of Heidegger's earlier theoretical views. The conclusion of the essay of 1935 is that the work of art has no origin because the work itself is an origin, inasmuch as a historical "opening" is instituted and announced for the first time by it, an opening in which the other phenomena constitutive of civilization will be eventually arranged.

These two conclusions (which we are disjoining from a larger discussion) correspond here to the elements that we have observed in the statement quoted in Heidegger's correspondence with Staiger. The work of art does not originate from a world; instead, it gives origin to a world in which the reader dwells and to which he belongs because the work is the institutive occurrence of this historical world. Like most of Heidegger's later essays, the words written in the letter addressed to Staiger clarify what had remained only implicit in "The Origin of the Work of Art": the work institutes and opens up a world, insofar as it is held and placed, in turn, onto a vaster background that remains unexpressed and that is identifiable with Being and with Being's "epochal" character.

## The Belonging of the Reader to the Work

There is no reason to go deeper into Heidegger's views because my current project is not a matter of following Heidegger but of drawing inspiration from him in order to formulate the relevant hermeneutic question. It seems to me more useful to hold and to work out the first of the two aspects that we have observed in Heidegger's statement in the letter to Staiger, the idea that the reader belongs to the work. This idea overturns the relationship customarily established between reader and work. As a matter of fact, it is clear that all "explanatory" and exhaustive hermeneutics imply the belonging of the work to the reader. The reader, in turn, has the capacity and the possibility of possessing fully the work, thereby resolving and dissolving it into the interpretation.

How can we conceive, more precisely, the belonging of the reader to the work? It seems to me that certain attitudes toward the work of art (or toward what presents itself as such) that are rightly regarded as inauthentic and "fallen" by common consciousness may supply useful indications. Before these attitudes criticism always assumes a position of exorcism or demythification. The most general case involves the identification between spectator or reader and the movie or cartoon hero. Critics tend to see in the hero the veiled expression of determinate characters of contemporary society and psyche; the more ingenious public assumes it as a behavioral model, as a life-ideal. It is plain enough that in this case criticism is right: it is true that the heroes of the *mass media* let themselves be completely dissolved into a psycho-sociological interpretation, and therefore this interpretation corresponds to them. And yet the attitude of the public is more right at bottom. Even the most sophisticated critic, in his concrete experience as a reader, originally behaves in the same manner. All of us draw near the work of art inasmuch as it is the original bearer of a certain human message, of a truth, of a moral statement that cannot be reduced to informing us of a certain historical or psychological situation nor to letting us formally enjoy stylistic expedients. (The fear that contemporary culture has toward Hegel, or to what in general is called representationalism [*contenutismo*], which, as I stated at the outset, is in part justified, drives criticism to refuse to recognize the determinant weight that the appeal to truth has in the work.)

Heidegger's view that the work of art institutes and founds a world refers precisely to this original experience. It is not the sign of a world that has always already constituted itself; it is not a voice from the past but the appeal of a world that is born with the work. There is a way in which this can be understood and illustrated by means of an example, from which we have to begin in order to become aware of the sheer impossibility and insufficiency of all reductive or *Erklärend* hermeneutic. The experience we generally have before a work of art is not of the kind that qualitatively changes our own world: instead the work of art may be regarded as an object of trade or as a physical entity worthy of chemical analysis. However, inasmuch as we experience what it is—a phenomenon not hastily pressed upon others, lived in its originality—the work does not slot itself into the world but changes it qualitatively. The work is not an object among others but a different light that is thrown upon them. In this sense, it has a personal character. It does not position itself as an element of our *Weltanschauung*; it is itself a *Weltanschauung* with which we have to dialogue.

Now reductive or explanatory criticism, be it psychological, sociological, or stylistic, attempts to exorcize the personal character of the work in order to make it a part of the world, thus placing it within a network of transparent relations. It is precisely for this reason that our experience of the personal character of the work, albeit rigorously thought and not hastily covered, should lead us to the conclusion that the work is an origin that founds a world. Such a world is not a pure event of the reader's consciousness but the domain in which the reader lives and moves.

It is clear that based on a certain prejudice, the founding character of the work could be interpreted instead as a purely emotional fact: the encounter with the work produces a certain emotion in the reader that transforms his *Stimmung* (i.e., the way in which he emotionally relates to the world). The work transforms the world by way of coloring in a variety of ways the lenses through which we look at it. The presupposition of this argument is that the work only exists in the "aesthetic sphere" or "aesthetic consciousness." Its characteristic—consider the theories of play—is that it has nothing to with the serious aspects of life, namely, with the distinction (see Croce) between true and false, good and evil, and so on. Now, it is not so much aesthetics as the poetics and criticism of the twentieth century that have done justice to aestheticist attitudes. While philosophers have continued to argue that the aesthetic moment lies on this side of any assumption of the real, poets and artists have defended in a decisive manner the ontological bearing of art: from the various forms of revolutionary engagement, to the metaphysical ambitions of expressionism, to the subversive will of those who, acting upon language, hoped to overturn consciousness, that is, the human mode of being in the world.

On the basis of these experiences it becomes easier to think of the founding character of the work, which arises as an appeal addressed to the future— not as future "aesthetic enjoyment," which would turn the beautiful into a product of decoration or entertainment—a claim to found the order of things and the position of the human being among them. The work's constitutive openness on the future comprises all the characters of the work that refer to its active presence in history—its value as bearer of moral and philosophical appeals in the founding of traditions, schools, styles, and tastes.

## History as Exegesis of the Work

Nonetheless, the most comprehensive model—the same model that inspired Heidegger's reflection on the hermeneutic problem[3]—for the relationship between the interpreter and the work of art in this light is that of the Western tradition to the Bible. For nonbelievers, this relationship could hold only as a significant historical example of the hermeneutic phenomenon, but its particular meaning actually is that it constitutes the hermeneutic phenomenon par excellence, not only in the historical sense but inasmuch as it is constitutive of man's existence as such as well. However one regards it, this relationship in its broadest sense is an example of the founding character of the work and of the interpreter's belongingness to the work to be interpreted. When we consider the relationship of the Western tradition to the Bible, even the second element that we observed in "The Origin of the Work of Art" becomes less obscure: the common belongingness of the interpreter and the work to a deeper background, namely, to the unsaid. It is only inasmuch as the work embodies a real prophetic character, instead of being a purely historical document of a past event, that the unsaid that lies in its background is not something provisionally concealed but constitutive. According to the Bible, God remains hidden, even though one can relate to him by working out the meaning of prophecies across the temporal field and above all by living in obedience to his commands. Here we stand before an absolutely original situation that is full of potentiality for the development of hermeneutics. For the specific scope of our inquiry, the validity of the relationship of biblical interpretation lies in indicating the horizon in which our observations about the problem of interpretation acquire their meanings.

In the case of the Bible, we stand before an entire civilization that constitutes and develops itself as the exegesis of a book. The history of the West is in its essential development the history of the interpretation of the Bible. To belong to this civilization signifies belonging to that specific text, and in this sense we should conceive of the belonging of the reader/interpreter to the work in its fullest form. To be sure, this model does create some difficulties when one attempts to apply it to the reading of works that are plainly less epochal. So it seems to be inapplicable to the interpretation and enjoyment of works of art which are held to be valid and yet deprived of the founding meaning of revealing a civilization or an epoch of spirit.

The difficulty is quite real and stems from attributing such a decisive and "original" function to aesthetic experience. Nonetheless, it can be resolved by considering that the "epochal" character of the artwork is a constitutive feature even when it has not been recognized as such; that a work can become the model around which determinate historical epochs actually position themselves and develop precisely because in itself it is capable of founding an epoch; and, in regard to works of art that common judgment views as minor art, then perhaps we should revise the concept of the individuality of the work. In other words, it may well be possible that the work, or at least some works, should be more organically set in the epoch they open up and to which they testify, since not every one of them deserves in equal measure the attribute of a founding character. In any case, it is not clear why aesthetics should not acknowledge that aesthetic enjoyment in its fullest sense is much more rare than one might think, that there are only a few authentic works of art, and that everything that we generally call art realizes only in part and analogically (think of the example of the hero who becomes a model of behavior in popular culture) what reflection recognizes as constitutive of the aesthetic phenomenon.

These are just hypotheses on the possible ways in which the difficulty can be resolved, which must be addressed if we are to take seriously the artwork as something that *operates* in history by virtue of its essential openness to the future without reducing it to a mere occasion for aestheticist play in which Spirit recognizes and is pleased with itself. The charge of aestheticism that one might raise against the hypothesis that I am putting forth here, the view that assigns to art a decisively privileged ontological position, can backfire against every reductive (*Erklärend*) view of aesthetic enjoyment—be it sociological, psychological, or stylistic—that regards enjoyment as a play whose value lies in discovering an increasingly dense network of references that ultimately close it upon itself and deprive it of any meaning apart from the heightening of experience (i.e., of humanity, mind, vital feeling, and so on) that Spirit has of itself.

Furthermore, every hermeneutic that dissolves the work of art into the play of reference necessarily implies that the work has no "active" character within history other than the sign of a becoming that fundamentally takes place outside of itself. When we consider that the representational function has been attributed as the proper function of other "forms" of Spirit (i.e., religion and philosophy), we see the extent to which the historicist attitude that supports these positions joins aestheticism with irrationalism and assigns man the task of recording and documenting the movement of which he is not the protagonist.

Note that these ideas are insufficiently elaborated here; in fact, they intend to remain mere indications of the radical problematization hermeneutic questions should undergo if they are to avoid being reduced to the level of pure technologies of reading.

The model of the Western tradition's relationship to the Bible refers to other elements that we will have to keep in mind to specify, more precisely, the meaning and forms of a hermeneutic that will not dissolve its object. Openness to the future confers upon the work of art a somewhat eschatological meaning, which could be formulated as follows: reductive criticism (in the sense in which the term has been employed here) is an arbitrary elimination of the anagogical meaning from the "four senses theory" elaborated by the Church Fathers and by the medieval interpreters of Scripture. The allegorical meaning, once separated from the anagogical, is still an a intraworldly reference: an event of the Old Testament prefigures those of the New Testament. But this link between events, as Auerbach has rightly observed,[4] does not subsist outside of their relationship to the suprahistorical event of salvation. Every technique of reading that is grounded on the exhibition of reference, on demythification and explanation, is always a form of intraworldly allegory. What for the Church Fathers was the eschatological expectation of salvation is now the *continuum* of history (the historicist background), but this, too, is an empty concept once all eschatological perspective is denied.

In the case of art, eschatology is the constitutive openness of the work onto the future, in the light of which all the intraworldly references (to the past, to society, and so on) detectable in it acquire their meaning. The important thing is to read the work as an announcement of and appeal to a new event, as the self-presentation of a truth, which is not exhaustively heard by finding an already constituted situation to which the work might refer, but as an appeal that demands an answer rather than an explanation.

This becomes clearer if we consider it on the plane of language. The language of the Bible, in the measure in which it is prophetic, is never the sign of something that is or wants to be "recognized" as such. The Word of God does not signify a preconstituted world; rather, it creates it. Something similar is characteristic of the work of art. Since the historical epochs are determinate openings of Being, original ways in which beings are arranged within the light that man—Dasein—projects, their event is above all linguistic. A historical world—a given order and "meaning" of beings and of man among them—is always born through the institution of language. The sign-meaning relationship can occur solely within an already instituted opening because the establishment of linguistic conventions always comes after the birth of language, which in its origin is never a sign but the becoming world of the world.

The eschatological character of openness onto the future is worked out by virtue of the artwork's founding a language and a world. Indeed, one of the most salient outcomes of modern aesthetics from Kant onward is precisely the recognition of the artwork's originality and irreducibility. The work founds a completely new legality, of which it is itself the first exemplary realization. It does not correspond to prefixed laws; instead it institutes them. If this originality is not to be understood as a purely clever

invention of the new—as simple originality in the banal sense of the term—
it will be necessary to recognize its ontological significance. The artwork,
in appealing to a world, does not arrange itself into the existing world but
instead founds one.

What could it mean, for interpretation theory and, more concretely, for
criticism to respect the work's founding and opening character ? It is a question that deserves more discussion both in the domain of philosophy and by
the critical methods.

It will be a matter of taking the truth appeal presented by the work more
seriously, drawing the line of demarcation between irrational/historicist aestheticism and a human vision of art that is precisely ontological.

# III *Truth*

# 8 Aesthetics and Hermeneutics

The outcome of recent philosophical hermeneutics has been the "recovery of the truth claim of art," to use Gadamer's expression. This recovery, in itself, is fundamentally polemical toward a large part of the twentieth century's philosophical aesthetics, whose inclination has been to redefine art by excluding its theoretical or practical bearing or, at best, by assigning to art a position of subordination according to which, even though art belongs to the field of truth, it is the task of other activities to take cognizance of the truth that art represents, by including it into a perspective that is vaster, more comprehensive, and therefore "truer." If the latter attitude can be exemplified by Lukacs's aesthetics (in all its phases, though with different tonalities), the former is shared by many theoretical trends that have made recourse against Hegel to the Kantian lesson of the *Critique of Judgment* and have attempted to define the specificity of art by bringing it back to an autonomous dimension of consciousness, cut off from any dimension that would have to do with truth and action. Neo-Kantianism is much more widespread than is generally believed because of the vast influence Cassirer has exercised upon American aesthetics, specifically on the work of Susanne Langer, who has brought it together in a kind of synthesis with Morris's semiotics. The meaning of the neo-Kantian presence lies in its defining aesthetic experience solely in reference to the dimension of consciousness, so that the reference to consciousness's other becomes totally unnecessary. The realm of things that can belong to the sphere of experience is not determined by the things themselves, but, rather, by the "attitude" of the subject. Anything can be the focus of aesthetic analysis (as is visible in the history of taste and of the sociology of art) as long as consciousness performs what Gadamer calls an "aesthetic differentiation" with respect to it. As is well known, these are the principles by means of which Gadamer develops his critique of "aesthetic consciousness" in *Truth and Method*.[1] Aesthetic consciousness, insofar as it constitutes the aesthetic quality of its objects with an attitude of contemplation, never really encounters anything other than itself. The museum understood as a social institution is only a correlation of aesthetic consciousness, its most significant incarnation. In the museum, too, objects are presented in the condition of absolute abstraction of the purely aesthetic stage. In other words, they are withdrawn from their concrete historical links (i.e., their religious, social, political, or everyday "uses") by means of an activity that situates all of them at the same level of the objects of a "taste," which in turn has become absolute and total.

Nevertheless, it may be observed that art history has often drawn from these kinds of activities a vital impulse for further developments. This was the case of the "importation" into Europe of African art at the turn of the century. Here, too, it was not a matter of works of art in the sense in which we understand that word. Instead, it had to do with objects that had had a religious or social function that once cut off from their own context became the object of a purely aesthetic contemplation. A valid objection to the aesthetic consciousness would be to point out the stimulating function these objects have had for European philosophical culture during the first decades of the twentieth century precisely on account of their uncanniness. This would show that cutting off certain products from their own original environment and collocation in order to set them into another world, where they have an essentially different function, may be the principle of a new history rather than a mummification, as the critique of aesthetic consciousness would have it.

In reality, the example of the driving force exerted on European art by the discovery of African art in our century (which is merely an example among many) does not demonstrate at all the legitimacy of "aesthetic consciousness" but rather serves to caution us about the possible equivocal meaning implicit in its critique. During the first decade of the twentieth century many European painters did not receive and elaborate the suggestions of African art with the attitude of aesthetic consciousness. The latter attitude is a more typical characteristic of the collector who pays an almost ritual attention to the object and who has no intention of becoming a producer or of continuing the process of development. The example of African art tells us something else of equal importance: it is not possible to escape from the abstractions of aesthetic consciousness by replacing it with what Gadamer calls "historical consciousness." Here we encounter the second largely diffused stance in nineteenth-century aesthetics: historicism, taken in its various nuances so as to include the most trivial sociological approach, often opposed to the aestheticism of pure contemplation. But a viable alternative to the leveling performed by the museum by means of "aesthetic differentiation," of the violent colonialist act of abstracting the artwork from its own world, is not to be found in a naïve historicism that believes itself capable of reading a classical work in its own truth solely by means of a punctual and exact reconstruction of the historical conditions in which it was produced and enjoyed (in *Truth and Method*, Gadamer gives the example of the performance of a music from the past with the instruments of the epoch). The historicist attitude would merely substitute one abstraction for another: in this view we would no longer cut off the artwork from its world in order to place it into our own; rather, we would attempt to place ourselves into the world of the artwork, thus forgetting that we belong concretely to our present history. As is well known, these are two attitudes that Hegel discusses and criticizes in depth in his *Lectures on Aesthetics*. So we cannot replace the attitude of aesthetic consciousness, which puts all its objects at the level of an "aesthetic quality" that is only recognizable by our taste, with a historical consciousness that is deemed to be more capable of bearing the truth. At first sight, the historicist attitude would seem to be capable of claiming adherence to the truth of things because it does not consider artworks as abstract supports of aesthetic quality but rather as the productions of an epoch, of a society, of a concretely situated individual. On the contrary, the historical consciousness that dominates Hegelian historicism and the late-nineteenth-century historicism of Dilthey does position the historical productions of an epoch in their own context, but it does so without in turn letting itself be implicated. Paradoxically, it affirms the historicity of everything it encounters except itself. This is a well known objection that has been often raised against Hegel's historicism. In fact, it is only from the viewpoint of the end of history that it would seem possible to assign to every past event its exact collocation and truth. But historical consciousness takes on the peculiar character of a fixed schema on which events, epochs, and figures of universal history are projected in late-nineteenth- and early-twentieth-century historicism that explicitly rejects Hegel's outcomes, too. In fact, historical consciousness has its own historicity only inasmuch as it is historiography, that is to say, the neutrally objective representation and contemplation of those contents.

The critique of historical consciousness's limits already delineates in some way the sense in which hermeneutics speaks of an experience of truth in the realm of art, and more generally what it means by truth. The experience of truth that takes place in art should not be understood as the recognition of the thing's aesthetic quality (summed up in the judgment: this thing is beautiful) or as the encounter with a historical production as historicism construes it. The rejection of the historicist attitude on the part of hermeneutics deserves to be discussed in more depth. It seems indeed that the thing (artwork, historical document, and so on) represents by virtue of its own concreteness an encounter with the other, namely the "thing itself," which interpretation theory has attempted to ground and secure against any attempt by the subject to reflexively fold upon itself. However, for historicism, as is sufficiently visible in Dilthey, the encounter with the thing is still thought on the model of empiricism or, in Heidegger's language, of metaphysics. Dilthey had in mind the model of the natural sciences and wanted to accomplish for historical consciousness what Kant had for Newtonian physics. Thus he was interested in seeking out the conditions of possibility (the a priori structures) that ground the objective validity of historiographical knowledge. These conditions can be reduced to one—as seems evident above all in the beautiful pages Dilthey wrote on the subject of autobiography[2]—namely, the historicity of existence in its historiographical nature. The historicity of existence may be reduced to the fact that our existence only gives itself as a continuous construction and reconstruction of its own past. It is everyday existence as such that is historiographical: the continuity of meaning, having the same structural basis of historiography, makes up the spiritual life of every human being. Whether or not one accepts Dilthey's hypothesis of reducing historicity to historiography, it still remains true that Dilthey is concerned above all with historical knowledge as objectively valid knowledge. This implies that the historian suspend, as it were, his own historicity from his own consciousness in order to let the thing itself (its historical content) appear in what is most characteristically its own, thereby assuming a purely contemplative posture. Hermeneutics would object that such an attempt to be objective, modeled as it is on the methodological ideal of the modern natural sciences, lets what is most characteristic of history escape from its view, not only the historicity of the "object" but also the historicity of the knowing subject.

But is not hermeneutic experience a matter of securing the encounter with the other? Is not the defense of the truth claim of aesthetic experience a reference to the effect that in enjoying the artwork we truly encounter "something" rather than the phantasm of (our) taste?

The demand to liberate aesthetics for an encounter with something other (i.e., the thing itself) in contemporary aesthetics was forcefully raised by Adorno. Indeed, for him what distinguishes a genuine experience of the work of art from the pure enjoyment of *Kitsch* and of ideologically charged products of entertainment in mass culture is precisely the irreducible alterity of the work over the subject's taste and expectations, which are always already compromised by the manipulations of the mass media. However, Adorno seems to bring the encounter with the thing itself back to a sort of mythical "use value" of the artwork, juxtaposed to an equally mythical "exchange value." Or at least so it appears in the *Introduction to the Sociology of Music* where Adorno juxtaposes the adequate listening of the expert, who likes the music because of its structural characters, to the inauthentic or ideological listening of those who like the performance only because they identify with the group of amateurs who enjoy a specific musical genre.[3] In other words, the pop song has no structural consistence that could justify its aesthetic evaluation. The success met by a song—if and when it happens— comes from the fact that it comes to constitute a site of recognition for vast groups, for reasons that may have to do either with its capacity to represent a certain taste or with the manipulation of the market by the channels of distribution. The radical example of the aesthetic experience of the mass that does not encounter "the thing itself" but rather the tastes of the consumers (those who enjoy it), would be another typical case of substitution of exchange value for use value. For Adorno, this substitution shows the self-assertion in the field of art or in what pretends to be art of the universal commodification of capitalist society.

Inasmuch as he remains bound to the formulation of the *Introduction to the Sociology of Music*, Adorno's thesis regarding adequate listening as structural listening (typical of the expert who knows how to read musical notes) brings the exigency of defending in aesthetics the encounter with "the thing itself" back to weak theoretical argumentations: above all an adequate structural listening may be justified only by virtue of its identifying a supposed "use value" of the work with its given organized and recognizable form. The thesis that this is the use value, that is, the primary value of the artwork, in opposition to other functions of the artistic product (be they emotional, psychological, or "gastronomic") has a precise historical and cultural collocation, namely, the distinctive mark of a group or society—the educated bourgeoisie that spent evenings playing music in private salons, which no longer exists under late capitalism—and therefore it is entirely reducible to exchange value. The exclusive appreciation of the structure is exhibition, recognition, and enjoyment of a distinctive mark of the group, too. (A similar mark is probably found in the entire asceticism permeating Adorno's aesthetics, up to its latest formulation.) In comparison with the most recent *Aesthetic Theory*, the reduction of the supposed use value of the work, understood as a structure to its "exchange value," seems to be valid, even though Adorno's insistence on the work as a social construct is not based on the idea that an approach is adequate only insofar as it is directed to the structure, but rather on the idea that the truth of the work may be given only through its collocation within a certain language and its techniques. There is no relation of the work to the history of Spirit, understood as the yet to be realized history of freedom, other than through the relation of the work to the history of the specific technical language in which it is formulated. What is encountered in the work is, once again, never the thing itself but the "truth content," namely a spiritual content, which is therefore historical in the larger sense of the taste of a group, of a class, of an epoch, too.

It seems difficult to speak of an experience of truth in relation to art without always recognizing and heightening the work's belonging to a historical world. The opposition of use value to exchange value, or the identification of the structural approach as the sole adequate approach in opposition to the purely gastronomic or ideological enjoyment of art, fails because there is no encounter with the work of art that is not an encounter with its own belonging to a social and historical world.

The exigency of recognizing aesthetic experience as an encounter with the thing itself cannot be satisfied on the basis of Adorno's categories, since even in his work they do not survive as alternative categories. In its defense of the truth claim of aesthetic experience, hermeneutics starts by recognizing that the kind of distinction made by Adorno between use value and exchange value makes no sense because these two values coincide completely. An encounter with a work of art can never signify encountering it as it is mythically in-itself, outside of the social mediations of which it is both an outcome and an active agency. It is a lesson that can be found unequivocally stated in Kant's *Critique of Judgment*, as long as one reads it with "hermeneutic" attention as, for example, Gadamer does in some beautiful pages of *Truth and Method*,[4] where the Kantian notion of "reflecting judgment" as the judgment of taste is revealed to be deeply bound to sociality. The Kantian judgment of taste awaits the consensus of all, though it does not lay claim to a universality that could be compared to the determined judgments of science. True, in its expectation of a shared agreement the aesthetic judgment appeals to the universal function of the cognitive faculties exactly like the determined judgment. But it remains also true that in matters of taste there are no irrefutable demonstrations. In the pages of *Truth and Method* just recalled, Gadamer is concerned with showing that the field of action of the reflecting judgment is extended beyond the borders of the beautiful of nature and art, to comprise questions that embrace both the moral life and concrete historical existence.[5] These are all fields where it is not enough to subsume a particular under a general concept, but that necessitate, rather, a "productive integration," which is precisely the work of the reflective judgment. For me, it is important to underscore that, even thought the Kantian judgment of taste is not reduced to passively following the canons that are empirically established by fashion, it is exercised with a view to a sort of ideal community that is always still in the process of constituting itself. From this perspective, in the light of the outcomes of twentieth-century philosophical hermeneutics, it is clear that philosophical discourse falls within the domain of the reflecting judgment, strictly understood. This view calls for the revision of the rigid separation between the "productive" activity of what appears to be proper to art and the purely reflexive activity that seems to be proper to philosophy and criticism.

What is interesting here is that the classical Kantian doctrine of aesthetic judgment, understood as reflecting judgment, points toward the reduction of aesthetic experience to sociality. To formulate an aesthetic judgment does not signify recognizing given qualities of the object but rather discovering, revealing, and heightening the fact of its belonging to a community, even if an ideal community. However, its ideal character is rooted in what the community to which we belong factually is. In other words, if we look more closely, the ideal is precisely the ideal that this community makes of itself. The two notions of verisimilitude and necessity that hold the chain of tragic events in Aristotle's *Poetics* may be legitimately read in this sense, too. What tragedy exposes to us is the course of human events, in its factual unfolding and in its having to be ideal. These two elements cannot be disjoined, otherwise tragic catharsis would never occur.[6]

According to Kant, whenever I enjoy the beauty of an object of nature or of art I am actually enjoying the right—that is, harmonious—functioning of the knowing faculties. However, the awareness that this functioning is "right" (approximately stated) always already comprises its communality for all human beings. What is pleasing in aesthetic experience is neither the object nor the individual's subjectivity, but rather its very communicability. If I aesthetically like something, it is because my knowing faculties operate as those of others, thereby guaranteeing every possible communication, including the objective universality of theoretical judgments.

Hence, Kant's theory of aesthetic judgment serves to confirm that if we are to defend the truth claim of aesthetic experience against aesthetic consciousness, we cannot suppose as possible an objective encounter with the artistic product, in the sense in which Adorno, for example, in his sociology of music speaks of an adequate listening insofar as it is directed to the musical work. If there is truth in aesthetic experience, it must be given within and through the mediations that always constitute such experience, rather than in a mythical immediacy that will not resist under critical scrutiny. An experience of truth, characterized in this way, is comprehensible only if we refer to the meanings that experience and truth take up in the reflection of hermeneutics. Here experience is understood neither as the stamping of the image of the thing on the *tabula rasa* of consciousness nor as the correspondence of the statement to a given state of affairs. There is an experience of truth when the person who undergoes the experience is truly changed as a result of it. Experience is thus understood in the sense illustrated by its resonance in the German word *Erfahrung*, which comprises a reference to *fahren*, to undertake a voyage, involving the accumulation of new knowledge, and above all a process of modification of the physiognomy of the subject, on whom the experiences and the encounters leave their mark. The fact that there is an experience of truth in art signifies above all that the encounter with the work and its earlier production are events that modify those who are involved in them. Thus art is an experience of truth because it is truly experience, namely an event in which something really happens. In *Truth and Method* Gadamer describes all this complex story of the happening of truth (let us not forget that Heidegger was the first to speak forcefully of the "happening" of truth) by making recourse to the notion of play as well as the "fusion of horizons," (*Horizontverschmelzung*) after having extended the model of aesthetic experience to historical experience in general. What occurs in the fusion of horizons and in aesthetic experience has as its model the dialogue. In dialogue, understanding each other is never merely to transmit to the other one's own viewpoint or to passively receive from the other her viewpoint. Instead, it is the birth of a *novum*, a common horizon in which the two interlocutors recognize each other not as they were before but as discovered *anew*, enriched and deepened in their being. In this sense, the model of dialogue entails a dialectical, Hegelian aspect: the *novum* that dialogue gives rise to is also elaboration, corroboration, return to itself of what already was. The experience of truth that is realized in this manner is placed under the sign of continuity: the other standing before me in a dialogue, just like the thing I encounter, initially is present as an agent of discontinuity, as the breakdown of an equilibrium. A dialogue is above all a kind of reckoning with this novelty, that is, with the alterity of the other, in order to reestablish the continuity he has interrupted. The situation of misunderstanding from which every interpretation starts, according to Schleiermacher, can perhaps be understood as the pure and simple otherness of the interlocutor, who insofar as he is other disturbs the equilibrium, produces a modification, thereby forcing one to readjust the equilibrium.[7]

The possibility that the other, or something new, will present itself is safeguarded only by its belonging to a domain that always already mediates it with whatever it enters into relation. If there were no communality between the two interlocutors, or between the observer and the artwork (and in general between the reader and any kind of text), dialogue would not even begin. The mediation, which takes place in the fusion of horizons, is in part always already given in the universal *medium* of language. This theory of language as universal medium of experience, whose theoretical foundation is in Heidegger's philosophy, has enabled Gadamer to resolve the problem of pre-understanding that is required by every process of interpretation. It would be beyond our task here to discuss the grounds and consequences of the fact that the universal medium of experience is precisely language. Instead, it is important to underscore that the continuity of hermeneutic experience is corroborated and more emphatically stressed, since the mediation of the fusion of horizons always already presupposes another mediation, that of language.

What is the meaning of this for the question regarding the truth of aesthetic experience? The question now is whether or not aesthetic experience, understood in terms of continuity, is not in danger of being thought as the pure and simple recovery of "aesthetic consciousness" from the critique of which hermeneutic reflection started. In this regard, I find illuminating the pages of *Truth and Method* that Gadamer devotes to tragedy, in the analysis of which he takes up many Aristotelian elements. Precisely by arguing polemically against the detached attitude of aesthetic consciousness, which is capable of enjoying tragedy only as a spectacle and as a perfect representation, Gadamer points out that the effect of tragedy upon the spectator is the "deepening of his continuity with himself. . . . In the event of tragedy the spectator meets himself once again, insofar as what he meets there is precisely his own world as he already knows it in its own religious or historical tradition."[8] We are not far away from the social and historical implications of the Kantian notion of taste as "common sense," recalled by Gadamer in the pages on Kant just mentioned. For Gadamer, the recovery of the self that happens in tragedy is diametrically opposed to the attitude of aesthetic consciousness, whose only preoccupation is to verify the product's abstract characters and formal qualities. However, if we stand by the definition of the experience of truth as an experience in which the subject comes out truly modified, then the recovery and deepening of continuity of the self with itself appears more akin to the fixed ahistorical nature of "aesthetic consciousness" than it is to the *becoming other* characteristic of every encounter with truth. Hermeneutics does start from the defense of the notion of truth as an experience that truly modifies the person who undergoes it. But the adoption of the model of dialogue seems to recall the Hegelian dialectics as a movement in which the conclusion finds what was already there at the outset, though more enriched and more deepened. Thus, the self-continuity that for *Truth and Method* is the dominant value of every hermeneutic experience, in the end seems to frustrate the notion of truth as becoming other, which had seemed most productive in resolving the aporias of empiricism and scientism.

To be sure, a lot of pages of *Truth and Method* point beyond the thesis that the "human condition" and its limits (meaning an encounter of the self with what he already was rather than a becoming other) are found at the bottom of aesthetic experience as hermeneutic experience, especially where Gadamer adopts play as the model of hermeneutic experience. Indeed, it is characteristic of play that it transcends the individual players, so that the players are expropriated as a result in a sense that goes back to Heidegger's notion of *Ereignis* (event) as expropriation (*Ent-eignen*) and trans-propriation (*Ueber-eignen*).[9] This means that despite his emphasizing continuity, in the end, there is a discontinuity/misidentification pole in Gadamer, too, which at least leaves open the tension between the two extreme poles of hermeneutic experience.[10]

Nevertheless, the danger of surpassing, and sublating into continuity the elements of novelty and becoming is quite real. It would seem that precisely against this danger we should raise the model of aesthetic experience, especially the characters that have been underscored and exalted by the avant-garde of the twentieth century. From the perspective that twentieth-century avant-garde intended to represent, of the break of continuity with tradition as well as with every *Bildung* understood as harmonious construction of unified totalities, that is, the formation of art works and subjects, the recovery of man in his own original dimension that Gadamer finds exemplified and still binding in the Aristotelian theory of tragedy appears to be bound up with a type of aesthetic experience that is no longer ours. The avant-garde (whose necessary, and therefore nonfortuitous relevance for the history of art has been shown by Adorno) did not want to be true in the sense of going back—on the part of art, of the artist, of the consumer—to a dimension of truth that is always available, albeit forgotten or covered up. On the contrary, it is understood in its own truth as the capacity to make something happen by means of scandals generated by linguistic innovations or by political and ideological engagements of various sorts. The happening of truth signifies producing differences, distances, discontinuities: to grasp this merely as a moment that has to be reabsorbed in the reconstruction of a continuity signifies taking up, once again, at least implicitly the model of Hegelian dialectics as the only possible conception of truth. We must recognize in this model of continuity that is always being reconstituted anew—and therefore in the immediate character of every return of the self to itself—the aestheticist limits that Kierkegaard saw embodied in the figure of the seducer. On the other hand, in the differences he continually produces as well as in the lacerations with which he pays for his curiosity for novelties, the seducer truly experiences a becoming other that is irreducible to the model of continuity.

The problem Jürgen Habermas posed to Gadamer with respect to the origin and meaning of the discontinuity that hermeneutics assumes as the datum from which to start (which is what Habermas ultimately expects, given his Hegelian and Marxist perspective), is not resolved by recognizing the historically given rifts at the root or at a specific moment of our European civilization, at the beginning of the Reformation when the question of hermeneutics was thematically addressed for the first time.[11] These rifts can be identified only in the light of a model of continuity, like the classical and Hegelian ideal of the Greek polis. The weight given to the notion of *application* in *Truth and Method* clearly shows that such a model of continuity is dominant not only in the Hegelian-Marxist objections to hermeneutics but also in the work of Gadamer. Gadamer calls application a sort of "lived interpretation," above all of the texts that stand as the models for the historical existence of a given society: for example, the Bible or, at a different level, the codes of law. If, on the one hand, application is productive inasmuch as it evinces the constitutive aspect of mediation with the present that every interpretation of texts, even the most remote, necessarily possesses. On the other hand, it runs the risk of leading to the idea that a nonhistoricist and nonaestheticist model of interpretation presupposes the texts' applicability to the present situation, or at least the attempt to reconstruct their conditions of applicability. It seems to me that from this point of view the notion of application always involves a possible proximity, which is tributary to the ideal of continuity. What we think we can "apply" is never truly distant. Nevertheless, in its proximity it loses all the density of meanings, be they aesthetic or auratic, that constitute its wealth as an eminent, high model of experience (an argument in need of elaboration with respect to the concept of the classic).

It is important to underscore that if hermeneutics has provided philosophy with the conceptual tools to rethink aesthetic experience as a genuine experience of truth, by virtue of its idea of truth as an encounter with the other hermeneutics, it is precisely the fidelity to the data of aesthetic experience as it has appeared in the light of the concrete unfoldings of the arts of our century that can enable hermeneutic reflection to abstain from falling into the logic of continuity and identity. Today it is precisely art that presents itself as the privileged site of the negation of identity, and therefore of the event of truth. This thesis can be illustrated in many ways, among which I shall elucidate what follows:

(a)  The crisis of representation, which may be considered emblematic of twentieth-century aesthetics, ranging from nonfigurative painting to the dissolution of narrativity in literature, is one of the most imposing forms of identity's negation, understood above all as the capacity to identify the artistic products themselves and the subject who produces them or to whom they are destined.

(b)  This crisis does not allow itself to be absorbed by resorting to perspectives that are intended to restore in some ways the mastery of identity, whether it is understood as the mastery of the structure or of the subject who is its correlate. For example, art cannot be described in terms of the Lacanian imaginary[12] in order to then observe that the play of identification and misidentification that occurs within its bounds functions, analogously to the psychoanalytical cure, as a means for reestablishing the borders between the real and the imaginary (somehow repeating what has traditionally been attributed to as the function of Aristotelian catharsis). It is a given that in much of contemporary art the crisis of representation is accompanied by a renewed capacity for phantasmagoria (it is a term used in Adorno's *Negative Dialectics*, though he sees it merely as an element of the situation of crisis that the avant-garde intends to overcome, rather than a phenomenon that could fall within such an overcoming). Such a capacity for phantasmagoria, deeply bound as it is with the tools of the technical reproducibility of the arts, above all of cinema, constitutes the basis for a new "explosion" of the imaginary that aesthetics cannot reabsorb into the models of continuity and identity. Rather, aesthetics must recognize it as the announcement of what may well originally constitute every aesthetic experience as an experience of truth, that is to say, alienation, becoming other, or the play of identification. All these are characteristics of aesthetic experience identified by Plato in the sections of the *Republic* dedicated to dramatic art, which he wanted to exclude from his ideal state precisely on account of them. Today art is the site of the happening of truth because in it more than in any other site, the subject is subjected to an expropriating summoning, forced, as it were, to undertake an analysis without the guide of any model of recomposition, deprived of the analyst-father who will guarantee that nothing bad will happen there.

(c)  Art is this site, even in the more compromised, institutional sense: museum, gallery, concert hall, theater, of course, next to the more recent institutions like cinema and the disco. The death of art, seen by many as a necessary outcome, has always been theorized from the point of view of the ideal of continuity and identity. However, such a death would be the death of art as a specific social form (subjected to the law of the division of labor) as well as the disappearance of art as an event of discontinuity, that is to say, as the event of truth.

# 9 Aesthetics and Hermeneutics in Hans-Georg Gadamer

## The Question of the Truth of Art

Hegel's philosophy of art illustrates very clearly the risk often faced by many theories of the truth of art, that is, of justifying the truth of art by means of a dialectical operation that recognizes art as a manifestation of truth only in the moment in which it is overcome and abolished by philosophy. The aesthetics that reproduce, albeit in different forms, this typical movement of Hegelian dialectics face two problems, which can hardly be overcome within the limit of their perspectives, whether they look at art as a substructure of economic developments in Marxist fashion or whether they look at it from the stance of psychoanalysis, as the work of unconscious archetypes (individual or collective).

On the one hand, if the point of grasping and enjoying the work of art is to understand its point of reference, the individuality of the work loses all its significance. What matters is the semantic reference, and the value of the work coincides more or less explicitly with its sign-function. The encounter with the work as such is a provisional moment; its truth is what it means rather than what the work concretely and physically is, the historical situation or the psychic structure of which it is a manifestation. On the other hand, the question of interpretation, which is concretely posed by art, has lost its meaning (this is always the consistent outcome of Hegelian dialectics). There is only one mode of grasping correctly the work in its truth, which will coincide with philosophy, psychology, and sociology depending on varied perspectives. The evaporation of interpretation as a specific problem shows clearly the Hegelian background of these two positions. In order to reveal the truth of art by dialecticizing it with social structures or unconscious archetypes, it is necessary to assume somehow the absolutist point of view that Hegel assigned to philosophy, which is the presupposition of every dialectical act.

It is precisely the abandonment of the Hegelian absolutist point of view, an abandonment carried out mainly by existentialism, that reproposes the problem of a philosophical theory of interpretation understood as a philosophy of the finitude of human existence. This is how, in his last work, Gadamer approaches the hermeneutic question within a perspective in which the phenomenon of interpretation is revelatory of the human condition.[1] In fact, the human condition can be identified as the hermeneutic situation. The interpretation of the work of art is only one of the modes in which the hermeneutic situation may be realized. The hermeneutic question is decisive also and above all for the historical sciences and for theology. Nevertheless, as we shall see, the question of interpretation of the work of art represents its fundamental aspect. Gadamer's work, then, contains much more than simple implications of or possible applications to the reflection on art, even though his book cannot be called a book of aesthetics.

Following Heidegger, Gadamer conceives of finitude as temporality. Interpretation is a historical event in which another event (i.e., the work to be interpreted) appears in its truth. The hermeneutic problem of this encounter exists only from the point of view of finitude, precisely because neither of the two moments resolves the other in itself, either by overcoming or by abolishing it as in Hegel's dialectics. Each one maintains its finite individuality, and yet the one makes itself present in and through the other. We can see here how with the abandonment of the Hegelian perspective there reemerges, together with the hermeneutic question, the other element of the individuality and autonomy of the work, which usually evaporates in Hegelian perspectives. Indeed, the hermeneutic question is reproposed precisely insofar as the irreducible individuality of the work and generally of the historical event is acknowledged. As a result, the first step toward a theory of interpretation is to reconstruct the ontological status of the work of art. Gadamer shows how the hermeneutic question and the autonomy of the work are indissolubly bound.

For example, the question concerning the multiple interpretations of a work and their legitimacy can be resolved positively only if we explicitly state that the various interpretations are legitimate insofar as they correspond to the *effective possibilities of being* of the work as such and do not depend exclusively on the subjectivities of the interpreters. With respect to this view, Gadamer states that he is in agreement with Pareyson's theory of formativity and with his emphasis on the intrinsic normativity of the work.[2] Insofar as it is formative, the work imposes itself to the author first, rather than to the interpreter, and therefore constitutes an actual experience of transcendence.

## The Crisis of "Aesthetic Consciousness"

According to Gadamer, the ontological status of the work of art can be reconstructed by means of a critical reexamination of the concept of "aesthetic consciousness."[3] The crisis of aesthetic consciousness, as key concept for defining the world of art and the very essence of the work, is an outcome of the whole history of post-Kantian aesthetics. The comprehensive meaning of this history, finely reconstructed by Gadamer in the first part of his work, is the gradual dissolution of the implicit ontological content that still functioned in Kant as a limit against the subjectivist meaning of the separation between taste and cognitive faculty, established by the *Critique of Judgment*. With the evaporation of a (albeit problematic) teleological view of nature, the autonomy of art increasingly became like an evanescent domain of experience without ontological roots.

This process culminates with the crisis of the concept of genius and the affirmation of aesthetic consciousness as the only possibility of defining the essence of art. While for romantic aesthetics art was still sufficiently distinguished as the work of genius, the concept of genius as unconscious production (rooted in nature already in Kant) no longer draws a following in the twentieth century, not even among the artists. Gadamer sharply points out that it is precisely in Valéry, the theorist of art as intellectual activity, who stands diametrically opposed to an aesthetics of genius as unconscious production, that one finds the second aspect of the crisis of the concept of genius: the crisis of the ontological *status* of the work of art, namely herme-neutic nihilism. With the extinction of the concept of genius, understood as the last possibility of giving an ontological qualification to art by establish-ing its link to nature, the work loses any individual consistence, so that the verses have only the meaning attributed to them by the reader, and the artis-tic product exists only as the correlate of instantaneous illuminations, the discontinuous *Erlebnisse* that constitute aesthetic consciousness. The concept of aesthetic consciousness, then, sums up the process of subjectivizing aes-thetics undergone by aesthetics after Kant and its crisis.

In Gadamer's analysis, aesthetic consciousness has the same character of instantaneity and discontinuity that Kierkegaard assigned to the aesthetic sphere, understood as a moral fact. If the work is not definable other than as the correlate of an aesthetic *Erlebnis*, a momentary illumination produced in the subject upon encountering it, then it loses every relation with its own world and ultimately every relation with the world at large. Hence, the expe-rience of the work no longer is an encounter with a historical individuality that is addressed to someone, but rather a fact that stands outside of the his-tory the work as well as outside of the subject's history, suspended, as it were, in a realm where all is born and evaporates in mysterious ways. We hear, once again, the echoes of Heidegger's critique of the historical con-sciousness of historicism:[4] for abstract aesthetic consciousness, just as for the historicist mindset against that Heidegger polemicizes, every work of art is equally graspable, since its social correlate is the museum, where the works are arranged next to one another, isolated from their own world, and offered to an aesthetic enjoyment that claims to grasp them in their eternal nature. On the contrary, by placing them and itself outside of temporal finitude, aesthetic consciousness ends up no longer understanding those works at all.

Instead, the viewpoint of the finite (i.e., temporality) is continuity. The work to be interpreted is a historical event that is linked to a certain world. An event is my own interpretation of the work, with all the difficulties im-plied by the mediation of my world with that of the work. The eternal nature of the work of art—assuming one still wants to speak in these terms—is nei-ther the atemporality of aesthetic consciousness nor the instantaneity of an *Erlebnis*. Rather, still following Kierkegaard, it is contemporariness as a task to be realized. Here aesthetics extends into hermeneutics because the en-counter with the work is an encounter with a truth that is already given as historical event, which demands to be understood by means of an act that understands it above all by understanding itself. The question concerning the truth of art is identical to that of the truth of the *Geisteswissenschaften*, that is to say, with the hermeneutic problem.[5]

## Ontology of the Work of Art: *Spiel*, Imitation, *Darstellung*

Gadamer reaches this conclusion not only by criticizing abstract aesthetic consciousness but also by examining more precisely the ontological *status* of the work of art. The running thread of this analysis is the concept of play, *Spiel*, chosen not only because of its proximity to the whole German tradition but also for the multiple possibilities of development contained by the term, more than the concept—and this is not surprising insofar as Gadamer is a Heideggerian thinker. In German, in fact, *spielen* is used to refer to the performance of a theatrical or musical work of art. The work fully realizes itself in its nature by virtue of its being performed (*gespielt*) and its being a *Spiel*, an act.

From the outset, Gadamer uses the concept of play differently than in the tradition: it is not introduced to illustrate the distance of art from the theoretical and practical interests that make up the texture of everyday existence. Instead, the natural character of play, which serves to make the nature of the work of art transparent, is the primacy of play over the player. The subject in a play is above all the play itself, since the player constitutes only one moment and an aspect of the play. The nature of play is fully realized when it is absolutely clear that the players are "in play" (at stake), insofar as they belong to a reality that transcends them and realizes itself in the players and in their play. This nature of play has its full actualization in art. The difference between play in the ordinary sense of the term and art lies in the fact that art is characterized by a "transformation in structure," a *Verwandlung ins Gebielde*—as Gadamer calls it. This indicates that the transcendence of play over the players in the work of art has acquired the consistence of an object that offers itself, in an exemplary manner, to enjoyment and performance in order to be played again and again, with the autonomy that the rules of ordinary games do not usually possess.[6]

The work as *Gebilde* (structure) realizes the nature of play in another way as well: by virtue of its self-presentation (*Selbstdarstellung*). Play is essentially manifestation, and precisely so in the playing of the players, who are the means of its manifestation. This appears more clearly if we pose the question concerning the relationship between the world of art and reality, a question that shows its non-sense as soon as it is posed, since the work itself is grasped and enjoyed as reality. Only abstract aesthetic consciousness distinguishes the work from reality within the instance of reflection, thus developing the concepts of dream and of aesthetic illusion. However, these concepts are evidently insufficient because they assign a negative meaning to aesthetic experience, defined only as something that does not possess the character of "'real' experience." Instead, what positively distinguishes the work from the reality given to us in everyday experience is that the work of art constitutes a totality of meaning, which is more definite and more accomplished than the chaos of unrealized possibilities characteristic of ordinary life.

According to Gadamer, to describe the relationship between the work of art and reality we need to recover the ancient concept of mimesis, abandoned after the triumph of the aesthetics of genius and of the scientific mindset because it did not appear to satisfy the exigency of the originality and creativity of genius or to coexist with a vision in which truth was reduced to the domain of the exact sciences. In actuality, once the concept of genius precipitated into crisis, imitation became once again the only term for determining the relationship between art and nature, and for defining more generally the ontological status of the work of art. As Aristotle already observed, imitation is not a copy or reproduction of reality, but rather a transposition of reality itself in its truth.[7]

Gadamer's argument about figurative arts—*Bild* as increase of being rather than copy of an *Urbild*—holds true in general for the concept of imitation.[8] In artistic imitation, which institutes forms, namely, totalities of meaning by means of which it distinguishes itself from the chaos characteristic of ordinary relationships, reality comes to light in its truth. To be the subject of a portrait, for example, is not an accidental fact. The being of the character portrayed in the portrait undergoes a transformation, increases in its being insofar as it reveals a new dimension, a new truth. This explains why, even in the case of portraits that appear to be slavish reproductions, the painting's value never sends us back to the represented subject. The portrait has a value of its own, even with respect to the character, because it constitutes a new reality in which the subject is presented in a new truth dimension. The relationship between *Bild* and *Urbild* is quite complex. It is possible to say that the *Urbild* is constituted as such by *Bild*, in the sense that it illuminates itself only in the image that art gives of it.[9]

The relationship between imitation and imitated "subject," together with its dialectical implication, serves more generally to illustrate the concept of art as *Darstellung* (presentation). Not only does the work represent an imitated reality, but also the performance in turn presents the work. What they share in common is that since there is no reciprocal determination between *Bild* and *Urbild*, insofar as the *Urbild* comes to light only in the *Bild*, it is never possible to compare these two terms. Similarly, since the work comes to light only in the interpretative performance, it is never possible to compare the work and the interpretation of it as if they were two objects that could be placed next to each other. Here the nature of *Darstellung* that is characteristic of play reveals its true meaning: presentation is always representation for someone and by means of someone; it is always a historically situated interpretative act, even though the autonomy and consistence of play and of the work of art becomes manifest only in interpretation.

This further clarifies the temporal character of the work of art as *Darstellung*. Insofar as it exists in the performance, the work is temporal in the sense that it is made in order to be performed. Thus, the temporality of the work constitutes its essential character. Furthermore, the work enjoys its infinity and transcends the very consciousness and intention of the author insofar as it is a historical event, which always re-presents itself in new ways and through the mediation of other events (i.e., the various performances). The effort to reconstruct these intentions or to re-present the work in the domain in which it was born (as if one were to perform ancient music with the instruments of the epoch) is merely an effort to forget the true hermeneutic question posed by the work. Interpretation is always a mediation between two worlds, that of the work and that of the interpreter, and is never reducible to the philological claim to transpose itself completely into the world of the work. The infinitude of the work lies in its historicity and event character, for the author sets the work into a play that he cannot forecast or control, in which the work acquires its own life.

## Aesthetic Experience and the Hermeneutic Situation

The previous discussion of aesthetic experience has shown that aesthetics cannot enclose itself; instead, it demands a more solid foundation in hermeneutics. Here, evidently, the term "hermeneutics" has a broader meaning than is traditionally intended. Every historical formation and so every work of art is a "text" to be interpreted, an object of *Verstehen*, and as such it is recognized in its truth, too. The truth of art does not lie in presenting contents that reflexive consciousness would have to illuminate and to make true once and for all. Rather, it is itself the becoming event of truth, namely a historical production that has its own meaning and its own consistence. Art presents itself in other historical events (i.e. interpretations) and therefore poses the hermeneutic question concerning the mediation between these different worlds.

What distinguishes the hermeneutic situation analyzed by Gadamer—through the reconstruction and discussion of the principal hermeneutic theories in modernity and in contemporary philosophy—is basically the same structure that we have recognized in aesthetic experience. The historian belongs as much to the tradition that makes up the document or event that he must interpretatively reconstruct, as the interpreter and the consumer of the work of art belong to the play that the work itself is. The historian's work involves the same process that takes place in the interpretation of art. The event to be interpreted is present only in interpretation, so it is impossible to compare event and interpretation objectively in order to guarantee the truth of the statement in a scientific manner, based on the supposedly true model of the exact sciences.

The circle, which is characteristic of the hermeneutic situation, is essentially linked to the finitude of human existence, and every hermeneutic theory ought to take it into account in its formulations. Gadamer places at the basis of his hermeneutics what he calls the principle of *Wirkungsgeschichte*, which indicates literally that in describing an event the historian's job is to keep the most remote consequences in mind. For example, in the case of a literary text, this implies analyzing its success in various epochs and domains in order to ensure that the event won't be isolated, abstracted, as it were, from its own temporal concreteness, but rather grasped in the historical flow to which it belongs. For Gadamer, however, the principle of *Wirkungsgeschichte* has a broader meaning: every hermeneutic theory must place at its basis the belonging of the interpreter to history.[10] This means: I stand before an event to be interpreted, but my position and the structure of my hypothesis are already in part determined by the event itself, which somehow exerts its pressure upon me even before I set out to interpret it. The possibility of interpreting a text or historical event consists in both text and interpreter originally belonging to a historical "horizon" that transcends and supports them both. The horizon's movement of expansion, or narrowing down or changing of perspectives, is not, above all, a fact of historical consciousness. Rather, "in it this motion becomes aware of itself."[11] Not only the work of art but the very historical becoming in its totality is definable as *Selbstdarstellung*, in which the interpreter belongs to the tradition to be interpreted, which makes itself visible through him, just as much as the consumer of art constitutes only one moment within the autonomous realization and presentation of the work.

The argument about aesthetic experience, therefore, constitutes not only one moment or aspect or simply the point of departure of Gadamer's inquiry. There are not two experiences, aesthetic and historical, that, placed next to each other, would be studied in order to construct a theory of extra-scientific truth; nor is aesthetics just a phase one leaves behind once the question is posed at the level of hermeneutics. On the contrary, the structure of aesthetic experience reveals itself as the type of the hermeneutic situation itself, which is identical with the human condition.

## Language as the Horizon of a Hermeneutic Ontology

It is not by chance that Gadamer underlines, in his introduction to *Ursprung des Kunstwerkes* ("The Origin of the Work of Art"),[12] the significant role that the reflection on art has had in the development of Heidegger's thought.[13] The same goes for Gadamer. In fact, after typifying man's relation to history, the relation of "belonging" between the interpreter-consumer and the work of art as *Spiel* ultimately becomes the model for conceiving the relation of belonging to Being. For this reason, Gadamer speaks of a "hermeneutic ontology" in the last part of his book. If we keep this in mind, we can account for the impression of circularity that the work awakens in the reader. In fact, Gadamer's argument never proceeds from premise to conclusion, by posing problems in search of a definitive solution. Rather, he proceeds along ever expanding circles within which clarity is to be sought. The circular structure corresponds to the content of the work and to its meaning. Even though he never explicitly uses this term, the epigraph from Rilke that Gadamer uses reinforces the central place in the overall work of the concept of *belonging* to the work as *Spiel*, to history, and ultimately to Being.[14]

The final transition occurs by means of an examination of the concept of language, where language is revealed to be the horizon of hermeneutic ontology. The relation to historical events or to works of art is always a dialogue, a *Gespräch*, hence it is a matter of listening and responding, and, above all, of interpreting or mediating the world of the work or of the event with one's own world, allowing the event or the work in question to come to light in the act of interpretation. This relation is always linguistic—and this is why it is compared to a *Gespräch*—even when the object to be interpreted cannot be identified at all with a statement written or pronounced by someone, or when historical events are presented as narrations or documents that stand in need of interpretation and translation. Interpretation, in turn, is always a linguistic event, which is made possible by the communality of language shared between speaker and listener, presupposed as the basis of any conventional institution of meanings.

The object of interpretation and the interpretative process are both linguistic events. The hermeneutic situation is distinguished by its being placed inside the horizon of language. The comprehensive historical horizon, which supports the varied permutations of historical horizons, is nothing other than the horizon of language. And just as much as it belongs to history, man belongs to language rather than possessing language as a tool. Thus every formalization of language, which claims to establish the limits and modalities of languages by means of rigorous conventions, always moves within an already existing language that makes it possible. Hence, no formalization can ever be total, for it never encompasses the entire linguistic horizon but rather always moves within it.

The primacy of language over particular languages, which has a kind of metaphysical preeminence, is quite lively in the Western philosophical tradition, as is visible in the history of the concepts of *logos* and *verbum*. The being of man coincides with his belonging to the world of language: "the original humanity of language signifies also the original linguistic nature of being in the proper world of man."[15] Here the world is not to be understood as *Umwelt* or milieu, as environment. On the contrary, language as comprehensive horizon of the singular horizons is precisely the possibility of overcoming every circumscribed *Umwelt* in order to build ever-new domains and institute new relationships.

The "belonging" of the interpreter to the work and to history characterizes even more broadly and more radically the relation of the interpreter to language. The interpreter is always already "thrown" into language, even before he decides to use it in order to interpret the singular linguistic productions that history hands him. In other words, belonging to the work and to the historical tradition itself is made possible by the communality of belonging to the world as linguistic horizon. Hence, the obvious need to extend aesthetics into hermeneutics, which coincides with ontology.

We could say, paraphrasing a motto that Heidegger takes up from Hölderlin, that man's being-in-the-world is "dwelling in language." To belong to this omni-comprehensive linguistic horizon means that the being of beings is similar to the being of the work of art, and in general of historical events. In other words, it consists in a *Sichdarstellen* (self-presentation) that has its constitutive nature in presenting itself in interpretation only. The linguistic horizon is that within which the singular historical events (persons, things, works) offer themselves to understanding, thus illuminating themselves and attaining their own "*Da*" ("there")—as Gadamer puts it in Heideggerian language—presenting themselves in the light of their own being. The horizon as such is never visible, since every understanding moves inside the horizon and is made possible by it.

Thus understood, language ultimately is identical with Being, in the Heideggerian sense of the light within which singular beings become visible; Being, in withdrawing from visibility, makes beings visible and reveals them. With respect to the identification of Being and language, it is important to observe that at the end of *Truth and Method* Gadamer recovers the ancient metaphysical concept of beauty as the universal character of being. The essence of beauty, established in the analysis of aesthetic experience, is self-presentation in the act of interpretation, a *Sichdarstellen* that always demands someone in whom or to whom it can realize itself. This is precisely what takes place in language, where every statement constitutes a use of language for a specific purpose as well as an interpretation of language itself, which reveals its constitutive dimension in its usages. Since the illumination of Being that renders beings visible occurs above all in language, it is possible to speak with good reasons of an identification of ontology and philosophy of language, though in a different sense than is commonly understood in contemporary philosophy. It is not a matter of dissolving Being into language, but rather of recognizing language as the *Word of Being* in which beings reveal themselves, and in which man always already has its collocation. This is an emphatically pronounced Heideggerian conclusion, which serves to understand the meaning of the etymological and poetic philosophy practiced by Heidegger in his latest writings, and a consistent development of Heidegger's thought.

The concept of belonging, which stands in the background of Gadamer's work, may generate the objection that Gadamer ultimately returns to a form of Hegelianism, while he had started off from the need to formulate the question of the truth of art in non-Hegelian terms. On the contrary, there is a radical difference between this position and Hegel's, and it is testified to by the emergence of the hermeneutic problem. Reason never encompasses the linguistic horizon, that is, Being, but is placed and held into it. It does not exhaust Being with any statement, and this is the reason why the question of interpretation arises. The recognition that the beautiful is the universal character of Being, says Gadamer at the end of the book, does not signify reposing in a self-satisfied aestheticism. The self-presentation of the work in the act of interpretation, of the performer or of the consumer as well as the interpretative reconstruction of history are unthinkable other than in relation to the finitude of man: "The event of the beautiful and the hermeneutical process both presuppose the finiteness of human life."[16]

Truth and method are closely bound in this perspective, not in the sense that the truth of a statement is identical with its verifiability, as if the method contained the truth. On the contrary, the validity of every method is conditioned by being originally placed inside an horizon of truth, understood as the light which makes beings visible. The human condition is thus definable as the "hermeneutic situation," and it is not only aesthetic experience but every search for truth that stands under the sign of interpretation.

# 10 The Work of Art as the Setting to Work of Truth

## 1. Work, Truth, World

From the perspective of ontology, Heidegger's most thorough definition of the artwork appears, as is well known, in the essay *Der Ursprung des Kunstwerkes* ("The Origin of the Work of Art"),[1] according to which a work of art is the "setting-itself-into-work of truth." Heidegger works out this definition with a view toward specifying the ontological meaning of art, but he does not do the same with aesthetic enjoyment.[2] This essay and the following Heideggerian works remain quite vague on the encounter between the reader/spectator and the work, on how to conceive of aesthetic enjoyment. To attend to this question we can draw some indications— though merely as starting points for a theoretical proposal that cannot in any way claim with any certainty to be "faithful" to Heidegger's teaching— from Heidegger's own practice as a reader and interpreter of poetic texts: ranging from the commentary on Hölderlin to the most recent *Unterwegs zur Sprache*.³ Accordingly, it is not so much a matter of interpreting his thought as it is of further developing and continuing it.

In regard to the literal meaning of the expression "setting-itself-into-work of truth," with respect to which the concept of aesthetic enjoyment is to be examined, I can only refer to the illustrations Heidegger himself provides in the essay mentioned above. Let me recall here that Heidegger is not speaking in any way of the setting-itself-into-work of truth as though to manifest or make known a truth that is already given, established, as he would if it were a truth about a situation or an actually present structure of the entity; instead, the setting-itself-into-work of truth for Heidegger has the same pregnant meaning as the Italian expression "putting a building to work" (*messa in opera di una costruzione*), where the meaning is that it has been put in a condition to function. The artwork sets-itself-into work in the same sense. Or to put it better: in the work, truth sets-itself-into-work in the same sense: in fact, the work opens a new "epoch" of being as an absolutely originary event, which cannot be reduced to what it already was, and it grounds a new order of relationships within beings, a true and actually new world. This is why, if there is a term that can define the encounter between the reader and the work, it is "*Stoss*," shock or quake: the artwork suspends in the reader all natural relationships, making strange everything that until that moment had appeared obvious and familiar.

It is clear enough, though, even from such a cursory description of the way in which Heidegger poses the problem, that such an encounter with the work—understood as the *Stoss* of encountering a new world—cannot be reduced in any way to the traditional concepts of aesthetic enjoyment.

## Representationalism and Formalism in the Concept of Aesthetic Enjoyment

The terms in which the encounter with the artwork has been conceived throughout the history of aesthetics are basically two: representationalism and formalism. Such an antithesis is not only and mainly a convenient polemical schema; rather, it is linked in the same manner with the way in which metaphysical thought (ontic thought) states (or fails to state) the question of truth. If the question of truth is not posed radically, when attempting to state it philosophically, and instead continues to be conceived in terms of correspondence with a "given" state of affairs or (a variation of the correspondence theory) of syntactic and formal correctness, it will always necessarily oscillate between representationalism and formalism.

If art's relationship to truth is emphasized but still conceived metaphysically, the value and meaning of art will consist in manifesting—making more visible on the plane of sensibility—a propositional truth that somehow would supply information regarding the "state of things," be it the emotional condition of a human being, the social configuration of an epoch, or the very structure of being. Instead, to the extent that one is willing to recognize for art an original function that is irreducible to knowledge, still metaphysically thought, art is viewed as a purely formal construction of objects that "impose" themselves and their validity. This is so because they are equipped with a structure whose recognition produces a delightful experience. In either case, pleasure has to do with recognition (a key term in Aristotle's poetics, which contains the two coexisting or oscillating meanings discussed here). In the first instance, it is a truth that is recognized insofar as it is already known by other means (hence the provisional and inessential character of art for all representational perspectives); in the second instance, it is a much more subtle fact that entails an evaluation of the successful outcome of the form: the beautiful structure gives pleasure because I "recognize" that it is what it should have been. Very often this sort of pleasure seeks to further ground itself without revising the metaphysical concept of truth, thus reducing itself to psychological or vitalistic positions.

While defending genuine demands, representationalism and formalism isolate (as they have to within the domain of metaphysics) and, therefore, reveal the internal contradictions and insufficiencies around which much of the history of aesthetics has busied itself. The basic difficulty of every representational attitude is the already mentioned provisional and inessential character of art. As is well known, these are the characters that art takes on in Hegel's thought, where it is justified precisely because it is *aufgehoben*, overcome and sublated, by philosophy. Now, what in Hegel's system happens to art as a form of Spirit—hence at the level of Spirit's history—in relation to philosophy occurs in every form of representationalism at the level of aesthetic enjoyment. If the work is only the manifestation of a truth, once I obtain the information it wants to give me, it no longer has any meaning for me. The persistence of such an interest could be justified only by the argument that the work has not been thoroughly understood. In fact, this is how a representationalist view accounts for the persistence of the living presence in history of the great works of art: they—it is argued—contain a truth that still remains to be understood. However, the fact remains that the ideal posits a condition for which no further interest in the work is either necessary or possible.

For representational views, there are multiple elements related to the inessentiality of the work. For example, if the work is the bearer of a message of truth, it will address itself principally to the intellect; all the interest drawn from the sensible and physical presence of the work—an interest that at different levels engages our sensibility—is once again something that is not essential, the provisional covering of a truth whose ambition, however, is to appear entirely in its pure abstraction and impersonality. I speak of impersonality because at the level of truth recognition for a metaphysical conception of truth as objectivity, the person can be put only in parenthesis, or at most revealed as a provisional and unnecessary instance. So a consistent representationalism would have nothing to say about the characters of individuality and personality of aesthetic experience.

Furthermore, the inexorable logical consequence of arguing that the work in its concrete physical nature is inessential proves the impossibility of theorizing aesthetic judgment in a satisfactory manner. What matters in the work is the truth of which it is a carrier, a sign, a mythical representation, a mystification, etc. Nothing else counts once such truth is recognizable. Now, to discuss the most popular and pervasive form of representationalim—sociological representationalism—it is beyond doubt that the truth concerning the social context of a given epoch can be revealed just as well by works that are universally held to be mediocre in comparison with the masterpieces. The only way out of this would be to refer to the lesser or stronger evidence or force by which such a truth is presented or manifested in the work. The outcome, though, would be the reduction of every aesthetic judgment to the level of rhetorical questions or psychology of persuasion.

The consequences of taking on a consistently formalist view are no less problematic. Formalism more often than not keeps returning to representational positions to the extent that it pretends to radically ground itself. For example, the pleasure supplied by a beautiful structure can be led back to the necessary way in which our intellect or sensibility works, or as certain positivist intellectuals have done, to the perceptual, intellectual, and evaluative habits that are induced in us as a result of our belonging to a determinate social group. In all these instances, the work is viewed as a more or less provisional incarnation of forms, which are otherwise given, and which only find in the work the occasion for recognizing and explicating themselves.

If it does not intend to go back to these positions, formalism must necessarily remain within the domain of an aesthetic of play (as we have seen in the preceding chapters, this aesthetics, too, can be linked back to a substantially vitalist scheme) that affirms the value of recognizing the beautiful form as a value as such, a value that is connected with the very exercise of our faculties. This is much more widespread than one might think among many critics whose reflection on the work lies basically in putting emphasis on certain mechanisms through whose knowledge—it is held—the work can be more fully enjoyed.

When these mechanisms are exhibited in a definitive manner, it is clear that the work cannot be exhausted by such manipulations. As in the case of representationalism, in formalism, too, there is a true insufficiency: it consists in the fact that after every *Aufhebung* and every analysis, once the truth of which it is the bearer has been recognized, the work presents itself as something that does not allow itself to be put into parenthesis; the work does not allow itself to be exhausted by analytical and structural considerations. Although it is not useless (in the domain of a "science of art," though not so much in that of criticism, which instead intends to be of service to the most enjoyment of the work), the analysis of the work's mechanisms does not explain nor above all does it suppress our always renewed and "vital" interest in the work. If such an interest really resided in the perception of a structural play, it could not but collapse once the mechanism on which the play is grounded were uncovered. As in a detective novel where the murderer is already known, when we read the novel the second time around we no longer have the same interest in it we once had. Indeed, the reader of detective novels who is not a grammarian, a stylist, or a theoretician of the mass media no longer reads it at all.

These, together with all the other insufficiencies and contradictions that are internal to formalism and representationalism do not arise, as I have already shown, because each view isolates its own defense in an exclusive manner, even though each does present valid demands. In fact, this way of isolating each demand is more deeply linked to metaphysical thought, and to its conception of truth. Representationalism and formalism cannot be "overcome" by means of their synthesis; rather, they can be overcome only by revising the presuppositions on which they are grounded.

## Form and Content in the Setting-Itself-Into-Work of Truth

It seems clear enough from an in-depth analysis of the concept of "setting-itself-into-work of truth" that for Heidegger it is not a matter of purely and simply synthesizing these two demands. Rather, the point is to state the problem in a new way. On the one hand, the idea that the work is inessential and provisional is constitutive of the representational attitude: since the truth is given prior to and outside of the work, the work itself is only a contingent manifestation or representation. The relationship between truth and the work's contingency, or that of every event, is linked, ultimately, to a perspective that continues to take truth as correspondence with the given, in order to guarantee the validity of knowledge and of the manifestations of truth because of its being fully given, established once and for all, subtracted from the event.

Now, Heidegger thinks of truth as event. To the extent that truth happens as the opening of historical horizons within which beings come to being, it has a "tendency to set itself to work," as Heidegger says.[4] Being at work is not a contingent feature of truth, and precisely because it is an event. As such, it must somehow happen, and it is nothing outside of or above this occurrence. If in the work of art truth happens, the work remains inexorably linked to it, just as truth remains linked to the work. It is possible to conceive at a certain moment of leaving the work only because of the supposition that truth is always already pre-given, independent of the work. The ontological concept of truth as event excludes every contingency of the incarnation of truth with respect to truth itself, and every possible *Aufhebung*. Truth is the truth of the work; therefore once the work is removed or forgotten, the truth that happened in it is forgotten as well.

This close link between truth and work could collapse into formalism at a certain point. If the truth that sets itself to work in the work belongs solely to the work, it could be confused with the pure and simple factuality of the work in its physical nature, with its own formal structure. However, what keeps Heidegger from falling into the dangers of formalism is his attempt never to lose sight of the ontological rooting. The work—he says in "The Origin of the Work of Art" (*Der Ursprung des Kunstwerkes*)—is a *Gestalt*, a form insofar as it is *gestellt*, that is placed, installed. The form does not define the thing in its particularity and isolation by enclosing it within its structural perfection. Nor are we to conceive of installation in a purely physical sense, as the dialectics of form and background in the terms of *Gestaltpsy-chologie*. This is not what Heidegger means. Instead, the work is form to the extent that it is placed in the *Riss*, the rift joining and separating world and earth, *Welt* and *Erde*.

In regard to the meaning of *Riss* and its related terms, Heidegger makes etymological and philosophical elaborations that I will not discuss here. More important than those elaborations are the coupling terms "world" and "earth." Here it should suffice to say that the world is the system beings give rise to within a specifically given horizon or opening of being.[5] The earth, which is not identical with nature (in contrast to the world as culture), represents the permanent ontological reserve of meanings, which makes is so that the work cannot be exhausted by interpretation. Every interpretation defines a world that is opened and founded by the work. However, the work as such is a permanent reserve of new interpretations, and for this reason Heidegger sees in it the presence of the earth, which is always given as that which withdraws and holds itself in reserve.

This definition of the form as installation of the work into the rift between world and earth serves to bring to light that the form is an opening of the world. The work is form precisely insofar as it happens as the first event of a world, which it opens and founds. On the one hand, since truth is inexorably linked to the work's happening as a specifically singular event, the work is not emptied of its individuality. On the other hand, such individuality does not close the work on itself nor reduce it to the level of a "thing," whose presence would be a formally perfect object offered to aesthetic enjoyment. By contrast, the form can be conceived solely by virtue of its being situated (*gestellt*) between world and earth. As an event, the work opens and founds a world. As a founding event that cannot be derived from other intraworldly events, the work has a privileged link to Being in that it connects the world to the earth as permanent reserve of meanings, and thus to Being itself in its originating force.

In this way, Heidegger defends the two demands of representationalism and formalism without making recourse to a simple synthesis, instead revising the metaphysical concept of truth. On the one hand, then, he renews the interest in the work's physical concreteness much more radically and much more productively than formalism would allow. On the other hand, he views the work as a genuine bearer of truth, one that is much more present when conceived as arising and instituting itself together with the work.

## The Problem of "Aesthetic" Enjoyment

Perhaps Nietzsche was one of the first thinkers to feel the cogency of the problem of a genuine synthesis of representationalism and formalism (and to attempt to find a solution for it at the ontological level). In the first chapter of *The Birth of Tragedy*, Nietzsche defines the man who is aesthetically sensitive as someone who feels the fascination of the definite apollonian form, lingering by it with overly caring and passionate attention; yet he is also able to see the same form as pure appearance. This dialectic—attending to the form and seeking out its meanings beyond it (though not in the same Schopenhauerian sense that Nietzsche saw it in)—is constitutive of aesthetic enjoyment, and Heidegger's idea of the work as the setting-itself-into-work of truth gives ontological reasons for it.

True, on the one hand, enjoying the work always implies or in some sense even comes to a head with an act of aesthetic contemplation, in which the work imposes itself by virtue of its formal perfection, without further referring to anything that might disturb the satisfaction and stillness connected with such a state. On the other hand, it is equally true that the encounter with a great art work always represents not only an "aesthetic" but also a theoretical, moral, and emotional experience, which engages the person at all levels and leads us to speak of art's truth, of its cosmic nature, and of its ontological meaning. Hence, in concrete experience the work resists being confined within the limits of the formalist view of beauty, it moves out of the "aesthetic sphere" in which it was enclosed and holds its truth appeal, in the broadest and fullest meaning of the word.

Heidegger's view of the work as the setting-itself-into-work of truth meets both demands, which were initially brought to light in the field of aesthetics, to be isolated and tightened under representationalism and formalism. At the same time, however, it runs the risk—if it really is a risk—of no longer being able to speak of "aesthetic enjoyment." On the other hand, this is precisely the meaning of Heidegger's polemic against aesthetics (and furthermore against ethics) understood as the attempt to isolate a type of experience in which the encounter with the artwork would be given in a very specific manner and that would be distinguished from experiences of a different kind, though equally specific, isolated, and specialized.

In regard to the enjoyment of the artwork, Heidegger speaks of dwelling in the opening opened by the work, that is to say, in the world that it founds.[6] Indeed, it is the artwork, in Heidegger's mature thought, that opens and founds historical worlds, which ultimately exist precisely to the extent that one makes an effort to live, interpret, and imitate it. For this, consider the epochal significance of some of the great masterpieces of art fostered by the Western tradition. After all, every artwork can have an epochal significance as testified to by the alternating history of taste, by the devaluations and reevaluations of works, authors, and styles that the history of art and of criticism is full of. To dwell in the world founded by the work is to live in the light of it. The history of an epoch is, in the end, solely an exegesis of one or more artworks, wherein a certain "epoch" of being was instituted and opened.

The aesthetic enjoyment outlined in this view is neither a pure enjoyment of the work in its formal perfection nor a movement beyond the work in search of the truth, of which it would be the manifestation or revelation. Nor is the work to be understood as pure form, to be suppressed or overcome by means of a theoretical act that would go beyond the work to absorb it completely in itself. Nonetheless, since dwelling in the world founded by the work signifies rearranging one's own existence and "vision of the world" in light of the disclosure of being that has happened in the work, this means also that the work should be conceived as an announcement of truth. And since the effort to understand and actualize the world founded by the work leads not so much to definitions as to clear-cut formulations in which an interpretation of such a world is given, the encounter with the work always is a consummation of, and aesthetic satisfaction for, the form.

However, what matters in this conception of the artwork is that both elements are always present. Just as, for Heidegger, the work is the setting-into-work of truth insofar as it stages the original conflict between world and earth, so is the enjoyment of the work—and history in its broadest meaning—an endless articulation of definite formulations that never exhaust the artwork (the epoch of being). Instead, they live precisely insofar as the work remains their *Boden*, their background that is never totally resolved into the stated foundation (*Grund*), which therefore still remains in need of founding.

Thus, on the one hand, Heidegger's view of the encounter with the artwork—understood as dwelling in the opening instituted by the work—offers a way out of the difficulties in which the traditional, that is, representationalist and formalist, perspectives of aesthetic enjoyment are entangled. On the other hand, however, there arises the problem of whether one can still speak of aesthetic enjoyment, and of an "aesthetic" experience as a something distinct and distinguishable from other kinds of "experiences." If the whole historical life of humanity comes to be seen as a movement in the light of the artwork, as an endless act of interpretation of poetry (and thinking is such only insofar as it dialogues with poetry), then it is no longer possible to isolate and describe the enjoyment of art in the same terms of aesthetics. Perhaps, though, it is the very notion of aesthetic enjoyment—in the narrow meaning in which the tradition attributes to this term—that we should renounce, in order to recover the possibility of more authentically understanding the "truth" of art.

# 11 The Truth That Hurts

The rise of artistic poetics in our century can be examined from the point of view of their stance vis-à-vis art and truth, specifically in their stated opposition to the philosophical aesthetics that, echoing the neo-Kantianism of the second half of the nineteenth century, sharply distinguished aesthetic experience from the domain of knowledge and action. From this viewpoint—which seems to me more reasonable and more productive than others for the arguments of criticism—Alfredo Jaar's oeuvre acquires the prominence he deserves because he stands in the line of continuity with the programmatic stance of poetics, and above all because of the particular interpretation he gives of this program. The defense of the truth appeal of art was the principal motivation in the experience of the historical avant-garde. This took the form of a direct effort to represent "modern" life as faithfully as possible, never abandoning the idea that the artist was able to grasp and communicate an objectively given truth. Think of futurism's obsession with machines, speed, and movement; the search for nonphenomenal structures of the real like the "spiritual" in the art of Kandinsky, which is grasped also by means of the occult (in Mondrian); and of the gradually emergent range of views from surrealism to the varied interpretations of expressionism, to the new politically inspired realism. Even when gestures of mockery and provocation prevailed (such as Duchamp's *Fountain*) over others, thereby radicalizing the revolt of all the avant-garde against tradition, there always survived a "realist spirit." In other words, the scandal the artist intended to provoke was thought out in the name of a program that was felt to be true insofar as it was based and legitimated by a foundation. Even the devil to whom Adrian Leverkuhn sells his soul in Thomas Mann's *Doctor Faustus* is a character stemming from traditional mythology. It presents a residue of the principle of reality that liberates the artist for its own creation by subjecting him to another power that is exterior to him.

In all these cases, art wishes to defend its own truth appeal in radical opposition to the truth of science and philosophy. Since science is subjected to the world of appearances and measurable phenomena, it is incapable of grasping the lived meaning of existence; philosophy floats in metaphysics' abstractions, according to which only being as being holds true, and thereby excludes the validity of concrete and historical dimensions.

This elementary objectivism, which in the experience of the late avant-garde took the form of an ideology of design, of a healthy and aesthetic systematization of the life-environment, was opposed solely by Bertold Brecht in his theatrical poetics. It is not by chance that today Brecht's theatrical poetics has been almost universally forgotten, together with his essays, which instead still deserve to be known and appreciated by a generation that has never seen his theater or possibly read his books. Naturally, the opportunity to forget Brecht was given by the dissolution of "socialist realism" and its ideology. No one today in aesthetics and literary criticism dares to speak of "socialist realism" any longer; even Lukacs's work is confined to the specialized domain of a few scholars. But Brecht was not a "realist," whether socialist or not. The key for understanding Brecht's timeliness (not exclusively from Jaar's viewpoint) is the idea of "epic theater," or of non-Aristotelian theater. According to this view, the task of art is not to represent the truth of the world but, rather, to take a stance in the name of a project of transformation. In his own poetics, Brecht affirms a notion of truth—which recuperates and radicalizes Hegelian dialectics, according to which truth is what changes us, what is happening in the life of the single individual and in that of society at large without leaving things intact as they were—through the denial of catharsis as the meaning of the artwork. Catharsis originally consisted of the purification of the feelings of pity and terror that tragedy awakens in its spectators; after Aristotle, however, it was extended to all the arts: pity and terror are existential feelings far too universal to be confined to tragedy. Oedipus's troubles are "accounted for" based on the observation that he has killed his father and married his mother, whether he was conscious of it or not does not really matter according to the "objectivist" vision of the Greeks. It may be indispensable to take cognizance of the order or disorder of the world in order to undertake its transformation, but truth lies in this transformation rather than in the representation of existence as it is—assuming that such an undertaking would be possible for someone living inside the specific order.

It could be pointed out that we stand far removed from the early decades of the last century. What happened since then to the visual arts, literature, and poetry? Exercising the same simplifying yet indispensable gesture of hermeneutic violence that has guided our reading of the avant-garde so far, we could say that the common thread in the adventures of the visual arts, literature, and poetry can be found in "the analytical trajectory of modern art," as Filiberto Menna called it in a brief and precious essay of 1975. It is the idea shared by many artists that art's relationship to truth consists in putting art directly in question, thereby raising the question of its limits, its tools, and its position in society. This was opposed by means of an effort to interpret the analytic attention as the means for a new "decorative" art that would feed itself with recollections of the art of the past and with a willingness to rediscover nature as material (i.e., stone, wood, light) for the artist's work, or as a new subject worthy of representation outside of the manifestations of an increasingly hermetic and languid avant-garde.

Many relevant figures in the contemporary artistic landscape have been left out in this rough outline, and yet it could be paradoxically defended precisely in the name of its generality. The outline is merely a background, which is nevertheless indispensable in order to look at the figures that are drawn into it as well as those that break off from it. Nothing more is intended. But it is precisely this background that Jaar evokes for us, lay readers or scholars coming from other disciplines.

He does so, above all, insofar as he introduces himself (www.alfredo-jaar.net) by citing the verses of William Carlos Williams: "It is difficult / to get the news from poems / yet men die miserably every day / for lack / of what is found there." I don't know whether William Carlos Williams understood the news in the contemporary sense of "news." Surely, though, Jaar understands it in this way; not as universal "truth" about nature or existence but precisely as news in its everyday sense. Wouldn't a newspaper be better? Or a televisual or photographic documentary? Jaar's works look exactly like photo reportages, like *Hàgase la luz* (Throw light) which is dedicated to the genocide in Rwanda, where a million people were massacred by the Hutu in about 100 days in 1994, at a rate of 10,000 per day while the international community could not reach an agreement to intervene in time to put an end to it.

The "Rwanda Project"—which took four years to develop beginning with Jaar's trip in August of 1994—is a book that tells the story of the project, illustrates the struggles between Hutu and Tutsi before the 1994 massacre, and shows photographs marking the different phases of the project. It is a story—with respect to the analytic line mentioned above—in the course of which Jaar puts on stage the very meaning of photography as a way of informing and awakening public consciousness about bloody events such as this (the genocide on the part of the Tutsi is third in number of victims among those that took place in the twentieth century, next to the Shoah and the slaughter of the Armenian people by the Turks at the end of World War I). However, Jaar does not interrogate the meaning and limits of photography with a view to grasping reality more faithfully. Understanding the truth of art as news rather than as the final revelation of human nature or of the world, is a way of abstaining from attributing eternal qualities to the monument and from blocking the images in Aristotelian fashion. As Heidegger would say, news is the truth insofar as it is *gewesen* instead of *vergangen*. In other words, it is a having been that does not present itself with the definitiveness of a stone from the past—which in Nietzsche rests on Zarathustra's shoulders, paralyzing him—but, rather as an open datum calling for an active interpretation and a practical intervention. The postcards that Jaar sends to his friends from Rwanda are not closed images but messages calling for a response. The point is to bring history back to its roots, that is, the news or reportage, rather than to Aristotle's philosophical poetics of history, which leaves out the details

of contingent events in order to represent their essentially rational character. Aristotle's view of history corresponds well to what Benjamin once
called the history of the winners, according to which what has taken place
is wholly rational and therefore must be accepted as such, insofar as it has
given place to their victory.

# *Notes*

*Introduction. The Hermeneutic Consequence of Art's Ontological Bearing*

1. S. Zabala, ed., *Weakening Philosophy: Essays in Honour of Gianni Vattimo* (Montreal: McGill-Queen's University Press, 2007).

2. G. Vattimo, *The End of Modernity*, trans. J. R. Snyder (Baltimore, Md.: John Hopkins University Press, 1988); *The Adventure of Difference*, trans. C. P. Blamires and T. Harrison (Cambridge: Polity Press, 1993); *Beyond Interpretation*, trans. D. Webb (1994; Stanford, Calif.: Stanford University Press, 1997); *Belief*, trans. L. D'Isanto and D. Webb (Cambridge: Polity Press, 1998); *After Christianity*, trans. L. D'Isanto (New York: Columbia University Press, 2002); R. Rorty and G. Vattimo, *The Future of Religion*, ed. S. Zabala (New York: Columbia University Press, 2005); J. D. Caputo and G. Vattimo, *After the Death of God*, ed. Jeffrey. W. Robbins (New York: Columbia University Press, 2007).

3. I should point out that the Italian Publisher Meltemi began, in the fall of 2007, to release the *Complete Works of Vattimo*, edited by Mario Cedrini, Alberto Martinengo, and S. Zabala.

4. G. Vattimo, *Dialogue with Nietzsche*, trans. William McCuaig (New York: Columbia University Press, 2004). *Dialogue with Nietzsche* is not only a collection of essays from the 1960s to the 1990s, as is this book, but also includes a book from 1967, *Ipotesi su Nietzsche* (Turin: Giappichelli, 1967).

5. G. Vattimo, *Nihilism and Emancipation: Ethics, Politics, and Law*, ed. S. Zabala, trans. W. McCuaig (New York: Columbia University Press, 2004).

6. R. Rorty and G. Vattimo, *The Future of Religion*, ed. S. Zabala (New York: Columbia University Press, 2005).

7. I am specifically referring to Marcel Duchamp's *Fountain* (1917), David Lynch's *Mulholland Drive* (2001), and Alfredo Jaar's photographs in *Let There Be Light: The Rwanda Project, 1994–1998* (New York: Actar, 1998).

8. A. C. Danto, *After the End of Art* (Princeton: Princeton University Press, 1997), 18.

9. See chapter 3, page 33.

10. An introduction to the history and meaning of weak thought can be found in my introduction to *Weakening Philosophy: Essays in Honour of Gianni Vattimo*, ed. S. Zabala (Montreal: McGill-Queen's University Press, 2007), 3–34.

11. M. Heidegger, *Being and Time*, trans. J. Stambaugh (New York: State University of New York Press, 1996), 22–23.

12. "Thrownness" refers to the fact that Dasein always finds itself already in a certain spiritual and material, historically conditioned environment; hence, in the world, in which the space of possibilities is always historically limited. It represents the phenomenon of the past as having-been.

13. Dasein's "fallenness" characterizes its existence in the midst of beings that are both Dasein and not Dasein.

14. Existence means that Dasein is potentiality-for-being, "*Seinkönnen*"; it projects its being upon various possibilities, especially the phenomenon of the future.

15. Heidegger, *Being and Time*, 16.

16. This is the title of an essay by Heidegger, "The Age of the World Picture" (1938), in *Off the Beaten Track*, ed. and trans. J. Young and K. Haynes (Cambridge: Cambridge University Press 2002), 57–85.

17. See A. C. Danto, *The Transfiguration of the Commonplace* (Cambridge, Mass.: Harvard University Press, 1981).

18. See chapter 6, page 95.

19. For a complete historical account of the different epochs of hermeneutics, see Jean Grondin, *Introduction to Philosophical Hermeneutics* (1991), trans. J. Weinsheimer, (New Haven, Conn.: Yale University Press, 1994); G. L. Bruns, *Hermeneutics: Ancient and Modern* (New Haven, Conn.: Yale University Press, 1992); and David Jasper, *A Short Introduction to Hermeneutics* (Louisville, Ky.: Westminster John Knox Press, 2004).

20. Evidence that hermeneutics has become the common language of contem-

porary philosophy can be found in G. Vattimo, "The Age of Interpretation," in *The Future of Religion*, ed. Santiago Zabala (New York: Columbia University Press, 2005), 43–54; and G. Vattimo, *Beyond Interpretation* (1994), trans. D. Webb (Stanford, Calif.: Stanford University Press, 1997); and also in the recent *Diccionario de Hermenéutica*, ed. A. Ortiz-Osés and P. Lanceros, Bilbao, Universidad de Deusto, 2006. Recent series dedicated to hermeneutics thought, such as Studies in Hermeneutics, ed. Joel Weinsheimer (Yale University Press); Hermeneutics: Studies in the History of Religions (SUNY Press); Studies in American Biblical Hermeneutics (Mercer University Press), The Interpretations Series (Melbourne University Publishing), and Hermeneusis (Anthropos Editorial), make up a very large library publishing not only the books of Heidegger, Pareyson, and Gadamer, but also contemporary authors such as J. Grondin, K. Eden, J. Sallis, J. Risser, and others.

21. A fine study on the historical grounding of modern hermeneutics is Kathy Eden, *Hermeneutics and the Rhetorical Tradition: Chapters in the Ancient Legacy and Its Humanist Reception* (New Haven, Conn.: Yale University Press, 1997).

22. M. Heidegger, *On the Way to Language* (1959), trans. Peter D. Hertz (New York: Harper & Row, 1982), 32.

23. Luigi Pareyson, *Verità e interpretazione* (1971; Milan: Mursia, 1985), 53.

24. Anticipating both Gadamer and Paul Ricouer, whose hermeneutic theses were exposed in the early 1960s, Pareyson had, in the early 1950s, already developed his theory of interpretation. His complete works are currently being published in twenty volumes by Mursia Publisher of Milan and are edited by Giuseppe Riconda, Giovanni Ferretti, Claudio Ciancio, and Francesco Tomatis. Robert Valgenti is translating volume 15 of Pareyson's complete works, *Truth and Interpretation*, for SUNY Press (forthcoming) and has published "The Primacy of Interpretation in Luigi Pareyson's Hermeneutics of Common Sense," *Philosophy Today* 49, no. 4 (Winter 2005): 333–41. Silvia Benso is currently translating Pareyson's later work, *Dostoevsky*, also for SUNY Press (forthcoming). Existing translations of Pareyson's work are limited to "The Unity of Philosophy," *Cross Currents* 4, no. 1 (Fall 1953): 57–69; and "Pointless Suffering in the *Brothers Karamazov*," *Cross Currents* 37, nos. 2–3 (Summer/Fall 1987): 271–86. See also H.T. Bredin, "The Aesthetics of Luigi Pareyson," *The British Journal of Aesthetics* (1966): 193–202; M.E. Brown, "On Luigi Pareyson's 'L'estetica di Kant,'" *Journal of Art and Art Criticism* (1971): 403–10.

25. Luigi Pareyson, *Esistenza e interpretazione* (1950; Genoa: Il Melangolo, 1985), 218.

26. H.-G. Gadamer, *Truth and Method*, trans. J. Weinsheimer and D.G. Marshall (London: Continuum, 2004), 164.

27. L. Pareyson, *Estetica. Teoria della formatività* (1950; Milan: Bompiani, 1988), 59.

28. Information on the production of the pilot and film can be found in http://www.lynchnet.com/mdrive.

29. See chapter 5, page 88.

30. M. Heidegger, "The Origin of the Work of Art" (1935–36), in *Off the Beaten Track*, ed. and trans. J. Young and K. Haynes (Cambridge: Cambridge University Press 2002), 1–56.

31. H.-G. Gadamer, *Gadamer in Conversation: Reflections and Commentary*, ed. Richard Palmer (New Haven, Conn.: Yale University Press, 2003), 55.

32. See chapter 9, page 143.

33. See chapter 7, page 121.

34. Gadamer, *Truth and Method*, 290.

35. Gadamer, *Truth and Method*, 291.

36. See chapter 11, page 162.

37. See chapter 11, page 164.

38. See chapter 11, page 164.

39. See chapter 10, page 158.


## 1. *Beauty and Being in Ancient Aesthetics*

1. J. Warry, *Greek Aesthetic Theory* (London: Methuen, 1963); E. Grassi, *Die Theorie des Schönen in der Antike* (Cologne: Dumont, 1962); W. Perpeet, *Antike Aestetik*, (Freiburg: Alber, 1961).

2. For example, see Warry, *Greek Aesthetic Theory*, 84.

3. Warry, *Greek Aesthetic Theory*, 18–20.

4. Warry, *Greek Aesthetic Theory*, 80.

5. Warry, *Greek Aesthetic Theory*, 150.

6. Warry, *Greek Aesthetic Theory*, 107.

7. However, Warry reaches this concept with a bit of confusion. See *Greek Aesthetic Theory*, 108–9.

8. Warry, *Greek Aesthetic Theory*, 123.

9. Grassi, *Die Theorie des Schönen*, 187–266.

10. Grassi, *Die Theorie des Schönen*, 93.

11. Grassi, *Die Theorie des Schönen*, 94.

12. Grassi, *Die Theorie des Schönen*, 143.

13. See for example for the author says in *Die Theorie des Schönen*, 148.

14. Perpeet, *Antike Aesthetik*, 112 n. 1.

15. Perpeet, *Antike Aesthetik*, 66–67.

16. Perpeet, *Antike Aesthetik*, 103.

17. Perpeet, *Antike Aesthetik*, 37.

## 2. *Toward an Ontological Aesthetics*

1. Though no less conclusively, since every introduction always implies the reprise of the general meaning of an argument.

2. For a more detailed interpretation of Heidegger's thought, I refer to my book *Essere: storia e linguaggio in Heidegger* (Turin: Marietti, 1963). The theses I am arguing here are more clearly understandable in light of my reading of Heidegger.

3. Heidegger theorized the epochal character of Being in the essay "Der Spruch des Anaximanders," published in *Holzwege* (Frankfurt: Vittorio Klostermann, 950), especially pp. 310 ff.; *Off the Beaten Track*, trans. Kenneth Haynes and Julian Young (Cambridge, Cambridge University Press, 2002).

4. The human being has a central role in the illumination of the horizon within which things come to being: this role is indicated by the word Dasein (Being-There), which Heidegger employs in *Being and Time* to refer philosophically to the human being; it is further clarified in the interpretation of the "there" of Being-There that Heidegger puts forth in the *Letter on Humanism Über den Humanismus* [Frankfurt: Vittorio Klostermann, 1946; 1949]). It is in and through the human being that the epochs of Being—the historical openings within which beings appear—are instituted.

5. I am using the term "metaphysics" in the sense Heidegger assigns to it beginning from the *Introduction to Metaphysics* (*Einführung in die Metaphysik* [Tübingen: Max Niemeyer Verlag, 1953]), a lecture course taught in 1935, re-elaborated and published in 1953; *An Introduction to Metaphysics*, trans. Ralph Manheim (New Haven, Conn.: Yale University Press, 1959–1987) to identify a type of thinking that is oblivious to the ontological difference and thus conceives Being on the model of beings.

6. From this perspective, every ontological proof of the existence of God that considers God as first cause, supreme entity, and so on falls into the purview of metaphysics and of ontic thought. In this respect, Heidegger speaks of the onto-theo-logical character of metaphysics in *Identität und Differenz* (Pfullingen: Neske, 1957); *Identity and Difference*, trans. Joan Stambaugh (New York: Harper and Row, 1969).

7. This is the conclusion by many of Heidegger's essays on the development of metaphysics in its final phase, which for him is emblematically represented by Nietzsche and his concept of the will to power. On this, Heidegger's most complete discussion is found in *Nietzsche*, 2 vols. (Pfullingen: Neske, 1961); *Nietzsche* (San Francisco, Harper and Row, 1979).

8. See especially Korsch, *Marxism and Philosophy* (New York: Monthly Review Press, 1973), which still represents a relatively orthodox phase of his thought.

9. See especially Lukacs, *Geschichte und KlassenBewusstsein* (Neuwied: Literatur Verlag, 1922); *History and Class Consciousness: Studies in Marxist Dialectics* (Cambridge: Cambridge University Press, 1971), which provides the basis for his later development, even though Lukacs rejected it afterward.

10. When this book was originally written only two volumes of Lukacs's *Heidelberger Ästhetik (1916-1918)* (Darmstadt: Luchterhand) had been published.

11. This is testified to, at the very least, by Jean Paul Sartre, *Critique de la Raison Dialectique* (Paris: Gallimard, 1960); *Critique of Dialectical Reason*, trans. Alan Sherida-Smith (London: Verso, 1991).

12. For a scholarly review of neo-Kantian aesthetics, and more generally for the presence of neo-Kantian thematics in subjectivist philosophies, see G. Woland, "Ueber Recht und Grenzen einer Subjektstheoretischen Aesthetik," *Jahrbuch u. allg. Kunstwissenschaft* 9 (1964): 28–48. For a more theoretical discussion, see Hans-Georg Gadamer, "Zur Fragwürdigkeit des aestetischen Bewusstseins" (On the questionableness of aesthetic consciousness), *Rivista di Estetica* 3 (1958): 347–83.

13. Edmund Husserl, *The Crisis of the European Sciences and Transcendental Phenomenology*, trans. David Carr (Evanston, Ill.: Northwestern University Press, 1970).

14. Husserl, *The Crisis of the European Sciences*, 112.

15. This direction is quite typical of the Italian school of phenomenology. On the interpretation of Husserl's Krisis, see Enzo Paci, *Funzioni delle scienze e significato dell'uomo* (Milan: Il Saggiatore, 1963); *Function of the Sciences and the Meaning of Man* (Evanston, Ill.: Northwestern University Press, 1972).

16. The conception of being as *Lebenswelt*, and as living background at work within the history of culture as a life that continuously renews the forms, is to be found in the works of M. Merleau-Ponty (e.g. *Phénoménologie de la perception* [Paris: Gallimard, 1945]); *Phenomenology of Perception*, trans. Colin Smith (London: Routledge and Kegan Paul, 1962). A substantial development of the notion of being in the later work of Merleau-Ponty is testified to by his posthumous work *Le visible et l'invisible* (Paris: Gallimard, 1964); *The Visible and the Invisible* (Evanston, Ill., Northwestern University Press, 1968) and especially by the notes on the question of truth, which are published in appendix to the volume, where some of Heidegger's themes are reexamined.

17. See Mikel Dufrenne, *Phénoménologie de l'expérience esthétique*, 2 vols. (Paris: Presses Universitaires de France, 1953); *Le poétique* (Paris: Presses Universitaires de France, 1963); *Jalons* (The Hague: Nijhoff, 1966). On Dufrenne, see G. Morburgo Tagliabue, *L'esthétique contemporaine* (Milan: Marzorati, 1960), and H. Spiegelberg, *The Phenomenological Movement*, vol. 2 (The Hague: Nijhoff, 1960), 579–85.

18. See Ugo Spirito, *Critica dell'estetica* (Florence: Sansoni, 1964), and A. Plebe, *Processo all'estetica* (Florence: La Nuova Italia, 1959).

19. See, above all, Heidegger, *Letter on Humanism*, 7, and the first part of *Was Heisst Denken* (Tübingen: M. Niemeyer, 1954); *What Is Called Thinking*, trans. J. Glenn Gray (New York: Harper and Row, 1968).

20. Heidegger explicitly theorizes silence in *Unterwegs zur Sprache* (Pfulligen: Neske, 1952), 152; *On the Way to Language* (New York: Harper and Row, 1971).

21. True, in paragraph 44b of *Being and Time* Heidegger speaks of violently "wresting" or tearing truth from beings, in the sense that it is necessary to leave out of the condition of "falleness" and inauthenticity in which thought is always already thrown. Nevertheless, it should be noted that in the later works, inauthenticity is increasingly linked, historically, to the event of metaphysics. Hence, metaphysics belongs to the epochal character of Being, too. One can no longer violently extract truth from inauthenticity as *Being and Time* argued, remaining bound to an essentialist vision of Being and truth.

22. For an integral reading of the art phenomenon, see Luciano Anceschi, "Che cos'è l'arte," *Rivista di Estetica* 2 (1962): 161–85; *Fenomenologia della critica* (Bologna: Marzorati, 1966).

23. A discussion of the ontological and ulterior character of philosophical thought is given by Luigi Pareyson, "Pensiero espressivo e pensiero rivelativo," *Giornale critico della filosofia italiana* 2: 177–90; and "Elogio della filosofia," *Le conferenze della Associazione Culturale italiana* 2 (1966–67): 43–58. On the ontological bearing of art, see also Pareyson, "Potere e responsabilità dell'artista," in *Teoria dell'arte* (Milan: Marzorati, 1965).

24. Here we should recall the famous passage from the Heidegger, *Letter on Humanism*, where he lays the basis for an authentic revision of the metaphysical notion of possibility, beginning as he always does with the etymology of the word (7–8?). There he shows that the possible is truly possible only if the relation between Being and beings is no longer conceived in terms of the foundation (which, instead, is typical of every thought that forgets the ontological difference), but in terms of a *mögen* that consists in the gift of "essence."

## 3. *The Ontological Vocation of Twentieth-Century Poetics*

1. On dodecaphony and its characteristic as an impure technical revolution, see the interpretations of T. Adorno, *Philosophy of Modern Music* (New York: Seabury Press, 1973) and T. Mann, *Doctor Faustus: The Life of the German Composer Adrien Leverkün* (1924; New York, Knopf, 1965). See also the material published in A. Plebe, *La Dodecafonia* (Bari: Einaudi, 1962); R. Vlad, *Modernità e tradizione nella musica contemporanea* (Turin: Einaudi, 1955), 185 ff; L. Rognoni, *Espressionismo e dodecafonia* (Turin: Einaudi, 1954); Rognoni, *Fenomenologia della musica radicale* (Bari: Garzanti, 1966); and the essays, translated into Italian, by Anton Webern, *Verso la nuova musica* (Milan: Bompiani, 1963) (*The Path Toward the New Music*, trans. Willi Reich [Bryn Mawr, Penn.: T. Presser, 1963]).

2. Luigi Pareyson has argued that Hegel's philosophy is characterized by ambiguity (on the basis of which one can understand the subsequent developments of

nineteenth- and twentieth-century philosophy). See Luigi Pareyson, *Esistenza e persona*, 3rd ed. (Turin: Taylor, 1966); see also the historical reconstructions of the question in the first edition of 1950, eliminated in subsequent editions.

3. Here I am not going to address the question whether it can be said that art is language and that the systems of signs on which artists work are precisely symbolic or, as Luigi Pareyson argues, that the they are not "matter" of art (see *Estetica. Teoria della formatività*, 2nd ed. [Bologna: Zanichelli, 1960], 28 ff). This is even more the case since this concept of matter entails that what the artist works on is laden with a history, involves internal rules of use and manipulation, and encloses given symbolic systems that the artist takes up into his work, to the extent that he adopts that matter. In this sense, too, one can speak of "languages" of art for the theory of formativity. A decisive objection against the "linguisticality" of art has been recently leveled by Mikel Dufrenne, "L'art est-il langage?" *Revue d'Esthétique* 19, no. 1 (January–March 1966): 1–42. Dufrenne especially argues that the discourse of art is not "informative" but "expressive," and thus expresses precisely through the very presence of the work in its own physical reality rather than referring somehow to a meaning. Furthermore, and for the same reasons, the artist is such not insofar as he observes the rules of a given grammar, but rather in that he violates them, creating the work. One could object to the last argument that the work constitutes a significant alteration within the context of a code, and therefore presupposes, uses it at least as a background.

4. On the links between art and play in Spencer, see, for example, the *Principles of Psychology*, vol. 2, 3rd ed. (New York: Appleton, 1897), 627. On Spencer, see also G. Morpurgo Tagliabue, *L'esthéthique contemporaine* (Milan: Marzorati, 1960), 7. The history of the concept of play in Kantian and post-Kantian aesthetics has been nicely placed in relation with the entire development of aesthetics between the Enlightenment and romanticism by V. E. Alfieri, "L'estetica dall'Illuminismo al Romanticismo fuori d'Italia," *Momenti e problemi di storia dell'estetica*, vol. 2 (Milan: Marzorati, 1959), 577–783.

5. See Tagliabue, *L'esthéthique contemporaine*, 577–783.

6. On neo-Kantian aesthetics, I refer to G. Wolandt, "Über Recht and Grenzen einer Subjektstheoretischen Aesthetik" *Jahrbuch u. allg. Kunstwissenshaft* 9 (1964): 28–48, and to the large bibliography published there.

7. For such an interpretation of pictorial impressionism, I refer to G. C. Argan, *Salvezza e caduta nell'arte moderna* (Milan: Il Saggiatore, 1964), especially 16 ff; however, Argan does not consider impressionism a traditional poetics as I believe one should when considering the programs with respect to figurative and representational reality. Instead, Argan sees impressionism as the first pictorial poetics that fully realizes the spirit of modern humanism. On the "realism" of the impressionists, in the specific meaning alluded to here, see also W. Hofmann, *Grundlagen der Modernen Kunst* (Stuttgart: Kröner, 1966), 181 ff; M. de Micheli, *Le avanguardie artistiche*

*del novecento*, 2d ed. (Milan: Schwarz, 1966), 200; see the anthology, too, by W. Hess, *Dokumente zum Verständnis der modernen Malerei* (Stuttgart: Rowohlt, 1956). On impressionism and expressionism in relation to poetry in German scholarship, see B. Markwardt, *Geschichte der deutschen Poetik*, vol. 5 (Berlin: De Gruyter, 1967), 367–461.

8. On cubism, in addition to the already cited volume by Argan, see especially M. De Micheli, *Le avanguardie artistiche del novecento*, 213 ff; on Picasso and his permanent links to the objectivity of the world, see especially 226 ff. See also the various documents gathered by de Micheli in the second part of his book. We have of Picasso the *Scritti*, in Italian, edited by De Micheli (Milano: Il Saggiatore, 1964). A detailed exposition of cubist poetics in its various stages of development is given in C. Gray, *Cubist Aesthetic Theories* (Baltimore, Md.: Johns Hopkins Press, 1953), which pays attention to the philosophical background of the movement, too. A philosophical interpretation of pictorial cubism, which is not in disagreement with the thesis I am putting forth here, is proposed in Jan M. Broekman, "Maleirei als Reflexion. Prolegomena zu einer Philosophie des Kubismus," *Jahrbuch f'aesth. U. allg. Kunstwissenchaft* 10 (1965): 35–64. Broekmann broadens the concept to include numerous artistic phenomena ranging from poetry to cinema, and reconstructs broad correspondences with the philosophy of the time, perhaps ending up ultimately with a very vague idea.

9. Futurist poetics has been documented in M. Drudi Gambillo and T. Fiori, eds., *Archivi del futurismo* (Rome: De Luca, 1958). Futurism's debts to the preceding art have been examined in G. Ballo, *Preistoria del futurismo* (Milan: Maestri, 1960). See also M. De Micheli, *Le avanguardie artistiche del novecento*; and W. Hofmann, *Grundlagen der modernen Kunst*, 225–304.

10. See Picasso, *Scritti*, 5 and 12, for example.

11. See G. Delfel, *L'esthétique de Stéphane Mallarmé* (Paris, 1951) with a preface by E. Souriau; on his relationship with Poe, see 46 ff. On Baudelaire, see H. Friedrich, *Die Struktur der modernen Lyrik* (Hamburg: Rowohlt, 1956), 27 ff; *The Structure of Modern Poetry* (Evanston, Ill.: Northwestern University Press, 1974).

12. On Valéry, see two essays by Luigi Pareyson, "Le regole secondo Valéry," *Rivista di Estetica* 2 (1962): 229–59; and "Suono e senso secondo Valéry," *Rivista di Estetica* 1 (1966): 56–98. Furthermore, see W. N. Ince, *The Poetic Theory of Paul Valéry: Inspiration and Technique* (Leicester: Leicester University Press, 1961).

13. This problem is posed more vehemently by the concrete products of surrealist and Dada art than it is by theoretical perspectives. The scandal triggered by pictorial and poetic works by surrealists and Dadaists is not merely the temporary scandal characteristic of every new language; these works radically refuse traditional forms of aesthetic contemplation. On surrealism, see: A. Breton, *Manifestes du Surréalisme* (Paris: J. J. Pauvert, 1962); M. Nadeau, *Histoire du Surréalisme* (Paris: Table Ronde, 1964); P. Waldberg, *Der Surrealismus* (Cologne: DuMont Schauberg, 1965); and

moreover, M. De Micheli, *Le Avanguardie artistiche del novecento*; W. Hofmann, *Grundlagen der modernen Kunst* (Munich: Haus der Kunst), 397. On Dada, in addition to the general texts cited above, see T. Tzara, *I manifesti del dadaismo* (Turin: Einaudi, 1964); H. Richter, *Dada. Kunst und Antikunst* (Cologne: Dumont Schauberg, 1964) (*Dada: Art and Anti-Art* [New York: Abrams, 1970]); and H. Hülsenbeck, *Dada. Eine Literarische Dokumentation* (Hamburg: Rowohlt, 1964). Philosophical interpretations of surrealism are given by F. Alquié, *Philosophie du surréalisme* (Paris: Flammarion, 1955) (*Philosophy of Surrealism* [Ann Arbor: University of Michigan Press, 1975]); A. del Noce, "Interpretazione filosofica del surrealismo," *Riv. Di est* 1 (1965): 22–54; and the essays by E. Castelli, F. Alquié, E. Zolla, J. Brun, M. Dufrenne, R. Giorgi, and M. M. Olivetti gathered in *Archivio di filosofia* 3 (1965), "Surrealismo e simbolismo."

14. See E. Zolla, in *Archivio di filosofia* 3:28. Only someone claiming to contemplate Duchamps's *Fontaine* (which is actually just a common igenic object) with the proper attitude of enjoyment of traditional art could be diagnosed with the illness of copro-filia, as Zolla does in the cited essay.

15. For example, Duchamp: see H. Richter, *Dada*, 92.

16. All the general works cited above contain large sections on expressionism. For the texts, see the essential anthology edited by P. Pörtner, *Literatur-Revolution, 1910–1925*, vol. 1, *Zur Aesthetik un Poetik* (Darmstadt: Luchterhand, 1960), vol. 2, *Zur Begriffsbestimmung der "ismen"* (Darmstadt: Luchterhand, 1961). More oriented toward literary expressionism is the anthology edited by H. Friedmann and O. Mann, *Expressionismus. Gestalten einer literarischen Bewegung* (Heidelberg: Wolfgang Scheunemann, 1956). For expressionist poetry, see the newly published edition of the classical anthology, and the new introduction by K. Pinthus, *Menschheitsdämmerung. Ein dokument des Expressionsmus* (Berlin, 1920; Hamburg: Rowohlt, 1959). For a recent account of expressionist art and poetics, see L. Mittner, *L'espressionismo* (Florence: Vallecchi, 1965), which contains an appendix on "L'espressionismo nella critica di oggi," 133–44, to which I refer for a broader bibliography. For this, see also R. Brinkmann, *Expressionismus. Forschungsprobleme, 1952–60* (Stuttgart: J. B. Metzler, 1961); and L. Mitnner, ed., *Il bilancio dell'espressionismo*, with essays by L. Mittner and V. Pandolfi, L. Rognoni, P. Bucarelli, G. C. Argan, and L. Chiarini (Florence: Vallecchi, 1965).

17. On this point, see the introduction by P. Chiarini in *Caos e geometria* (Florence: La Nuova Italia, 1970) and that of O. Mann in Brinkmann, *Expressionismus*. Of the numerous texts available, I will mention only Y. Goll, "The Appell an die Kunst," in *Literatur-Revolution*, ed. P. Pörtner, vol. 1 (Darmstadt: Luchterhand, 1960), 144–45.

18. Gegen, "Lyrik," in *Literatur-Revolution*, ed. P. Pörtner, vol. 2 (Darmstadt: Luchterhand, 1961), 218–20.

19. G. Benn, "Die Dichtung der neuen Generation," in *Literatur-Revolution*, ed. P. Pörtner, vol. 2 (Darmstadt: Luchterhand, 1961), 241–45.

20. W. Kandinsky, *Essays über Kunst und Künstler* (Stuttgart, 1955), in *Complete Writings on Art*, vol. 2 (1922–1943) (Boston: G. K. Hall, 1982), 215.

21. Kandinsky, *Essays*, 214.

22. Kandinsky, *Essays*, 233–34.

23. W. Kandinsky, "Every Spiritual Epoch," in *Complete Writings on Art*, vol. 2 (1922–1943) (Boston: G. K. Hall, 1982), 842.

24. W. Kandinsky, *Essays*, 232.

25. See Argan, *W. Gropius e la Bauhaus* (Turin, 1951); in addition to his essays published in *Progetto e destino* (Milan: Il Saggiatore, 1965), which examines the question of architecture in the context of the art of our century. On the relationship between architecture and the avant-gardes of our century, it is useful to look at the documents collected in U. Conrads, *Programme und Manifeste zur Architektur des 20. Jahrhunderts* (Frankfurt: Bertelsmann, 1964) (*Programs and Manifestoes on Twentieth-Century Architecture* [Cambridge, Mass.: MIT Press, 1970]). Theoretical writings by Gropius are translated into Italian: *Architettura integrata* (Milan: Il Saggiatore, 1963) (*Scope of Total Architecture* [New York: Harper, 1955]). What has been said here about the Bauhaus should be extended to the group of De Stijl, emphasizing the mysticism connected to the project of a human world. On this group, in addition to the general works already mentioned above, I refer to G.C. Argan, *Studi e note* (Rome: Fratelli Bocca, 1955), 155–72; and H. Jaffe, "Die niederländische Stijl-Gruppe und ihre soziale Utopie," *Jahrbuch f. Aesth. U. allg. Kunstwiss.* 10 (1965): 25–34.

26. See Pareyson, *Estetica*, 223; Pareyson, *Teoria dell'arte* (Milan: Marzorati, 1965), 128–29.

## 4. *Art, Feeling, and Originality in Heidegger's Aesthetics*

1. Heidegger himself speaks of a "turning" in his thought in *Letter on Humanism* (*Brief über den Humanismus* [Frankfurt: Klostermann Verlag, 1946; 1949]), 17. For a discussion of the various interpretations of Heidegger's turning, I refer to my book *Essere, storia e linguaggio in Heidegger* (Turin: Marietti, 1963), especially chapters 1 and 4.

2. On this, see Moritz Geiger, *Zugänge zur Aesthetik* (Leipzig: Der Neue Geist Verlag, 1928), who links his analysis of the aesthetic fact to the exhibition of the aesthetic *Erlebnis*.

3. Martin Heidegger, *Being and Time*, trans. Joan Stambaugh (New York: State University of New York Press 1996), 152.

4. For Heidegger's view of metaphysics, see chapter 2, note 4.

5. See *Letter on Humanism*, 29.

6. See chapter 4 of my book *Essere, Storia e linguaggio in Heidegger.*

7. From the point of view of an ontology of emotions and more generally of the psychic life, the outcomes of existential psychoanalysis (the *Daseinsanalyse* of Binswanger and M. Boss) are more negative than positive. The psychoanalysts who refer to Heidegger were compelled by force of circumstances to make the terms of the existential analytic of *Being and Time* more rigid than they were in order to apply them to their fields of investigation.

8. These two essays go back to 1935–36. The first, "Der Ursprung des Kunstwerkes," is included in the volume *Holzwege* (Frankfurt, 1950), partially reedited in the Stuttgart edition of 1960; the second, "Hölderlin und das Wesen der Dichtung," is published in the volume *Erläuterungen zu Hölderlins Dichtung*, 2nd ed. (Frankfurt: Klostermann, 1951) (*Elucidations of Holderlin's Poetry*, trans. Keith Hoeller [State College: Penn State University Press, 1991).

9. Here I am using the term in the sense specified in L. Pareyson, *I problemi dell'estetica* (Milan: Marzorati, 1966), 71.

## 5. Pareyson: From Aesthetics to Ontology

1. I refer here to my essay "Hermeneutics as Koine," *Theory, Culture, and Society* 5, no. 2 (1988): 399–408.

2. Luigi Pareyson, *Estetica. Teoria della formatività* (1954), 4th ed. (Milan: Bompiani, 1988).

3. Friedrich Nietzsche, "The Convalescent," in *Thus Spake Zarathustra*, trans. R. J. Hollingdale (London: Penguin Classics, 1961).

4. Pareyson, "Arte e conoscenza. Intuizione e interpretazione," in *Filosofia* 2 (1950); a more complete version was published in *Teoria dell'arte* (Milan: Marzorati, 1965), 45–52, from which I am citing.

5. On this see his autobiographical notes in *Verità e interpretazione* (Milan: U. Mursia, 1971), 238.

6. See Heidegger, *Being and Time*, 238.

7. For a broader discussion of this point, see my essay, "The Truth of Hermeneutics," in *Beyond Interpretation: The Meaning of Hermeneutics for Philosophy*, trans. David Webb (Cambridge: Polity Press, 1997), 75–96.

8. See "The Truth of Hermeneutics."

9. I am thinking above all of the essays published in the volume on Dostoevski, 1993, and those Pareyson published in various volumes of his *Annuario filosofico* (Milan: U. Mursia) from 1985 onward, in addition to the *Filosofia della libertà* (Genoa: Il Melangolo, 1989).

10. On this, I refer to my essay "History of Salvation, History of Interpretation," in *After Christianity*, trans. Luca D'Isanto (New York: Columbia University Press, 2002).

## 6. *From Phenomenological Aesthetics to Ontology of Art*

1. For a more extended discussion of this Aristotelian theme and its meaning for aesthetics, I refer to my book *Il concetto di fare in Aristotele* (Turin: Università di Torino, 1961).

2. On Spencer, see chapter 3, note 4.

3. See especially *L'estetica e I suoi problemi* (Milan: Marzorati, 1961); now it is available in its third edition in three volumes: *Teoria dell'arte* (Milan: Marzorati, 1965); *L'esperienza artistica* (Milan: Marzorati, 1974); and *Conversazioni di estetica* (Milan: U. Mursia, 1966).

4. Roland Barthes, *Critique et verité* (Paris, 1966), 55 (*Criticism and Truth*, trans. and ed. Katrine Pilcher Keuneman [Minneapolis: University of Minnesota Press, 1987]). With the increasingly marked recognition of the "objectivity" of language, the fact that it speaks "in" us, the *nouvelle critique* has gradually acquired a more or less open Heideggerian tonality, whose precedent can be found in one of the masters of the new critics, M. Blanchot, *La part due feu* (Paris: Gallimard, 1949); *L'espace littéraire* (Paris: Gallimard, 1955); *Le livre à venir* (Paris: Gallimard, 1959).

5. Luigi Pareyson, *Esistenza e persona*, 3rd ed. (Turin : Taylor, 1966).

6. Mikel Dufrenne, *Phénoménologie de l'expérience esthétique* (Paris: Presses Universitaires de France, 1953), 1:256 and passim.

7. In this perspective, Brecht's observations on the Aristotelian concept of catharsis and on the necessity of non-Aristotelian drama are quite relevant for highlighting the aestheticism latent in the entire aesthetic tradition of the West. See, for example, Brecht, "Breviario di estetica teatrale," in *Scritti teatrali* (Turin: Einaudi, 1962), 96–97; his note on "la madre," in *Scritti teatrali*, 27; and furthermore, *Schriften zum Theater* (Frankfurt: Suhrkamp,1963), 3:68–69, 97, 100, 271–72.

8. See Heidegger, "Der Ursprung des Kunstwerkes" in *Holzwege* (Stuttgart: Reclam-Bibliothek, 1960), 75 ("The Origin of the Work of Art," in *Poetry, Language, Thought*, trans. Albert Hofstadter [New York, Harper and Row, 1971], 163–86).

9. See W. Kandinsky, *Essays über Kunst und Künstler* (Stuttgart: Hatje, 1955), in *Complete Writings on Art*, vol. 2 (1922–1943) (Boston: G. K. Hall, 1982).

## 7. *Critical Methods and Hermeneutic Philosophy*

1. These observations on the hermeneutic question are raised in the context of the general question of interpretation formulated by Luigi Pareyson in the essays cited

in previous chapters (see also "Filosofia della persona," in the volume *Esistenza e Persona*, 3rd ed. [Turin: Taylor, 1966], 185–201); and of the investigations, still within the domain of existentialism, carried out by some of Heidegger's disciples, especially Hans Georg Gadamer (*Truth and Method*, trans. Joel Weinsheimer and Donald G. Marshall [New York: Continuum, 1993]).

2. It seems necessary to quote from the original text: "Lesen aber, was ist anderes als sammeln: sich versammeln in der Sammlung auf das Ungesprochenes im Gesprochenen?" (in E. Staiger, *Die Kunst der Interpretation*, 2nd ed. [Zurich: Atlantis Verlag, 1957]), 48). A philosophical elaboration of the etymology of reading (*lógos, léghein, legere, lesen*) can be found in many Heideggerian texts, for example, in *Vorträge und Aufsätze* (Pfullingen: Neske, 1963), 270.

3. See M. Heidegger, *Unterwegs zur Sprache* (Pfulligen: Neske, 1959), 96 (*On the Way to Language*, trans. Peter D. Hertz and Joan Stambaugh [New York: Harper and Row, 1971]). On the importance of the Bible for Heidegger's reflection on hermeneutics, see the observations in O. Pöggeler, *Der Denkweg Martin Heideggers* (Pfullingen: Neske, 1963), 270 (*Martin Heidegger's Path of Thinking*, trans. Daniel Magushak and Sigmund Barber (Atlantic Highlands, N.J.: Humanities Press, 1987), 218.

4. See Erich Auerbach's essay "Figura," in *Neue Dante-Studien* 5 (Istanbul, 1944): 52. For a discussion of the relationship between allegorical and anagogical meaning and the questions related to it, see H. de Lubac, *Exègèse Mediévale* (Paris: Cerf 1993).

## 8. *Aesthetics and Hermeneutics*

1. H-G. Gadamer, *Truth and Method*, trans. Joel Weinsmeier and Donald G. Marshall (New York: Continuum, 1993), 89.

2. W. Dilthey, *Plan der Fortsetzung zum Aufbau der geschictlichen Welt in den Geisteswissenschaften* (Stuttgart: Teubner, 1927).

3. T. Adorno, *Einleitung in die Musiksoziologie* (Frankfurt: Suhrkamp, 1962), chap. 1 (*Introduction to the Sociology of Music* [New York: Seabury Press, 1976]).

4. Gadamer, *Truth and Method*, 30.

5. Gadamer. *Truth and Method*, 39.

6. On this, see my book, *Il concetto di fare in Aristotle* (Turin: Giappichelli, 1961), chap. 4.

7. F. D. Schleiermacher, *Hermeneutik*, ed. Heinz Kimmerle (Heidelberg: Winter, 1959); in English, *Hermeneutics: The Handwritten Manuscripts*, ed. Heinz Kimmerle, trans. James Duke and Jack Forstman (Missoula, Mont.: Scholars Press, 1977).

8. Gadamer, *Truth and Method*, 132.

9. See Heidegger, *Vorträge und Aufsätze* (Pfullingen: Neske, 1954), 45 and 119.

10. Unless the subject recognized himself with the *id rather than the ego*, in the sense in which Lacan interprets Freud's statement "Wo Es war, soll Ich werden." See, for example, Lacan, *Ècrits* (Paris: Editions du Seuil 1966).

11. J. Habermas, *The Logic of the Social Sciences* (Cambridge, Mass.: MIT Press, 1988).

12. As argued by Octave Mannoni, *Clefs pour l'imaginaire; ou l'autre scène* (Paris: Editions du Seuil, 1969).

## 9. Aesthetics and Hermeneutics in Hans-Georg Gadamer

1. I shall examine here the last work of Gadamer, *Truth and Method*, trans. J. Weinsheimer and D. Marshall (New York: Continuum, 1975). See also Gadamer, "Che cos'è la verità," *Rivista di Filosofia* 3 (1956): 251–66, and his introduction to Heidegger, *Der Ursprung des Kunstwerkes* (Stuttgart: Reclam-Bibliothek, 1960). Important critical observations on Gadamer's work are found in Oskar Becker, "Die Fragwürdigkeit der Transzendierung der ästhetischen Dimension der Kunst (H. G. Gadamer)," *Philosophische Rundhschau* (October 1962): 225–38.

2. Gadamer, *Truth and Method*, 111.

3. On this see Gadamer, *Truth and Method*, part 1, and "Die Fragwürdigkeit des ästhetischen Bewusstseins," *Rivista di estetica* 3 (1958): 374–83.

4. See Heidegger, "Die Zeit des Weltbildes," in *Holzwege* (Frankfurt: Vittorio Klosterman, 1959), 60–104 ("The Epoch of the World Picture," in *The Question Concerning Technology and Other Essays*, trans. William Lovitt [New York: Harper and Row, 1977], 115–54), and *Vorträge und Aufsätze* (Pfullingen: Neske, 1954).

5. Gadamer, *Truth and Method*, 100.

6. Gadamer, *Truth and Method*, 110.

7. Gadamer, *Truth and Method*, 111, 113.

8. Gadamer, *Truth and Method*, 137.

9. Gadamer, *Truth and Method*, 137.

10. Gadamer, *Truth and Method*, 300.

11. Gadamer, *Truth and Method*, 304.

12. Gadamer, *Truth and Method*, 300 ff.

13. Heidegger, *Der Ursprung des Kunstwerkes*, 119.

14. "Solang du Selbstgeworfnes fängst, ist alles / Geschicklichkeit und lässlicher Gewinn/ erst wenn du plötzlich Fänger wirst des Balles, / den eine ewige Mitspielerin / dir zuwarf, deiner Mitte, in Genau / gekonnten Schwung, in einer jener Bögen / aus Gottes grossem Brückenbau: / erst dann ist Fangen-können ein Vermögen,— / nicht deines, einer Welt [Catch only what you've thrown yourself, all is mere skill and little gain; but when you are suddenly the catcher of a ball thrown by an eternal partner with accurate and measured swings towards you, to your center, in an arch

from the great bridgebuilding of God: why catching then becomes a power—not yours, a world's]" (Rilke, cited in the epigraph to Gadamer's *Truth and Method*).

15. Gadamer, *Truth and Method*, 363–79.

16. Gadamer, *Truth and Method*, 486.

## 10. *The Work of Art as the Setting to Work of Truth*

1. See the 1960 edition, Heidegger, *Der Ursprung des Kunstwerkes* (Stuttgart: Reclam-Bibliothek, 1960) ("The Origin of the Work of Art" in *Poetry, Language, Thought*, trans. Albert Hofstadter [New York, Harper and Row, 1971]).

2. Heidegger dedicated an important addendum to show the ontological implications of his argument. Such an addendum appears only in the recent editions of *Holzwege* (the volume in which the essay was originally published). In the 1960 Reclam-Bibliothek edition, 95–101.

3. Heidegger, *Unterwegs zur Sprache* (Pfullingen: Neske, 1959).

4. Heidegger, *Der Ursprung des Kunstwerkes*, 67.

5. For a broader discussion of the topic, see chapter 3 of my *Essere, storia, e linguaggio in Heidegger* (Turin: Marietti, 1963). On the idea of the work as *Gestalt* installed in the rift, see Heidegger, *Der Ursprung des Kunstwerkes*, 79 ff.

6. Heidegger, *Der Ursprung des Kunstwerkes*, 75.

# Index